WAYWARD GOVERNANCE

Australian Studies in Law, Crime and Justice

Forthcoming

Insider Trading in Australia, by Roman Tomasic and
Brendan Pentony

Wayward Governance:

Illegality and its Control in the Public Sector

P.N. Grabosky

Australian Institute of Criminology

National Library of Australia
Cataloguing-in-Publication entry

Grabosky, Peter N. (Peter Nils,). 1945-
  Wayward governance : illegality and its control in the public sector.

  Includes bibliographies.
  ISBN 0 642 14605 5.

  1. Abuse of administrative power - Australia. 2. Government liability - Australia. 3. Administrative responsibility - Australia. 4. Policy corruption - Australia. 5. Misconduct in office - Australia. I. Australian Institute of Criminology. II. Title.

350.9'9'0994.

Typeset by Australian Institute of Criminology

Printed in Australia by Renwick Pride Pty Ltd

Cover design by Arthur Stokes

But what is government itself but the greatest of all reflections on human nature? If men were angels, no government would be necessary. If angels were to govern men, neither external nor internal controls on government would be necessary. In framing a government which is to be administered by men over men, the great difficulty lies in this: you must first enable the government to control the governed; and in the next place oblige it to control itself.

James Madison, 1751-1836
President of the
United States

ACKNOWLEDGEMENTS

This book would not have been possible without the advice and assistance of people too numerous to mention.

The author is most indebted to the staff of the J.V. Barry Memorial Library of the Australian Institute of Criminology for assistance rendered over the course of the project. Additional support was provided by libraries of the Department of Aboriginal Affairs and the Australian Institute of Aboriginal Affairs.

Each of the case studies was read by someone familiar with the case in question or with the area of government activity which it entailed. David Biles, John Braithwaite, Brent Fisse, Tom Molomby, Cynthia Stohl, Michael Stohl, Bruce Swanton, Grant Wardlaw and Paul Wilson read and commented constructively on the entire manuscript.

Maggie Brady was particularly helpful with those chapters relating to Aboriginal affairs. Roger West and the Public Interest Advocacy Centre kindly granted me access to their files on the Social Security Conspiracy Case; Bill Luchetti allowed me to peruse the voluminous correspondence of the Yass Shire Council regarding their waste disposal difficulties; Alison Ziller permitted a review of the proceedings of the Jane Hill case; Peter Loof shared his insight of the Deputy Crown Solicitor's Office; Bob Brown provided me with materials on the Lea Tree incident, and Bob Ellis with guidance relating to Aboriginal sacred sites.

Special thanks are due to Irena Le Lievre, who typed the entire manuscript, and to Angela Grant, whose unsurpassed editorial guidance and indexing skills greatly facilitated the final stages of this project.

The introductory and concluding chapters were written during a period of temporary asylum kindly granted by the Department of Political Science, Northwestern University. Professor Wesley Skogan deserves special thanks for introducing me to personal computing, and for his tolerance and forbearance when I broke his machine.

The introductory and concluding chapters formed the basis of papers presented to annual meetings of the American Political Science Association, the Law and Society Association, and the Australian and New Zealand Society of Criminology. An earlier version of Chapter 5 was published in *Race and Class*, vol. 29, no. 23, 1988.

CONTENTS

FIGURES

Chapter 1

INTRODUCTION

This book seeks to develop a theory of government illegality, and to specify measures by which breaches of law by agents of the state may be prevented and controlled. Under what circumstances are governments more likely to abuse those powers which they command? What factors predispose public servants and elected officials to engage, with intent or through negligence, in unlawful activity? What political, organisational or administrative structures are best suited to discourage official misconduct? What form of remedial responses are best suited to deter future abuses, to make whole the injured citizen, and to restore the rule of law? These are among the questions which the following pages will begin to answer.

The theory is not intended to be universally applicable. Conceived within the context of western parliamentary democracies, and based on data from the Commonwealth of Australia, its usefulness to totalitarian systems, autocracies, and lesser dictatorships is questionable.

Australians are fortunate to live in a society which is basically well governed. As far as one can discern, political dissidents are not tortured and murdered by members of the defence forces, as they have been in Argentina (Amnesty International 1981). Public health authorities do not conduct grotesque experiments on unwitting subjects, as they have in the United States (Jones 1982; Bowart 1978). Postal officials do not pass on mail illegally to law enforcement agencies as they have in Canada (Canada 1981). Australian intelligence agents do not detonate explosive devices in friendly foreign harbours, as have the French (Shears & Gidley 1985). Managers of Australia's nuclear reactors have not, through their negligence, caused a catastrophic accident as have their counterparts in the Soviet Union.

Notwithstanding their relatively good showing by world standards, agencies within the Australian public sector are far from faultless. As the following chapters will demonstrate, they are capable of inflicting considerable harm.

In 1977, a judicial inquiry in Queensland found that fabrication of confessions, perjury, and planting of evidence by police were pervasive (Queensland 1977). Eleven years later, press reports of the Fitzgerald inquiry indicate that many of the practices may have persisted. In 1978, the *Beach Inquiry* in Victoria found that police routinely concocted evidence and testified falsely in court. The inquiry also concluded that, among other things, police assaulted suspects in the course of interrogation, and that information regarding injury to persons in police custody had been suppressed and distorted (Victoria 1978).

The failure of the Australian government to regulate the safety of imported medical devices adequately has contributed to death and injury. At least five people died after receiving artificial heart valves which were defective (Everingham 1984). One woman in Australia has died and thousands of others sustained permanent injury from the notorious Dalkon Shield contraceptive device (Cashman 1989).

Other harms which have resulted from the action or inaction on the part of government agencies or their officers include death and injury suffered by public sector employees at work, serious environmental pollution, and gross waste and inefficiency in the expenditure of public funds.

The focus of this book is on criminal or otherwise unlawful conduct by agencies in the Australian public sector or by officers of these organisations acting in the course of their employment.

Initially, it was intended to exclude corruption and other misdeeds for personal gain from the analysis, and to focus exclusively upon illegal conduct in the line of duty - in furtherance of government policy. This initial intention proved to be misconceived, however. Many illegal acts of an exclusively personal nature flow from some of the same organisational pathologies which give rise to or facilitate crime within the scope of employment. Moreover, the distinction between conduct for personal gain and that in furtherance of policy is often vague and ambiguous. An over zealous public official may break the law because of mixed motives - desire for individual recognition and personal advancement on the one hand, and fervent dedication to organisational goals on the other. Altruistic and self-interested acts often occur in a common constellation of events (Doig et al. 1984, pp. 28-9). Maurice Punch (1985, p. 10) provides an excellent illustration in the police setting, but the situation is to be found throughout the public sector. Perjury and conspiracy to pervert the course of justice are common techniques of covering up illegal acts committed in the course of implementing public policy, just as they are used to cover the tracks of the corrupt.

Not all of the incidents analysed in this book entail criminal conduct strictly defined. Indeed, the acts in question vary widely in terms of their moral blameworthiness. Some were, and remain, shocking to the public conscience, and are all but universally condemned. Others reflect a considerable degree of moral ambiguity. Whilst some arose from calculated intent or recklessness, most stem from negligence rather than venality.

To limit the coverage to strict criminality would narrow the scope to only those cases which resulted in convictions having been recorded in a court of law. Needless to say, in the public sector as on the streets, not every crime which is committed results in the conviction of the perpetrator. Indeed, in some instances, Australian governments are able to escape criminal liability altogether by relying upon the archaic doctrine of crown immunity. At times, authorities with the discretion to prosecute public sector offenders exercise their discretion not to do so.

Similarly, to exclude civil wrongs, that is, harms arising from tortious conduct, would also be unduly restrictive. The line between civil negligence and criminal negligence is fine indeed. Our task is not to belabour whether a particular injury arose from a public servant's unreasonable failure to be aware of the risk posed by his actions or those of his subordinates, whether the oversight was so unreasonable as to warrant the framing of criminal charges, or indeed, whether there was recklessness, a conscious disregard of the impending risk. The distinction is not insignificant, for the legal consequences can be profound. But our concern lies as much with the antecedents of harmful official actions as with precise calibrations of culpability.

For present purposes, government illegality has been defined rather broadly. The book will focus on criminal or otherwise unlawful conduct, proven or alleged, occurring in the

Australian public sector. This will include the breach of any law - civil, criminal or administrative - which renders those in breach liable to penalties.

Government illegality deserves our attention for a number of reasons. The size of the Australian public sector and the scope of its activities are great, and destined to remain so. An active and ubiquitous state carries that much more potential for abuse.

Of great concern to public officials in the current climate of fiscal crisis is the fact that breaches of the law by governments can entail very great cost, in financial as well as in human terms. The incidents analysed in this book resulted in loss of life, in severe physical injury and psychological trauma, and in hundreds of millions of dollars in lost revenue. Remedial measures in the aftermath of these incidents involved millions of dollars in investigative expenses, and further millions of dollars in eventual compensation to victims.

As a result of these incidents and their consequences, public servants and elected officials suffered acute personal embarrassment. Governments sustained considerable political damage, which in some cases contributed to their eventual electoral defeat.

A number of the incidents in this book entailed less tangible costs as well. The basic rights of Australians to privacy, to freedom of association and to freedom of expression were violated, and in some cases, perhaps irreparably eroded.

On another level, a number of incidents discussed below represented attacks on the rule of law. The government, after all, is the ultimate moral exemplar. When the government breaks the law, the legitimacy of the legal order is threatened. As Brandeis (1928) so eloquently put it

> In a government of laws, the existence of the government will be imperilled if it fails to observe the law scrupulously. Our government is the potent, the omnipresent, teacher. For good or ill it teaches the whole people by its example. Crime is contagious. If the government becomes a lawbreaker, it breeds contempt for the law; it invites every man to be a law unto himself; it invites anarchy.

The purpose of this book is not to engage in exposé social criticism, to hang out Australia's dirty linen, nor to indulge in simple hand-wringing. It was written in the belief that one can learn from the mistakes of the past. The analysis of each of the cases is intended to illustrate what went wrong, and how a repetition of the incident in question might be prevented in future.

Previous studies

There is not a great body of literature on government illegality and its control in Australia. This book, which combines case studies with analysis, is the first of its kind. Among the overseas examples of case studies in this area are the American collections by Becker and Murray (1971), Lieberman (1972), Douglas and Johnson (1977), and Ermann and Lundman (1987), which deal with a variety of misconduct on the part of a range of agencies, and that of Wise (1976), which focuses primarily on misconduct by police and security agencies. Corruption in British government has been the subject of a book by Doig (1984).

A more common *genre* includes those works which focus on a specific incident or pattern of misconduct. In addition to those works cited in the chapters to follow, the Australian literature includes such discussions of alleged police misconduct as that connected with the Ananda Marga conspiracy case (Molomby 1986), and the Mickelberg prosecution (Lovell 1985). Among the more noteworthy American examples are Hersh's (1970) study of the My Lai massacre, Bernstein and Woodward's review of Watergate, and Garrow's (1981) study of the FBI campaign against Martin Luther King.

Generic studies of abuses of power in Australia include Harding's (1970) work on police killings, illegalities by agencies of the criminal justice system (Basten et al. 1982; Zdenkowski et al. 1987) and Grabosky and Sutton's (1989) collection which includes various examples of nonfeasance by Australian regulatory agencies.

Studies of remedies for government illegality are also rare. Available Australian remedies have been the subject of works by Aronson and Whitmore (1982), Finn (1977; 1978) and Baker (1985). Institutions of government and their accountability are discussed by Cranston (1987). The major American work on government liability is that of Schuck (1983).

A more general discussion of public law remedies in Australia is that of Goldring (1985); in England, that of Birkinshaw (1985). These include references to such institutions as judicial review of administrative decisions and ombudsmen. Hurwitz (1981) discusses these in comparative perspective. The use of civil litigation directed specifically against abuses by Australian police authorities has been addressed by Churches (1980) and Goode (1975). An American overview is that of del Carmen (1986), and British perspectives have been provided by Harrison (1987), and by Clayton and Tomlinson (1987).

A number of articles deal generally with the jurisprudence and sociology of public sector misconduct and its control. The best Australian source is that of Fisse (1987) which discusses the choice between individual and corporate liability for government illegality. Comparable American works are those of Stone (1982; 1985), Doig et al. (1984) and Thompson (1985).

Finally, a few scholars in the field of public administration have addressed the issue of bureaucratic accountability and control. In Australia, the major contributions are those of Cranston (1987), Spann (1979, Ch. 18), Smith and Weller (1978) and Hazlehurst and Nethercote (1977); in Britain, that of Dunsire (1978). United States contributions range from the landmark general treatise on bureaucracies by Downs (1967) to the study of communications within public agencies by Kaufman (1973), to the descriptive overview of accountability machinery in the U.S. civil service by Rosen (1982), to more recent work by Gruber (1987).

Selection of cases

The cases selected for analysis in this book were not chosen randomly. Admittedly, this will inhibit one's ability to generalise from the observations which are made. But it should not stand in the way of greater understanding of government illegality, its causes, and means for its control.

The cases were selected in order to present as broad a landscape as possible of public sector illegality in Australia. The incidents described below occurred in federal, state and local government jurisdictions. The organisations involved include not only agencies of criminal justice, but other departments of state and statutory authorities. They involve allegations of the use of excessive force by police and prison officers, gross waste and inefficiency in the expenditure of public funds, environmental pollution, and danger to the health and safety of public sector employees. The incidents affected a variety of types of victim - both individual and collective. They include clients of the agency, its employees, individual citizens, ethnic communities, taxpayers, the natural environment, and in one case a foreign government.

Incidents were also chosen to reflect variation in the degree to which the practices in question were embraced by the agencies under whose auspices they occurred. Some of the conduct was institutionalised policy - officially endorsed if not publicly heralded. In other cases, the practices, although in furtherance of policy, were recognised as illegal, but unofficially condoned. In others still, the illegal conduct in furtherance of policy was officially condemned. And finally, there was conduct undertaken exclusively for personal gain.

Another criterion for selection was whether the incident in question, or at least its legal and political consequences, occurred in the relatively recent past. In some cases, matters were not entirely finalised at the time of writing. But in every case, there is enough of a tale to tell to warrant inclusion.

In the choice of cases, there may be a slight bias toward more highly publicised sensational matters. Some were major scandals. A number of the incidents were the subject of royal commissions, and have become household words to most Australians conversant with current affairs. There are no discussions of traffic offences by drivers of state-owned buses, or of accidents involving government motor vehicles whose drivers may have been negligent. Other cases, however, were nonetheless obscure; some went all but unnoticed outside the locale in which they occurred, and others have begun to fade dimly into history. Nevertheless, each contains an object lesson.

Theoretical foundations

There exists a paucity of theory on government illegality in particular, and on white collar crime in general. Without canvassing the entire history of western political thought, it might be instructive to begin with brief reference to America's founding fathers. Acutely sensitive to the potential for the abuse of power which resides in a highly centralised government, they deliberately set about designing a political system in which powers were dispersed (Wills 1981). The principles of separation of powers, checks and balances, and the fundamental statement of individual rights enshrined in the United States Constitution provided a model for subsequent democratic governments.

Whilst Lieberman (1972), in his review of various American cases, does not purport to develop a theory of government lawbreaking, he does proffer a number of explanations for the phenomenon. These include the absence of strict legal controls, shortcomings in the oversight of agency activity, lack of systematic planning, and inadequate monitoring within the organisation. Illegality is further facilitated by pressures to discourage dissent by officers of the agency, and by the low probability of punishment in the event that official misconduct is detected.

Other insights on government illegality may be gleaned from works with a specialised focus. Perhaps the most extreme form of government illegality is the use of terroristic violence for purposes of political repression (Stohl & Lopez 1984; 1986). Theorists of state terror have observed that societies characterised by heterogeneity and stratification, where political power is centralised and a tradition of democratic principles and institutions is lacking, are more likely to experience terroristic governance. The risk is compounded when the regime faces external threat or challenge from within (Gurr 1986).

Further material for a theory of government illegality may be drawn from the literature on police misconduct.

Among the explanations for police deviance are the temptations presented by opportunities for illicit activities, the cohesiveness and insularity of police which provide support and reinforcement for 'bending the rules', and the failure of both internal and external control mechanisms (Sherman 1978; Shearing 1981; Punch 1985). Nevertheless, police are a very specialised agency of government. Whether explanations of misconduct in the police context are applicable throughout the public sector is a matter worthy of exploration.

American sociologist Edwin Sutherland, with whom the term 'white collar crime' originated, focused primarily on individual-level explanations of business misconduct. Central to these is the theory of differential association, which holds that attitudes and techniques conducive to illegality are learned from those with whom one interacts on a daily basis (Sutherland & Cressey 1978). This has been further developed into a subcultural theory of corporate crime. For example, Geis (1967) has shown how young executives learned to co-operate with their competitors in heavy electrical equipment industry to fix prices, and how they came to rationalise this as an acceptable practice.

Kriesberg (1976) discusses three models of decision-making which may lead to corporate crime. The first, that of the rational actor, entails the systematic canvassing of options to maximise profits or whatever other values might be salient to the corporation. Corporate crime thus results from the rational calculus that an illegal course of action is most advantageous from the point of view of the organisation.

The second model, that of organisational process, involves adherence to pre-existing organisational routines and established procedures. Illegality results from the absence of standard operating procedures to deal with a new situation, or with the persistence of existing procedures which mandate or permit illegal action. Central to this model is inadequate monitoring on the part of knowledgeable or authoritative officers within the organisation.

The third of Kriesberg's models, that of bureaucratic politics, presents corporate conduct as the result of bargaining within the organisation. Decisions which eventuate are often the product of conflict and compromise, and may therefore be vague. Illegality which flows from bureaucratic politics can

9

result from the acquiescence of some members of the organisation, or from the tendency to insulate oneself from knowledge of wrongdoing.

Kagan and Scholz (1984), in presenting three models of corporate misconduct, distinguish between corporations as amoral calculators, political citizens, and organisational incompetents. Amoral calculators, motivated essentially by profit considerations, rationally assess the costs and the benefits of a course of illegal action. If the probability of detection and the anticipated penalty are low in relation to the likely amount of ill-gotten gains, an illegal course of action will be adopted.

Political citizens, on the other hand, are inclined to comply with the law, but will violate laws which they regard as arbitrary or unreasonable. When they perceive their regulatory environment as excessively legalistic or nit-picking, they tend to develop a 'subculture of resistance'. Illegality thus becomes a gesture of principled disagreement and ultimately one of defiance.

Illegality arising from organisational incompetence is a reflection of management failure, rather than malevolence. To quote from the *Robens Report* on occupational health and safety in the United Kingdom:

> Relatively few offences are clear cut, few arise
> from reckless indifference to the possibility of
> causing injury, few can be laid without qualification
> at the door of a particular individual. The typical
> infringement . . . arises rather through carelessness,
> oversight, lack of knowledge of means, inadequate
> supervision or sheer inefficiency (Robens 1972,
> p. 82).

The above theories of corporate crime beg the question of whether their explanatory reach is necessarily limited to the private sector. Are businesses qualitatively different organisations from government agencies? Does the relative absence of the profit motive and the lack of a competitive market setting in the public sector require a separate theory of government illegality? The image one has of public servants is one of risk aversion, while business people are perceived to be risk takers. Nevertheless, Stone (1982; 1985) has queried the extent to which the public/private distinction is relevant to issues of organisational illegality and its control. He observes that the line between public and private sectors, never distinct, is becoming increasingly vague, as private contractors deliver government services and as government enterprises compete directly with the private sector.

Recently, a number of scholars have advanced theories which purport to explain variations in organisational deviance generally, across public and private sector entities alike. Whilst these have tended to be grounded primarily in evidence from the literature on corporate crime, their extension to the public sector has been fruitful.

One of the first attempts at a general theory of organisational crime is the work of Finney and LeSieur (1982). They focus on performance emphasis, that is the strength of goal orientation within an organisation. Workers under pressure for greater output are more likely to offend, especially when confronted by barriers to the attainment of their desired performance. Their inclination to deviance may be reinforced or constrained by the moral climate established by top management. A variety of organisational properties, including complexity, centralisation, stratification, and the absence of participatory management may induce alienation among employees, and thus a greater willingness to employ illegal procedures in the course of their work.

Vaughan (1983; 1986) also looks to organisation theory to explain organisational deviance. Among the predisposing factors to illegality which she identifies are the organisation's competitive environment, the complexity of an organisation and the complexity of transactions in which it is engaged, and the absence or weakness of countervailing mechanisms of control. To the extent to which an organisation is unable to attain its goals by lawful means, the greater the pressure to rely upon extralegal methods. The more complex the organisation, the more numerous the opportunities for illegality. The lower the risk that illegality will be detected, the greater the likelihood that it will be practised. The potential for organisational misconduct is further enhanced by the presence of normative support for illegality within the organisation, and by the availability of means to carry out illegal acts.

11

Coleman (1987) seeks to combine individual and structural level explanations in an integrated theory of white collar crime. The basic factors which he specifies are motivation and opportunity. The culture of competition places considerable pressure on both organisations and individuals to achieve. In the face of this competitive pressure organisations and individuals must choose between legitimate and illegitimate means of achievement. Normative restraints are learned; ethical standards are acquired in association with persons who define law-abiding behaviour favourably, and in isolation from those who define law-abiding behaviour unfavourably. Decisions to engage in illegal activity reflect the perceived certainty and severity of punishment in the event of detection.

Braithwaite's (forthcoming) theory of organisational crime builds upon much of the foregoing in its attempt to explain variations in illegality across public and private sector entities. Organisations are more likely to break the law if legitimate opportunities for goal attainment are blocked, and if alternative illegitimate opportunities exist. Illegality is more likely in organisations which have developed a strong subculture of resistance to law-abiding conduct. The formation of such a subculture may be facilitated when the organisation is viewed with hostility and distrust by authorities responsible for oversight; it may be inhibited by the threat of adverse publicity ('potent shaming') in the event that misconduct is detected. Organisations with active self-monitoring systems, and whose specialised compliance units are endowed with power and influence, are less likely to offend; so too are those with open communications procedures. Organisations in which responsibility is compartmentalised, and in which officers are isolated in 'sealed domains' of activity, are at greater risk of offending.

Analytical framework

Each of the case studies has been based on a standard framework. The chapter begins with a description of the illegal conduct in question, and the extent of harm which resulted. In some cases this was death, in others physical injury. The first section also analyses the incident, to explore the questions of responsibility and culpability. Did the harm in question result from personal malice, or from carelessness? Where on the continuum between deliberate premeditation and honest mistake does it lie?

Another consideration is whether the incident entailed purely individual conduct, or whether it was essentially a collective act - a manifestation of organisational behaviour. Certainly, individuals do not exist in a social vacuum, and organisations are comprised of people. But some cases are obviously the product of organisational processes and others more the work of a person acting mainly on his or her own. Doig et al. (1984) discuss the degree to which responsibility for an illegal act may be shared by executives and subordinates. A manager who clearly and openly directs his or her subordinates to engage in illegal behaviour is clearly responsible. Short of this, an executive may set goals which can only be attained by extralegal means, without authorising their use. Liability may also rest with a manager who has reason to suspect that illegal means are being employed in pursuit of organisational ends, but who fails to take steps to investigate. The relative contribution of senior executives, middle management and rank and file will also be discussed, as will the question whether the incident followed a discrete policy decision or rather the exercise of individual discretion.

The second part of each chapter will address the organisational pathologies which may have contributed to the incident in question. The issue at hand here is different from the question of individual versus collective action, for the misdeeds of a particular individual may still have an organisational basis. The characteristics of organisations can affect the behaviour of their members. To use a very awkward metaphor, the shape and composition of a barrel can facilitate or inhibit the decay of the apples contained therein.

At perhaps the most basic level, one may readily appreciate how shortcomings in organisational procedures for recruiting and training personnel may lead to misconduct. Inadequate supervision, whether by managerial personnel within an organisation or by responsible authorities external to the organisation, may also contribute to misconduct. Bad management and ineffective leadership generally may have adverse consequences for an agency's behaviour.

Overall, the book will test the theories outlined above, and will explore any apparent linkages between the characteristics of an organisation and the misconduct under review. Are large organisations more likely to go astray than small ones? Are agencies in which decision-making is decentralised more prone to misconduct than those in which decisions are made at the top?

A key consideration relating to the organisational bases of government illegality is the flow of communications within the organisation (Downs 1967, Ch. 10). If policies and procedures are inadequately communicated from management down to the operating personnel, the likelihood of their deviating from these standards is that much greater. Alternatively, if adverse information is not communicated upward, management may not become aware of an impending problem in time to take preventive or ameliorative measures (Hall 1982, pp. 196-7; Guetzkow 1965). Other problems may arise when an organisation is deluged with information - a phenomenon known as 'overload' (Katz & Kahn 1978, pp. 449-55).

An issue related to both supervision and communications within an organisation is the extent to which delegation and decentralisation shield top management from knowledge of misconduct on the part of their subordinates (Finney & LeSieur 1982, p. 266). If one believes the accounts given by principals in the Iran-Contra affair, President Reagan remained ignorant of the diversion of funds which had been engineered by the staff of the National Security Council.

Organisations also interact with each other in the course of their daily affairs, and where co-ordination of activities is important, a failure of communications can have unfortunate consequences. The extent to which an agency goes astray on its own, or rather as a result of dependence on another organisation will also be explored.

Environmental pressures may also contribute to official misconduct. Pressures on an organisation to produce results may invite officers to take foolish risks, or to deliberately transgress the law. The legal and political environment can be similarly influential. Where laws governing acceptable conduct are perceived as ambiguous and where public pressures do not appear intense, agencies may engage in conduct that would otherwise be unthinkable.

Interaction between environmental and structural properties may also contribute to government illegality. In the case of the Challenger space shuttle disaster, pressures to adhere to a tight launch schedule, combined with the reluctance of technical personnel to advise senior management about the risk of a cold weather launch, produced a decision with fatal consequences (Rogers 1986; Romzek & Dubnick 1987).

The third part of each chapter discusses how the incident was detected, and how the law was mobilised in consequence. In some cases the misconduct in question was self-consciously clandestine, whilst in others, the nature of the incident was such that it came almost immediately to public attention. In the former context, the illegality may have been disclosed by a victim, by a third party, or by a whistleblower within the organisation itself. The circumstances of public disclosure are an important consideration, as they bear significantly upon issues of deterring similar conduct in future. The role of the news media in detecting official misconduct or in according persistent publicity to an incident in its aftermath is often crucial to the outcome of a matter.

The term 'mobilisation of law' refers to the choice of legal action taken by the injured citizen and/or the government in response to the incident in question (Black 1973). In some instances, this entailed criminal prosecution alone. In others, a criminal prosecution was undertaken by the state, and civil action for damages brought by individual plaintiffs. Some remained exclusively in the domain of civil law, and others still involved various administrative remedies. In one case, no legal action eventuated. In a number of cases, these prosecutions and civil actions were preceded, accompanied, or followed by judicial or parliamentary inquiries.

At the same time as the public and other government agencies may respond to public sector illegality, the wayward organisation may engage in 'damage control', seeking to 'neutralize, weaken, or redirect' the public reaction (Finney & LeSieur 1982, p. 285). This may involve developing a legal defence, or attempting to distract public attention from the incident in question. In some instances, an agency or government may 'stonewall,' in the hope that any unfavourable public attention may subside. In others, it may engage in an aggressive counter-offensive, seeking to discredit its critics or to re-capture public support.

Where the incident resulted from a collective decision, the dynamics of the decision-making process will be described to the extent that they are visible. In addition to the predispositions of decision-makers, and the selectivity with which they seek out and process information, decisions are affected by group dynamics (Janis & Mann 1977). A decision-maker who is surrounded by sycophants and yea sayers may not reach the same conclusions as one who is willing to listen to devil's advocates or to those with deeply held contrasting views. Decision-makers are also inclined to take risks in group settings which they would not do when acting alone - a phenomenon known as the 'risky shift' (Cartwright 1973).

The fourth section of each chapter will describe the outcome of those legal processes which were mobilised. For those cases which involved criminal prosecutions, the verdict and penalty, if any, are noted. Where the action taken was civil or administrative, the outcome of the case and damages or costs assessed against the government are discussed.

The fifth and final part of each chapter summarises the long-term consequences of the incidents in question. It reviews any changes in organisation and practice which may have taken place within the agency as a result of the matter, as well as any changes to external oversight procedures and accountability mechanisms which may have been introduced. Where legislative changes were introduced, these too are noted.

The book's conclusion seeks to identify any common patterns running through the various case studies, and to suggest topics or issues which warrant further investigation. It then discusses the remedies which may be available to redress wayward governance. As the case study chapters demonstrate, the diversity of official misconduct in Australia is such that there is likely to be no one intervention which can serve as a general solution to the problem of government illegality. Indeed, the goals of redress are so varied that they require an array of remedies. As readers work their way through the case studies, they may wish to pause and contemplate the extent to which the outcome of each case conforms to the following ideals.

The first goal of a system of response to governmental wrongdoing is deterrence. Stated simply, the individuals or organisation (or both) who are responsible for a breach of the law should be discouraged from repeating their transgression. In addition, other individuals and organisations alike should be discouraged from following in their footsteps. In other words, there should be a credible threat that future misconduct will be met with unambiguously undesirable consequences for the individual or organisational perpetrators. The rationale for a deterrent to official misconduct should be patently obvious. If public agencies and public officials can go about their business with impunity there exists an open invitation to the abuse of power.

The second goal is that of rehabilitation. Where the incident in question has arisen from some shortcoming within the organisation, the shortcoming should be remedied. When, for example, negligent conduct within an organisation may be traced to an inadequate training program or unsatisfactory communication of standard operating procedures, an appropriate remedy would require rectification of these problems. Rehabilitation, of course, may apply to individuals as well as organisations. Where an officer's wrongs have arisen from insufficient training, he or she should be given remedial instruction. The rationale for rehabilitation is also uncomplicated. By reforming an organisation, one reduces the likelihood of the same wrongs being inflicted repeatedly upon the public.

The third goal is that of victim compensation. Briefly stated, those who suffer injury as a result of official wrongs should be entitled to reimbursement for their losses. Where costs, be they financial, physical or psychological, are wrongfully inflicted upon the public, they should be borne by the perpetrator, or at least spread across society as a whole.

The fourth goal is that of denouncing the misconduct in question and of reaffirming the rule of law. This is especially important in light of the argument above that the government, as moral exemplar, threatens the legitimacy of the legal order when it breaks the law. It is of great importance that a common sense of anger and indignation be forcefully expressed, and that the collective conscience of the public be reaffirmed. Response to government illegality must remind society that no individual or organisation is above the law.

A final consideration in fashioning remedies for official misconduct is the avoidance of 'overkill'. Public servants already enjoy a reputation for being risk averse. Should they experience the threat (or the reality) of draconian punishment, they may be inhibited to an even greater degree from vigorous execution of their duties. Others may be discouraged from seeking or remaining in public employment altogether. To devise just remedies without such a chilling effect on public administration is no small task.

References

Amnesty International 1981, *Torture in the Eighties*, Amnesty International Publications, London.

Aronson, Mark & Whitmore, Harry 1982, *Public Torts and Contracts*, Law Book Company, Sydney.

Baker, D. 1985, 'Maladministration and the Law of Torts', *Adelaide Law Review*, vol. 10, pp. 207-53.

Basten, John, Richardson, Mark, Ronalds, Chris, & Zdenkowski, George (eds) 1982, *The Criminal Injustice System*, Australian Legal Workers Group and Legal Service Bulletin, Sydney.

Becker, Theodore & Murray, Vernon 1971, Government Lawlessness in America, Oxford University Press, New York.

Bernstein, Carl & Woodward, Bob 1974, *All The President's Men*, Warner Publishing, New York.

Birkinshaw, Patrick 1985, *Grievances, Remedies and the State*, Sweet and Maxwell, London.

Black, Donald 1973, 'The Mobilization of Law', *Journal of Legal Studies*, vol. 2, pp. 125-49.

Bowart, Walter 1978, *Operation Mind Control*, Fontana, London.

Braithwaite, John (forthcoming), 'Toward a Theory of Organizational Crime', submitted to *Criminal Justice Quarterly*.

Brandeis, L. 1928, *Dissenting opinion, Olmstead v. United States* 277 U.S. 438, p. 485.

References

Canada 1981, Commission of Inquiry Concerning Certain Activities of the Royal Canadian Mounted Police, *Third Report: Certain R.C.M.P. Activities and the Question of Governmental Knowledge*, Canadian Government Publishing Centre, Ottawa.

Cartwright, D. 1973, 'Determinants of Scientific Progress: The Case of Research on the "Risky Shift"' *American Psychologist*, vol. 28, pp. 222-31.

Cashman, Peter (forthcoming), 'The Dalkon Shield' in *Stains on a White Collar: Case Studies in Corporate Crime or Corporate Harm*, eds P. Grabosky & A. Sutton, Federation Press and Century Hutchinson, Sydney.

Clayton, Richard & Tomlinson, Hugh 1987, *Civil Actions Against the Police*, Sweet and Maxwell, London.

Churches, Steven 1980, "Bona Fide' Police Torts and Crown Immunity: A Paradigm of the Case for Judge Made Law', *University of Tasmania Law Review*, vol. 6, pp. 294-315.

Coleman, James W. 1987, 'Toward an Integrated Theory of White Collar Crime', *American Journal of Sociology*, vol. 93, no. 2, 406-39.

Cranston, Ross 1987, *Law, Government and Public Policy*, Oxford University Press, Melbourne.

del Carmen, Rolando 1986, 'Civil and Criminal Liabilities of Police Officers' in *Police Deviance*, eds T. Barker & D. Cartter, Anderson Publishing, Cincinnati, pp. 300-24.

Doig, Alan 1984, *Corruption and Misconduct in Contemporary British Politics*, Penguin Books, Harmondsworth.

Doig, Jameson, Phillips, Douglas & Manson, Tycho 1984, 'Deterring Illegal Behavior by Officials of Complex Organizations', *Criminal Justice Ethics*, vol. 1, pp. 27-56.

Douglas, Jack, & Johnson, John 1977, *Official Deviance: Readings in Malfeasance, Misfeasance, and Other Forms of Corruption*, Lippincott, Philadelphia.

Downs, Anthony 1967, *Inside Bureaucracy*, Little Brown, Boston.

Dunsire, Andrew 1978, *Control in a Bureaucracy*, Martin Robertson, Oxford.

Ermann, David, & Lundman, Richard 1987, *Corporate and Governmental Deviance*, 3rd edn, Oxford University Press, New York.

Everingham, Roland 1984, *Deadly Neglect: Regulation of the Manufacture of Therapeutic Goods*, Australian Federation of Consumer Organizations, Canberra.

Finn, Paul 1977, 'Public Officers: Some Personal Liabilities', *Australian Law Journal*, vol. 51, pp. 313-18.

------------ 1978, 'Official Misconduct', *Criminal Law Journal*, pp. 307-25.

Finney, Henry, & Le Sieur, Henry 1982, 'A Contingency Theory of Organizational Crime', in *Research in the Sociology of Organizations*, ed S. B. Bacharach, JAI Press, Greenwich, Conn. pp. 255-99.

Fisse, Brent 1987, 'Controlling Governmental Crime: Issues of Individual and Collective Liability' in Grabosky & LeLievre, pp. 121-44.

Garrow, David 1981, *The F.B.I. and Martin Luther King, Jr.*, Penguin Books, Harmondsworth.

Geis, Gilbert 1967, 'The Heavy Electrical Equipment Antitrust Cases of 1961' in *Criminal Behavior Systems*, eds Marshall B. Clinard & Richard Quinney, Holt, Rinehart and Winston, New York.

Goldring, John 1985, 'Public Law and Accountability of Government', *Federal Law Review*, vol. 15, no. 1, pp. 1-38.

Goode, Matthew 1975, 'The Imposition of Vicarious Liability to the Torts of Police Officers: Considerations of Policy', *Melbourne University Law Review*, vol. 10, pp. 47-58.

Grabosky, P. & LeLievre, I. (eds) 1987, *Government Illegality*, Australian Institute of Criminology, Canberra.

Grabosky, Peter & Sutton, Adam (eds) 1989, *Stains on a White Collar: Case Studies in Corporate Crime or Corporate Harm*, Federation Press and Century Hutchinson, Sydney.

Gruber, Judith 1987, *Controlling Bureaucracies: Dilemmas in Democratic Governance*, University of California Press, Berkeley.

Guetzkow, Harold 1965, 'Communications in Organizations' in *Handbook of Organizations*, ed J. G. March, Rand McNally, Chicago.

Gurr, Ted Robert 1986, 'The Political Origins of State Violence and Terror: A Theoretical Analysis' in *Government Violence and Repression: An Agenda for Research,* eds Michael Stohl & George A. Lopez, Greenwood Press, New York, pp. 45-72.

Hall, Richard 1982, *Organizations: Structure and Process*, Englewood Cliffs, Prentice Hall.

Harding, Richard 1970, *Police Killings in Australia*, Penguin Books, Ringwood.

Harrison, John 1987, *Police Misconduct: Legal Remedies,* Legal Action Group, London.

Hazlehurst, Cameron & Nethercote, John (eds) 1977, *Reforming Australian Government: The Coombs Report and Beyond*, Australian National University Press, Canberra.

Hersh, Seymour 1970, *My Lai 4: a Report on the Massacre and its Aftermath*, Vintage Books, New York.

Hurwitz, Leon 1981, *The State as Defendant*, Greenwood Press, Westport CT.

Janis, Irving, & Mann, Leon 1977, *Decision Making*, Free Press, New York.

Jones, James 1982, *Bad Blood: The Tuskegee Syphilis Experiment*, Free Press, New York.

Kagan, Robert & Scholz, John 1984, 'The "Criminology of the Corporation" and Regulatory Enforcement Strategies' in *Enforcing Regulation Kluwer-Nijhoff,* eds Keith Hawkins & John Thomas, Boston, pp. 67-96.

Katz, Daniel & Kahn, Robert 1978, *The Social Psychology of Organizations*, rev. edn, John Wiley and Sons, New York.

Kaufman, Herbert 1973, *Administrative Feedback*, The Brookings Institution, Washington.

Kriesberg, Simeon 1976, 'Decisionmaking Models and Corporate Crime', *Yale Law Journal*, vol. 85, pp. 1091-129.

Lieberman, Jethro 1972, *How the Government Breaks the Law*, Penguin Books, Baltimore.

Lovell, A. 1985, *The Mickelberg Stitch*, Creative Research, Perth.

Molomby, Tom 1986, *Spies, Bombs and the Path of Bliss*, Potoroo Press, Sydney.

Pennock, J.R. & Chapman, J.W. (eds) 1985, *Nomos XXVII*, New York University Press, New York.

Punch, Maurice 1985, *Conduct Unbecoming: The Social Construction of Police Deviance and Control*, Tavistock, London.

Queensland 1977, *Report of the Committee of Inquiry into the Enforcement of Criminal Law in Queensland*, Government Printer, Brisbane.

Robens, Lord 1972, *Report of the Committee on Health and Safety at Work*, Her Majesty's Stationery Office, London.

Rogers, William 1986, *Report of the Presidential Commission on the Space Shuttle Challenger Accident*, U.S. Government Printing Office, Washington.

Romzek, Barbara & Dubnick, Melvin 1987, 'Accountability in the Public Sector: Lessons from the Challenger Tragedy', *Public Administration Review*, vol. 47, no. 3, pp. 227-38.

Rosen, Bernard 1982, *Holding Government Bureaucracies Accountable*, Praeger, New York.

Schuck, Peter 1983, *Suing Government: Citizen Remedies for Official Wrongs*, Yale University Press, New Haven.

Shearing, Clifford 1981, *Organizational Police Deviance: Its Structure and Control*, Butterworths, Toronto.

Sherman, Lawrence 1978, *Scandal and Reform: Controlling Police Corruption*, University of California Press, Berkeley.

Shears, R. & Gidley, I. 1985, *The Rainbow Warrior Affair*, Unwin Paperbacks, Sydney.

Smith, R.F.I. & Weller, Patrick 1978, *Public Service Inquiries in Australia*, University of Queensland Press, St Lucia.

Spann, Richard 1979, *Government Administration in Australia*, Allen & Unwin, Sydney.

Stohl, Michael & George A Lopez (eds) 1984, *The State as Terrorist: The Dynamics of Governmental Violence and Repression*, Greenwoood Press, Westport, Conn.

------------- 1986, *Government Violence and Repression: An Agenda for Research*, Greenwood Press, New York.

Stone, Christopher 1982, 'Corporate Vices and Corporate Virtues: Do Public/Private Distinctions Matter?', *University of Pennsylvania Law Review*, vol. 139, 1441-509.

------------ 1985, 'A Comment on "Criminal Responsibility in Government"', in Pennock & Chapman.

Sutherland, Edwin & Cressey, Donald 1978, *Criminology*, 10th edn, Lippincott, Philadelphia.

Thompson, Dennis 1985, 'Criminal Responsibility in Government' in Pennock & Chapman, pp. 201-40.

Vaughan, Diane 1983, *Controlling Unlawful Organizational Behavior: Social Structure and Corporate Misconduct*, University of Chicago Press, Chicago.

------------ 1986, 'Organizational Misconduct: The Connection Between Theory and Policy', Paper presented at the Annual Meeting of the Law and Society Association, Chicago, Ill., 29 May-1 June 1986.

Victoria 1978, *Report of the Board of Inquiry into Allegations Against Members of the Victoria Police Force*, (Mr B.W. Beach), Government Printer, Melbourne.

Wills, Garry 1981, *Explaining America: The Federalist*, Doubleday, New York.

Wise, David 1976, *The American Police State*, Random House, New York.

Zdenkowski, George, Ronalds, Chris & Richardson, Mark (eds) 1987, *The Criminal Injustice System*, 2nd edn, Pluto Press, Sydney.

Chapter 2

THE ABUSE OF PRISONERS IN
NEW SOUTH WALES 1943-1976*

The punishment of convicted criminals is an issue which has indelibly marked the two hundred-year-old history of European settlement in New South Wales. Indeed, a central purpose of the original colonisation in 1788 was to relieve overcrowded conditions in British prisons. For its first thirty years, the colony of New South Wales was little more than a military prison.

Although the severity with which the convicts were punished for various breaches of penal discipline defies precise analysis, such limited statistics as do exist depict a regime of grim brutality. Over 42,000 floggings (with an average of more than 40 lashes per flogging) and 240 executions by hanging were officially recorded for the period 1830-37 (*Historical Records of Australia*, vol. I, no. 19, p. 654).

A century later, penal methods had evolved substantially - at least in theory. The beating of prisoners was proscribed by law. But well into the second half of the twentieth century, many ugly vestiges of British colonisation were still recognisable in the prisons of New South Wales.

Grafton

During World War II, increasing tensions in the state's prisons, and a number of serious assaults on prison officers, led the then NSW Prisons Department to use Grafton Gaol to house the state's most intractable prisoners. The penal methods implemented there over the following thirty-three year period were described by a Royal Commissioner as a 'regime of terror', '. . . brutal, savage and sometimes sadistic'. The Commissioner referred to the period in question as 'one of the most sordid and shameful episodes in NSW penal history' (New South Wales 1978, p. 108).

He concluded:

> It is the view of the Commission that every prison
> officer who served at Grafton during the time it
> was used as a gaol for intractables must have
> known of its brutal regime. The majority of them,
> if not all, would have taken part in the illegal
> assaults on prisoners (New South Wales 1978,
> p. 119).

The practices in question consisted of the systematic
beating of prisoners upon their arrival at Grafton,
euphemistically termed a 'reception biff', and further physical
assaults in the event of breaches of gaol rules during their
subsequent incarceration there. In other instances, beatings
were administered on a more or less random basis. In most
cases, the assaults took place without violence or provocation
by prisoners (Zdenkowski & Brown 1982, pp. 181-2 and 240-1).

Prisoners arrived at Grafton customarily attired in
overalls and slippers, their arms strapped to their sides by a
security belt to which their wrists were handcuffed. In the
words of Mr Justice Nagle:

> In some instances, the beatings began even before
> the security belt and handcuffs were removed. The
> beatings were usually administered by three or four
> officers wielding rubber batons. The prisoner was
> taken into a yard, ordered to strip, searched, and
> then the biff began. The word biff by no means
> describes the brutal beating which ensued. A
> former prison officer, Mr J.J. Pettit, described it:
> 'sometimes three, four or five of them would
> assault the prisoner with their batons to a condition
> of semi-consciousness. On occasions the prisoner
> urinates, and his nervous system ceases to function
> normally'. If most of the prisoners are to be
> believed, the officers had no compunction about
> beating them around their backs and heads; nor
> were they averse to kicking them when they were
> on the ground. They invariably abused them while
> they were hitting them, calling them 'bastards',

'cunts' and other abusive names. Sometimes they threatened to kill them (New South Wales 1978, p. 110).

The Royal Commissioner went on to quote a former Grafton prisoner, a local resident who had served a short term for failing to meet maintenance payments, and who was thereby spared violent treatment:

> Later one afternoon . . . I heard a commotion coming from an adjacent cell underneath in the 'trac' section. I could hear a lot of screaming and shouting and also the sound of thuds hitting against something. It went on for at least three minutes, I then heard the sound of a cell door slamming. The intense screaming then continued and its direction appeared to be moving. I then heard the same screaming coming from the yard. It lasted for some time further, and finally disappeared. The next morning at about 7.00 am I and other prisoners went into that yard. I saw what appeared to be pools of blood of considerable quantity on the concrete as well as on the path leading to the wood-heap.

He described the second incident in the following manner.

> One afternoon . . . I was marching through a walkover near a small yard, and looking towards the pound. I saw officer Wenczel and a prisoner, who was against a wall. Mr Wenczel was flogging him with his baton across his back and shoulders. I saw five to six blows, and the prisoner turned and was struck heavily across the head. Blood spurted from his forehead which was split. He fell on to the ground. The prisoner had his shirt off and blood was appearing on his body. I walked away from the scene (quoted in New South Wales 1978, p. 115).

It was clear, moreover, that the beatings in question were in furtherance of departmental policy; prison officers who testified before the Royal Commission conceded as much (Findlay 1982, p. 46). Departmental correspondence referred to the desirability of 'robust officers' to staff the institution, and for thirty-three years prison officers at Grafton were paid a 'climatic allowance' (New South Wales 1978, p. 108) - certainly an ironic euphemism, as the climate in the Grafton area is arguably the most equable in Australia.

Bathurst 1970

Although the regime at Grafton was most notorious, the more dramatic and certainly the more visible incidents occurred at Bathurst in 1970 and in 1974. Situated 100 miles west of Sydney, the prison was built in the last quarter of the 19th century. Those who seek to equate imprisonment with motel accommodation are ignorant of Bathurst Gaol as it existed in 1970.

Mr Justice Nagle's words are evocative.

In common with all maximum security gaols built last century, Bathurst has no glass in the windows. Prisoners, who spent about eighteen hours a day in their cells, frequently had their bedding wet by rain and sleet. There was no heating in the cells despite the extreme cold experienced in Bathurst. The cells could be stifling in summer. Screens were not permitted on the windows, and the piggery operated by the gaol outside its southern wall (between towers 4 and 6) contributed to the flies and insects and all types of odorous smells which invaded the cells in summer.

Sewerage created health problems when lavatories regularly overflowed or cisterns jammed.

Prisoners were permitted only two or three showers a week and the water-heating facilities were inadequate (New South Wales 1978, p. 45).

In addition to these physical conditions, prisoners complained about rancid food and had to endure a Dickensian system of trivial regulations:

Jumpers were not allowed in summer, no matter how cold; shirts were not to be removed in summer, no matter how hot. Prisoners had to remain fully dressed even in their cells, again no matter how hot, until 5 pm each day (New South Wales 1978, p. 46).

Dissatisfaction over these conditions intensified, and in October 1970 a number of prisoners staged a protest sit-in. Some days later, upon conclusion of the protest, the prison officers exacted retribution. In the words of the Queen's Counsel appearing at the Royal Commission for the prison officers union:

Some prison officers participated in a systematic flogging of a large number, if not all, of the prisoners in the gaol (New South Wales 1978, p. 55).

The Royal Commissioner himself described a number of the incidents in more graphic detail.

Prison officer Atkins also saw Prison officer Best assaulting prisoner Dowd on the top landing of A wing. Best kept repeating to Dowd 'call me sir' and hitting him as he shouted this at him. Dowd did call out 'sir', but Best continued to hit him. There had been no provocation on Dowd's part, nor any resistance when he was hit. Dowd's nose was broken. The blood on Best's shirt has already been referred to. Atkins described Best as having worked himself into a lather of sweat and frothing at the mouth, shouting and screaming (New South Wales, 1978, p. 61) . . .

. . . Then the cell door opened again. Prison officer Wilcox entered with a number of other officers. He said to Meaney: 'Come out here you little black bastard where I can get a go at you'. Wilcox hit Meaney with his baton from the front while Prison officer R.P. Morgan hit him from the other side. Prison Officer Paget used his baton on Meaney's legs. Morgan admitted having used his baton on Meaney, but alleged that he had to do so because Meaney 'offered resistance' because 'he refused to come out from behind the bed'. Morgan was unable to see whether Meaney had any weapons.

Meaney was a small man, about 5 feet 3 inches tall. Prison officer Paget was over 6 feet tall. Prison officer Morgan was also a much larger man than Meaney.

A fourth officer, W. Aitken, then entered the cell and hit Clark on the side of his head. As Clark doubled up, he hit him twice more, breaking the baton. He called for another baton and proceeded to hit Clark with his fists in the stomach and ribs. Clark was also a slightly built man. Prison officer Aitken was a big man, weighing over 15 1/2 stone. He was handed another baton and struck Clark on the spine (New South Wales 1978, p. 58).

The Royal Commissioner concluded, 'the whole episode was a disgrace in terms of ordinary human behaviour and repellent to any standard of decency to be expected of a prison system' (New South Wales 1978, p. 61).

Following the 'Bathurst Batterings' as they came to be known, the Department conducted an inquiry. Although the officer who conducted the investigation concluded that a prima facie case existed against prison officers generally at Bathurst, this was not communicated to the Minister. The Department, and the Minister, continued to dismiss allegations of misconduct as unfounded (Zdenkowski & Brown 1982, pp. 159-62; Findlay 1982, pp. 21-31).

Bathurst 1974

By February 1974, a little more than three years after the 'Bathurst Batterings', conditions at the prison had changed little. Tensions heightened once again, and rumours of a riot began to circulate. On a Sunday afternoon, petrol bombs were thrown into a number of buildings in the prison complex. Prison officers were issued with arms, and without having been so ordered, began firing on the prisoners. The Nagle Royal Commission found that 'there was an indiscriminate use of firearms, with no proper instructions given or understanding gained of when or where to use them' (New South Wales 1978, p. 93). The shootings were, moreover, in direct contravention of instructions sent from departmental headquarters.

> A few prisoners inside B Wing had been wounded and these were assisted to surrender. One of them was Bugg, who was carried by two other prisoners (Von Falkenhausen and Harrison) under a white flag. They were fired on by officers in the tower (New South Wales 1978, p. 93).

> Soon after 6 pm the prisoners sheltering in B Wing began negotiations for their surrender. The two prisoners mainly involved in these negotiations were Wally Bishop and Carson. Bishop carried a white flag and a prison officer's whistle. Despite the white flag, he was fired on and shot in the back (New South Wales 1978, p. 95).

> Subsequent medical examinations revealed that just under twenty prisoners were wounded by gunfire, some of them seriously. One (Bugg) is now a paraplegic, having been shot in the back from a .22 rifle. The bullet passed through a lung before lodging in his spinal cord. Another

33

(Connors) received injuries to his lung, liver and stomach through a bullet which entered the low rib region, passed through his lung and entered his abdomen. Other prisoners were found to have wounds in the forehead, in the parietal area at the side of the head, in the skull behind the ear, in the jaw, shoulders, arms, upper and lower back, spinal area, abdomen, knees, legs and ankles. Some were from pellets, others from the .22 rifles. A few wounds were superficial (New South Wales 1978, p. 93).

Following the shootings, when 'order' had been restored to the prison, a number of prisoners were subjected to brutal beatings:

Saric received a bashing that can be described only as savage. When seen by Dr Doust a short time later, he had three lacerations to the side and back of his scalp and at least thirty lineal weals four to six inches long and one to one and a half inches wide on the back of his body, on his shoulders and on the back of his upper arms. These lineal weals were in a geometric, criss crossed pattern, which the doctor thought was consistent with the prisoner running through a gauntlet of officers wielding wooden batons. It was suggested at one stage that the prisoners might have inflicted injuries of this type on each other with bricks or iron bars during the riot. Dr Doust said that the injuries were not consistent with such suggestions (New South Wales 1978, p. 101).

Bathurst had been gutted by fire. It would cost over $10 million to rebuild. The NSW Police were called in to investigate any offences which may have been committed by prisoners. A Royal Commission was heralded, but the Minister, Mr Maddison, announced that its appointment would be deferred until criminal charges against prisoners had been disposed of. The Department made no inquiries into the allegations of misconduct on the part of its officers

(Zdenkowski & Brown 1982, pp. 235-40; Findlay 1982, pp. 32-6). Indeed, Maddison had instructed the Commissioner of Police not to investigate allegations against prison officers (Whitton 1987, p. 331).

The circumstances which facilitated the systematic abuse of prisoners in New South Wales over more than three decades were many and varied. The *Nagle Report* was scathingly critical of the management practices of the Department of Corrective Services and its Commissioner, Mr McGeechan. Mr Justice Nagle criticised the lack of any clear or consistent penal policy on the part of the Department, described those aims and objectives which it did have as 'obscure to both prison officers and prisoners alike' and called the Department's future planning 'confused and incomplete' (New South Wales 1978, p. 36).

The lack of direction and guidance not only produced a demoralised work-force, but was to have brutal consequences as well. The trade union representing prison officers on at least one occasion explicitly requested formal instructions on the use of force against prisoners. The Department failed to comply with the request. Moreover, even after the 1970 Bathurst batterings, the Department failed to issue any directions condemning the use of force against prisoners (New South Wales 1978, pp. 156-7).

Managerial ineptitude took many forms. Administrative records were sorely inadequate. The Department failed to follow up to ensure the implementation of rules and directives. In its submission to the Royal Commission, the Department complained of inadequate resources. The conditions of incarceration to which the Bathurst prisoners were subjected was noted above. But even while the Royal Commission was sitting, the Department proposed to build stables for quarter-horses at Cessnock Corrective Centre at a cost of $250,000 (New South Wales 1978, p. 273).

Mr Justice Nagle was also critical of what he termed the Department's 'obsessive secrecy'. The Department had no public relations officer. Whilst public access to prisons must necessarily be strictly controlled, a number of persons were prohibited from visiting New South Wales prisons. These included Members of Parliament, members of the legal profession, prison administrators from interstate, and 'reputable private citizens'. There was, moreover, an almost absolute bar on the media (New South Wales 1978, p. 152).

The regime of secrecy so criticised by Mr Justice Nagle enabled the Department to deceive not only the public but also limit the information reaching the responsible Ministers. Mr McGeechan's report in the aftermath of the 1970 Bathurst allegations 'bore little relationship to the facts - either as Mr McGeechan knew them or as they happened' (New South Wales 1978, p. 73).

The low profile which the Department consciously adopted prevented the kind of external scrutiny which would inhibit the emergence, or certainly the institutionalisation, of systematic abuses.

These organisational pathologies were compounded by the hierarchical structure of the Department and by the management style of the Commissioner. In the words of Mr Justice Nagle:

> It would appear that an attempt was made to create an organization in which Mr McGeechan would be the head; that no proper delegation of authority was to be permitted; that there was no real provision for consultation; and that all decisions were to be Mr McGeechan's. Not only did this throw too much work and responsibility upon Mr McGeechan, but it did not permit an administrative hierarchy with well-defined areas of responsibility for the staff at each level. It has been recommended elsewhere that, in future, there should be a Commission of five persons in lieu of a commissioner. It is enough here to mention that the present organization of the Department is ineffective and does not properly use the capabilities of its senior officers (New South Wales 1978, p. 162).

The desirability of an independent inspectorate for the prisons system of New South Wales was noted in 1861 by a Select Committee under the chairmanship of Sir Henry Parkes. The recommendation, however, was never implemented. As a result, 117 years later, Mr Justice Nagle was forced to conclude:

One of the most serious criticisms that can be levelled against the Department's administration has been the failure by Mr McGeechan and his Head Office staff to appreciate exactly what was happening within the system. No attempt ever seems to have been made by Mr McGeechan or the Head Office staff to see that their instructions and orders were adopted and followed within the various gaols. Despite its apparent investigations, the Department says that it failed to detect improper actions by custodial officers, and at times it was apparently oblivious to them (New South Wales 1978, 188).

The dearth of whistleblowers (persons within the prisons system who might have called public attention to the malpractices going on), can be attributed to a number of factors. The victims of official misconduct, the prisoners themselves, lacked sufficient credibility and sympathy. Until the overwhelming evidence placed before the Royal Commission necessitated a general concession by the prison officers' trade union that some abuse of prisoners had taken place, prison officers had a substantial vested interest in concealing their own criminal acts from public view.

Those members of the Department who did call public attention to departmental shortcomings were dealt with harshly. One prison officer, who was also the secretary of the prison officers' trade union, called for a Royal Commission to inquire into allegations against Bathurst and into the Department as a whole. The Commissioner of Corrective Services, Mr McGeechan, recommended that he be charged with misconduct under the *Public Service Act 1902* (NSW). Subsequently, he was dismissed after an allegation that he had left a cell door open. He was later reinstated at a lower rank (New South Wales 1978, p. 157).

Four psychologists wrote to McGeechan following the 1970 Bathurst batterings expressing their wish to be dissociated from the 'systematic and calculated brutality' which had been practised by some officers. They were threatened with less desirable job assignments by departmental management, and none of the four were still employed by the Department by the end of 1971.

Apart from these examples of victimisation, personnel management practices were abysmal. Recruitment and training of staff resulted in a workforce largely unsuited to the task. Promotion to senior positions was based on seniority rather than competence. The *Nagle Report* criticised 'the poor calibre of many superintendents' (New South Wales 1978, p. 170), and maintained that the failure to remove the superintendent of Bathurst Gaol cost the state an estimated $5 million (New South Wales 1978, p. 162).

A consequence of poor management was an environment of poor industrial relations. The life of a prison officer has traditionally been stressful and unrewarding. The establishment of a trade union for the prison officers of New South Wales was an understandable response, as was the use of their industrial power to improve their conditions of employment. All too often, however, improvements in the living conditions of prisoners were resisted as incompatible with the working conditions of prison officers. On numerous occasions, the failure to introduce necessary and desirable reforms was rationalised by McGeechan in terms of his fear of provoking an industrial dispute (New South Wales 1978, p. 184). The Royal Commissioner criticised both the union and the Department for the confrontationist postures which each routinely adopted. Mr Justice Nagle implied that the Department failed to keep prison officers fully informed of its policies as they affected the workforce, and relied insufficiently on conciliation to resolve differences.

Ministerial responsibility

The degree to which cabinet ministers of the day bear some responsibility for the misconduct of the Department and its officers merits some consideration in the present context. Under the traditional Westminster model, the responsible minister is just that - he or she must bear responsibility for the achievements or shortcomings of subordinate officers. If John Maddison, the minister in question for most of the early 1970s, was aware of any offences against prisoners, his steadfast refusal even to concede the existence of malpractice in his Department would make him an accessory after the fact. The Royal Commissioner, who explicitly noted that his terms of reference did not extend to the actions of Maddison as Minister (New South Wales 1978, p. 27), concluded that Maddison's testimony before the commission was truthful, and that the Minister had been deceived by his Department. Thus, the most charitable characterisation of Maddison's handling of the prisons portfolio is that of gross incompetence. For him to have remained unaware of the managerial disaster described by Mr Justice Nagle is inconceivable. For him to have tolerated such poor management is inexcusable. And yet, when the administration of prisons in New South Wales came under criticism in Parliament or in the press, Maddison's standard response was to denigrate the critic as one who sought to erode authority (Zdenkowski & Brown 1982, p. 161). It was the classic cover-up reaction. He apparently never sought an outside review or independent assessment of his Department's operations. He explicitly directed the Commissioner of Police not to inquire into allegations of misconduct against prison officers. Rather, he placed his faith in and reaffirmed his support for a permanent head whose veracity and competence were consistently called into question by the Royal Commission. The numerous organisational pathologies canvassed in the *Nagle Report*, and the ministerial shortcomings which the Royal Commissioner failed to address, combined to produce an environment which fostered, then tolerated, brutality, which avoided internal investigation, and which consistently discouraged scrutiny from external sources.

Prisons, in New South Wales as elsewhere, serve the function of warehousing those defined by the authorities as undesirable. There, society's losers are kept out of sight, out of mind; as pariahs, their plight often fails to arouse the sympathy, or even the attention, of the general public. So it was that the regime at Grafton was able to continue for thirty years. Indeed, the 'high tech' facility which was designed to replace Grafton as the state's ultra high security prison, was conceived and planned in strict secrecy. Katingal, as it came to be called, was condemned as an 'electronic zoo' by Mr Justice Nagle (Stein 1981; Zdenkowski & Brown 1982, p. 182).

Neither public servants nor elected officials like to air their dirty linen in public. Penal reform has never been a vote-getter. Labor oppositions in New South Wales were thus reluctant to criticise a regime which was instituted under a Labor government in 1943. Events in 1970 began to erode this, however. The dramatic social divisions occasioned by the Vietnam War led many to question traditional institutions of society, prisons among them. A few principled men from 'respectable' social backgrounds were sent to prison for resisting conscription to national service. There they were able to see first hand the conditions and abuses which had hitherto remained invisible. These circumstances were then related to a member of state Parliament, George Petersen, who began to raise questions publicly. The media attention accorded these initial allegations elicited even more accounts of brutality from ex-prisoners, as well as attracting the attention of other concerned citizens. The anonymous publication in 1971 of an account of the 'Bathurst Batterings' placed the issue of the New South Wales prison system on the media agenda (Zdenkowski & Brown 1982, pp. 80-1 and pp. 158-9). The 1974 burning of Bathurst Gaol further heightened public debate. As a result of this episode some 46 prisoners were charged with various offences relating to property damage and riotous assembly. Police investigation and subsequent proceedings saw prison officers become the subject of a number of complaints of assault, most of which were supported by medical evidence. These made a Royal Commission inevitable.

The then Liberal government, however, sought to postpone the inevitable as long as possible. As late as 1975, John Maddison's successor as responsible minister, in dismissing calls for a Royal Commission, is quoted as having said 'we have one of the best prison systems in the world and there is no need for a witch hunt' (Zdenkowski & Brown 1982, p. 166).

At long last, on the eve of the 1976 state election, the Liberal government sought to neutralise further criticism by appointing a Royal Commission. With the change of government, new letters patent were issued. The Royal Commissioner was Mr Justice J.F. Nagle of the Supreme Court of New South Wales. As noted above, the *Nagle Report* found widespread breaches of the criminal law had been committed by officers of the New South Wales government. That His Honour regarded this abuse of power with the greatest revulsion is evident in a number of the above quotations from his report. He nevertheless chose not to recommend that criminal charges be laid against the identifiable perpetrators, suggesting instead that the decision be left to the 'appropriate authorities' (New South Wales 1978, p. 119).

Mr Justice Nagle did, however, recommend disciplinary action in two cases. In addition to the removal of Mr McGeechan from his position, the Royal Commissioner recommended that disciplinary proceedings be brought against one prison officer who was alleged to have made non-violent homosexual advances to prisoners. Some consider it indicative of a double standard that Mr Justice Nagle regarded such conduct as more worthy of disciplinary intervention than 'brutal, savage and sometimes sadistic violence' (Zdenkowski & Brown 1982, p. 256).

After some delay, the government announced that it had decided against prosecuting any of the prison officers for offences which they may have committed. One former prisoner sought to proceed by way of private prosecution; the magistrate found no case to answer, and awarded costs to the amount of $30,000 against the complainant. The New South Wales government gave no considerations to redress by way of monetary compensation to those who may have been injured as a result of misconduct by government officers; prisoners were largely unable to seek civil damages in a court of law (Zdenkowski 1980).

The release of the *Nagle Report* in 1978 provided the Wran Labor government with an historic opportunity to achieve fundamental reforms in the NSW prison system. The creation of a five-person corrective services commission, as had been recommended in the *Nagle Report*, and the appointment of a progressive Chairman, Dr Tony Vinson, seemed to herald a dramatic departure from the pre-Nagle era. Indeed, most of the 252 recommendations from the *Nagle Report* were implemented. These ranged from a relaxation of restrictions on cell decorations, to improvements in amenities for prison officers, to a formalisation of regulations on the use of force. The recommendation that Katingal be closed was accepted, but only after a campaign over a period of months (Zdenkowski & Brown 1982, pp. 86-90).

The Commission under Vinson demonstrated profound concern for the rights of individual prisoners, and permitted prisoners to communicate their grievances directly to the Chairman. Vinson sought to maintain a high profile, making frequent visits, often unannounced, to correctional institutions throughout the state. An inspectorate was created within the Department, and four investigators were seconded to the unit from the state police. Disciplinary actions were taken against thirty-two prison officers during Vinson's term as Chairman, for reasons as varied as the use of excessive force and the possession of drugs in prison (Vinson 1982, p. 97).

But abuses were to continue. In 1979, a number of inmates at Goulburn Gaol alleged they had been beaten by prison officers. A magistrate's inquiry found evidence of assault by four officers. The events resulted in disciplinary proceedings under the Public Service Act. Findings of misconduct were made in two cases, but no criminal charges were laid (Zdenkowski & Brown 1982, pp. 197-206).

In October 1980, prisoners at Parramatta Gaol staged a peaceful sit-down strike to protest against the decision of the Wran government not to proceed with criminal charges against those prison officers named adversely in the *Nagle Report*. At least fifteen prisoners were injured; a police prosecution against one prison officer was dismissed. The government's response was to publish new regulations governing the use of firearms by prison officers (Zdenkowski & Brown 1982, pp. 206-10).

Vinson sought to introduce a means of identifying prison officers that would permit the identification of individual miscreants while preventing fabrication of allegations and the scapegoating of particular officers. Industrial resistance proved too great, however. Prison officer work stoppages became more numerous, and arose not from disputes relating to the traditional concerns of wages and working hours, but from such issues as amenities for prisoners, and prisoner classification and parole decisions (Zdenkowski & Brown 1982, pp. 117-18 and pp. 126-8).

The resulting disruptions to the NSW prisons system created hardships which were borne most heavily by the prisoners themselves. The Vinson era proved to be short-lived. Prison officers, traditionally intolerant of reform, experienced increasing frustration at the pace and direction of the current and anticipated changes to penal administration. Emboldened by the government's reluctance to bring criminal charges against those who were implicated in the abuses at Grafton and Bathurst, they used industrial action to slow the pace of change.

The Wran government, although at the peak of its popularity, saw prison officer strikes as increasingly embarrassing. The government originally endorsed the Nagle blueprint for reform and supported Vinson, but soon withdrew and allowed him to be pilloried. Trivialised media coverage of penal issues, including references to colour television, piped music, and escalating escape rates, reinforced by criticism from opposition benches, elicited the government's fundamental conservatism. Vinson was forced to resign in 1981.

The strategy embraced by Vinson's successor, the use of automatic remissions of sentence and discretionary early release, was designed to facilitate the management of prisoners by providing them with incentives for compliant behaviour. Although some degree of success was achieved, the provisions for release on licence were severely restricted when allegations were made that the then Minister for Corrective Services, Mr Jackson, had accepted payments in return for granting early release to certain prisoners. Mr Jackson was later convicted of criminal charges relating to such allegations and imprisoned.

The institution of an independent inspectorate external to the Department, first proposed over 125 years ago by Sir Henry Parkes and endorsed in 1978 by Mr Justice Nagle, has yet to be implemented. That such a body might have served to lessen mindless industrial confrontation appears to have been lost on the government. A system of official prison visitors, established in the early 1980s, provides a certain degree of external oversight of prison conditions.

Mr Justice Nagle's recommendation for an independent prison ombudsman was similarly rejected by the government. Instead an assistant ombudsman was assigned the responsibility of investigating complaints against the Department. Such a reactive institution, mobilised only in response to complaints received, would appear to be less of a safeguard against departmental malpractice than would an office with proactive powers of unilateral investigation. Even the scrutiny of the assistant ombudsman proved a bit too close for the Department's liking, however. In 1982 the Department requested changes to the ombudsman's legislation, which would prevent the ombudsman's office from inquiring into the allegations against prison officers (Vinson 1982, p. 221). By the mid 1980s these tensions had subsided, and the ombudsman was able to refer to a co-operative relationship between his office and state prison authorities.

A greater degree of industrial peace has also been achieved, in part as a result of more astute management practices. When work stoppages have occurred, the extraordinarily co-operative demeanour of prisoners has enabled senior management to keep the institutions running without major disruption.

In the decade since the *Nagle Report* was published, the general public has become increasingly unsympathetic to the state's prisoners (Brown 1987). The social processes which generate crime and produce offenders are unlikely to abate. As more convicted offenders are sentenced for longer terms, facilities become overcrowded and tensions mount. Whether unrest on the part of prisoners or prison officers will again reach the boiling point remains to be seen. In the event that it does, official misconduct would be inhibited less by departmental safeguards than by the scrutiny of the press, concerned citizens, and by such independent institutions as the ombudsman's office.

*The author is indebted to the previous contributions of Findlay (1982), Nagle (1978), Vinson (1982), Zdenkowski and Brown (1982). Any errors of fact of interpretation remain the author's responsibility.

References

Brown, David 1987, 'Preconditions for Sentencing and Penal Reform in New South Wales: Some Suggestions Towards & Strategy for Contesting an Emerging Law and Order Climate' in *Sentencing in Australia*, ed I. Potas, Australian Institute of Criminology and Australian Law Reform Commission, Canberra, pp. 341-61.

Findlay, Mark 1982, *The State of the Prison: A Critique of Prison Reform*, Mitchellsearch Ltd., Bathurst.

Historical Records of Australia, vol. I, no. 19, Library Committee of the Commonwealth Parliament, p. 654.

New South Wales 1978, *Report of the Royal Commission into New South Wales Prisons*, (Justice J. F. Nagle, Royal Commissioner), Government Printer, Sydney. References are to the reprint (Parliamentary Papers 1976-77-78 No. 322) which consolidates the original three volumes of the Report.

Stein, Paul 1981, 'The New South Wales Royal Commission into Prisons' in *Decisions: Case Studies in Australian Public Policy,* eds S. Encel & P. Wilenski, Longman Cheshire, Melbourne, pp. 206-24.

Vinson, Tony 1982, *Wilful Obstruction*, Methuen Australia, Sydney.

Whitton, E. 1987, *Can of Worms II: A Citizen's Reference Book to Crime and the Administration of Justice*, The Fairfax Library, Sydney.

Zdenkowski, George 1980, 'Judicial Intervention in Prisons', *Monash University Law Review*, vol. 6, no. 4, pp. 294-330.

------------ 1983, 'New South Wales Prisoner Denied Court Access', *Legal Service Bulletin*, vol. 8, no. 2, p. 88.

Zdenkowski, George & Brown, David 1982, *The Prison Struggle: Changing Australia's Penal System,* Penguin Books, Ringwood.

Chapter 3

TELEPHONE TAPPING BY THE
NEW SOUTH WALES POLICE

Norman Allan, a policeman of the old school, served as the
New South Wales Commissioner of Police from 1962 to 1972.
In recognition of his services to the state, Her Majesty the
Queen created him a Companion of the Order of St Michael
and St George.

In his first *Annual Report* after assuming office, Allan's
successor, Fred J. Hanson, paid tribute to the former
Commissioner and highlighted some of the notable advances
that were achieved during the Allan decade.   Amongst
references to substantial increases in police personnel and to
the increased mobility of police resulting from the provision of
additional motor vehicles, there is reference to 'the developing
use of scientific and technical aids in police work' (New South
Wales 1973, p. 5).   It seems unlikely that Commissioner
Hanson was referring to the innovation for which Allan might
best be remembered: the introduction of illegal telephone
interceptions by New South Wales Police.

About midway through his decade as Commissioner,
Allan summoned Sergeant D.R. Williams, a senior technician
serving in the police communications branch, to his office in
downtown Sydney.   Expressing dissatisfaction with such
traditional methods of criminal intelligence gathering as the
use of paid informants, Allan directed his communications
specialist to begin exploring techniques of electronic
surveillance based on listening devices ('bugging') and the
interception of telecommunications ('wiretapping').

Sergeant Williams returned some weeks later with a
prototype device for intercepting telephone calls.   The
Commissioner was pleased, and agreed to the formation of a
small group to work specifically in the area of surveillance
technology.

Initially called the Electronics Section, the group was
placed   under   the   administrative   control   of   the
Communications Branch.   For operational purposes, however,

it came under the control of the Superintendent in Charge of the Criminal Investigation Branch. In 1980, the unit underwent a change of name to 'Technical Support Group'. Two years later, when it became part of the Bureau of Criminal Intelligence, it was given the even more cryptic name of 'Technical Survey Unit'. What the unit did in its various incarnations over sixteen years was engage in illegal wiretapping. By the time they ceased operations, personnel of the unit had undertaken over 200 separate interceptions. However useful the information gleaned from these wiretaps may have been, they were all quite illegal. The fact that the New South Wales Police were themselves engaged in systematic criminal conduct was known not only to the technical specialists themselves, but also to the vast majority, if not all, of the Criminal Investigations Branch, to a senior executive of the New South Wales Police Association, and to five successive commissioners of police.

The system for intercepting telecommunications was refined over the years to become a highly sophisticated operation. The wiretapping devices, small transmitters each about the size of a cigarette packet, were assembled by police technicians from materials available at retail outlets. Police officers, often disguised as Telecom technicians, installed the devices after normal working hours. The officers applied for and were paid overtime for their criminal efforts. They travelled in surplus Telecom vans purchased at auction from the Australian government, and bearing Commonwealth of Australia number plates. The vehicles were registered under false names, using the home addresses of officers in the Technical Support Unit. Official insignia were obtained from Telecom, ostensibly for the purpose of lawful undercover surveillance. The officers carried leather toolbags, specially made facsimiles of those used by Telecom technicians.

The actual interceptions were achieved in one of two ways. The most common involved installing the transmitting device to the appropriate connections in the Telecom wiring pillar on the footpath near the target telephone. Signals from the transmitter were received in a motor vehicle parked unobtrusively nearby. Additional police were stationed in vehicles at nearby vantage points in order to warn the officers installing the intercepts of any risk of detection. Initially recordings were made manually. As technology improved, the receiving device was commonly attached to a voice activated tape recorder. Further developments in technology enabled police to determine the number dialled from the telephone under surveillance.

The second method of interception, known as 'hardwiring' involved the direct wiring of the target telephone to a telephone service in nearby premises rented by the NSW Police. This method was preferred for surveillance over a longer term, or where there was greater risk of detection of the target by surveillance, by neighbourhood residents or by Telecom authorities.

Indeed, Telecom authorities became unwitting accomplices in the criminal enterprise. A list of telephone numbers dialled from the telephone under surveillance was forwarded to Telecom by police along with a request for details of the subscribers to those numbers. Telecom were told that the numbers in question were obtained in the normal course of investigations, not through illegal intercepts.

Mr Justice Stewart, himself a former police officer and not generally unsympathetic to the police and their mission, was stern in his condemnation:

> By all current standards of justice and fairness it is clearly intolerable that persons may be brought to trial as a result of activity of police officers which is flagrantly in breach of the law. Alarming as it may be to acknowledge that convictions for undoubtedly serious offences by major criminals would not otherwise have been achieved without the use of the interception of telephone conversations, it is nevertheless unacceptable by community standards for persons to be apprehended as a result of unlawful conduct by police (Australia 1986a, p. 167).

Although a number of the illegal intercepts were effected for the purpose of investigating unsolved crimes, there appear to have been other more sinister motives. In the words of the Stewart Royal Commission:

The initial interception of the telephone conversations of Ryan was made because of conversations heard during the continued interception of the telephone conversations of Roy Bowers Cessna after his arrest on 14 March 1979. The Commission did not obtain a satisfactory explanation as to why the interception of Cessna's telephone conversations had continued and there is a basis for suspicion that the telephone interception might have been continued in order to ascertain details of Cessna's defence (Australia 1986a, p. 136).

The Stewart Royal Commission observed that the Technical Survey Unit was requested to install an interception device on the telephone service of a Sydney solicitor on 18 March 1979 (Australia 1986a, p. 147). Because of the clandestine nature of these illegal interceptions, there is no record of the reasons which underlay the wiretap request. Police may well have overheard conversations between lawyer and client; if so, they would have violated not only the law, but also one of the fundamental principles of British/Australian justice.

Other interceptions made during the search for escaped prisoner Raymond Denning continued subsequent to his recapture. Mr Justice Stewart was unable to obtain an explanation of these events. Another interception was continued some six weeks after a suspect was charged with an offence relating to drug trafficking.

Article 17 of the International Covenant on Civil and Political Rights, to which Australia is a signatory, states 'no one shall be subjected to arbitrary or unlawful interference with his privacy'. More specifically, the interception of telephone communications, except in narrowly defined circumstances, is a violation of Australian law.

The Telecommunications (Interception) Act 1979 is both explicit and stern:

7(1)   A person shall not -

(a) intercept

(b) authorise, suffer or permit another person to intercept; or

(c) do any act or thing that will enable him or another person to intercept a communication passing over a telecommunications system.

Penalty: $5,000 or imprisonment for 2 years.

7(4) A person shall not divulge or communicate to another person, or make use of a record, any information obtained by intercepting a communication passing over a telecommunications system . . .

The ability to communicate in confidence is one of the basic criteria of a free society. Recognition of the value of privacy in communication is by no means limited to dreamers and romantic idealists. In the words of the Commissioner of the Australian Federal Police:

. . . I have maintained my stance that the preservation of one's right to an expectation of privacy when using the telecommunications system, is of primary importance and not to be lightly cast aside (Australia 1986b, p. 131).

An even more eloquent statement was made over a quarter of a century earlier by the then Attorney-General of Australia, Sir Garfield Barwick. In introducing legislation which deliberately excluded the power from police and customs authorities to intercept telephone communications he said:

Mr Speaker, eavesdropping is abhorrent to us as a people. Not one of us, I am sure, would fail to recoil from the thought that a citizen's privacy could lightly be invaded. Indeed, many citizens no doubt feel that far too many intrusions into our privacy are permitted to be made in these times with complete impunity. Many things which might fairly be regarded as personal and of no public consequence appear in print without the citizen's permission and without his encouragement, but in particular all of us, I think, dislike the feeling that we may be overheard and that what we wish to say may reach ears for which we did not intend the expression of our thought. Much of our normal life depends on the confidence we can repose in those to whom we lay bare our sentiments and opinions, with and through whom we wish to communicate (House of Representatives, *Debates*, vol. 27, 5 May 1960, p. 1423).

During subsequent debate on the same legislation, a Liberal Senator stated the position of the Menzies government:

This Government says that telephone tapping is abhorrent and is contrary to the character and will of the Australian people. We believe that the privacy of citizens should be guarded at all times (Senate, *Debates*, 18 May 1960, p. 1040).

The potential for abuse of electronic surveillance was clear to another Liberal backbencher:

To every fair-minded person in Australia, the idea of eavesdropping or listening in unknown to another's conversation is normally repugnant. The idea of using the forms of interception available over the telephone for purposes such as detection of subversion, crime or offences against our fiscal or tariff legislation is not really acceptable because of the possibility that the innocent remarks of some unfortunate telephone user might be dragged from their context and used against the person, or that advantage might be taken of information obtained by interceptions to the detriment of a person whose conversation was recorded (House of Representatives, *Debates*, vol. 27, 11 May 1960, p. 1613).

The illegal interceptions were not the work of a few 'rotten apples' or 'rogue police'. As was noted, initial impetus for the enterprise came from the Commissioner of Police himself. Not only were the interceptions condoned by five successive Commissioners, but they were common knowledge among experienced detectives and were known to at least one former president of the NSW Police Association.

It is perhaps instructive to contrast the New South Wales situation with that faced by the Victoria Police. Although they too might have benefited from the use of illegal methods in criminal investigation, the Chief Commissioner of the Victoria Police decreed explicitly that his officers were not to engage in illegal wiretapping (Australia 1986a, p. 177).

The cult of secrecy which surrounds policing in Australia explains in part how such a criminal enterprise can persist for so long. Admittedly, policing has traditionally involved an element of stealth. There are aspects of policing which depend for their efficacy on invisibility. But secrecy and mystification carry political advantages as well. Police use these tools to shield themselves from critical scrutiny. They employ them creatively to enhance both their resources and their autonomy.

Governments have shown traditional reluctance to probe too deeply into police affairs. Criticism of governments by police or police associations can be electorally disadvantageous if not fatal. The risk of being accused of political interference in police matters is too great in all but the most obvious crises. It is often convenient to regard abuses of power by police with a knowing blind eye. So it is that police ministers in New South Wales were content to let the police manage their own affairs.

As the criminal enterprise became institutionalised, an element of bureaucratic inertia may also have characterised the persistence of criminal conduct. In the words of one former commissioner:

> Well, this had been a practice before I became Commissioner and so far as I was aware it was being conducted without any complaint as far as any person was concerned . . . I just let the practice continue . . . it did not occur to me to cut it out (quoted in Australia 1986a, p. 116).

The persistence of illegal wiretapping in Sydney was facilitated by the tolerance of other organisations which might otherwise have been in a position to disclose the criminal conduct.

First of these was Telecom Australia, or its predecessor, PMG. As early as 1968, a PMG employee discovered an interception device in a distribution pillar. The device was not removed, and no action was taken by PMG. Again in 1977 a device was found by Telecom employees in a distribution pillar in Sydney's eastern suburbs. Originally assumed to be a bomb, it was subsequently determined by Army Ordnance disposal specialists to have been an interception device. The instrument was then delivered to the Acting Chief Investigating Officer of Telecom, who was soon thereafter contacted by the NSW Police Technical Services Unit. The Telecom official advised the officers that the device was illegal, returned the hardware to them, and warned that it should not happen again. He took no further action.

The Australian Federal Police (AFP), the body responsible for enforcing the Telecommunications (Interception) Act 1979 also manifested considerable nonchalance in the face of apparent criminal conduct. In 1983, another interception device was found by Telecom employees at Bondi. A senior investigator at Telecom informed Superintendent Shepherd, officer in charge of the Bureau of Criminal Intelligence, of the discovery. Shepherd in turn advised that he could be of no assistance. Finding this response unsatisfactory, Telecom authorities referred the matter to the AFP in March 1984, nearly one year after the initial discovery. A report was prepared and forwarded to the Assistant Commissioner (Investigations) which suggested that the device operated at a frequency assigned to state police bureaus of crime intelligence.

Telecom was not advised of the outcome of AFP inquiries until February 1985, when the Assistant Commissioner who commanded the AFP's Eastern Region replied 'Inquiries completed 10 August 1984. No suspect identified, and no information available to assist inquiries further' (quoted in Australia 1986a, p. 233).

Another device found by Telecom workers in 1984 was referred to the AFP for investigation. An internal report

mentioned that it was almost certain that the device 'was
planted by or for a police organisation (the New South Wales
Police Force)' (Australia 1986a, p. 234). In reply to a query
from Telecom, the Assistant Commissioner Commanding the
Eastern Region of the AFP replied 'Inquiries completed 10
August 1984. No suspect identified, and no information
available to assist inquiries further' (Australia 1986a, p. 234).

Even the Commissioner of the AFP, Sir Colin Woods,
was aware that the NSW Police were systematically violating
the laws of Australia. According to one of his deputy
commissioners 'Sir Colin approved the receipt of tape
recordings of conversations obtained but directed that AFP
officers should not themselves carry out the intercepts'
(Australia 1986a, p. 202).

Woods did not testify before the Stewart Royal
Commission, but provided a sworn statement:

> He decided not to launch an investigation into the
> illegal activity because he concluded that there
> would be little likelihood of identifying NSW
> officers involved and because the public interest
> was better served by adopting the course which had
> been recommended to him. He believed that the
> activity was beyond his capacity to influence or
> control and that worthwhile information could be
> gained from the interceptions (quoted in Australia
> 1986a, p. 203).

It might also be argued that the criminal wiretaps, and
much police crime in general, is implicitly encouraged by
Australian courts. Illegally obtained evidence has been
traditionally admissible in Australian courts at the discretion of
the trial judge. Whilst those who obtain such evidence remain
liable to criminal prosecution, seldom, if ever, does this occur.
Meanwhile the fruits of these acts are often accepted.

Australian courts have traditionally taken a lenient
attitude toward police illegality. Their failure to affirm the law
more forcefully may thus be interpreted as a subtle if perhaps
unintentional, invitation to police crime. With neither Telecom
nor the Australian Federal Police inclined further to pursue
the illegal wiretapping matters coming to their attention, the

enterprise might have continued indefinitely. But some of those involved in the illegal interceptions or with access to tapes and transcripts thereof saw an opportunity at the very least to discredit political enemies through selective disclosure of materials. Selectivity was indeed the principle. Although police were aware by means of an illegal intercept that a senior NSW detective had warned a suspected drug dealer, Robert Trimbole, to leave Australia as he would otherwise soon be arrested, no action was taken, lest the existence of illegal intercept operations be disclosed. Trimbole left Australia seven days later.

In 1983, a small number of tape cassettes and 524 pages of ostensible transcriptions of telephone conversations were given to the press. From the publication of *The Age* articles in February 1984 which disclosed existence of illegal telephone intercepts, public attention focused not on the question of criminal activity by the NSW Police, but rather on allegations of improper conduct on the part of Mr Justice Murphy of the High Court of Australia.

At the beginning of February 1984, the Editor of *The Age* delivered copies of tapes and transcripts in his possession to Senator Gareth Evans, then Attorney-General of Australia. On 21 February 1984, Evans appointed the newly appointed Director of Public Prosecutions, Ian Temby Q.C., to be Special Prosecutor under the provisions of the *Special Prosecutors Act 1982* (Cwlth).

A set of *The Age* materials was also delivered to the Attorney-General of New South Wales, who referred it to the state Solicitor-General for advice. She recommended that state police be requested to co-operate with Federal police in any subsequent investigations, and that state police be disciplined should it be established that they were involved in any unlawful telephone interceptions.

In September 1984 the Stewart Royal Commission of Inquiry into Drug Trafficking requested that the New South Wales police supply details of telephone interceptions conducted during the period January 1980 to June 1981, including the names of those personnel who may have been involved in the operations. A number of serving and retired officers were interviewed, all of whom denied any knowledge of the interception of telephone conversations.

With *The Age* disclosures, a cover-up of substantial proportions was arranged within the New South Wales Police. Fearing the eventual mobilisation of the Federal Police and the execution of a search warrant, officers of the Bureau of Criminal Intelligence and the Technical Survey Unit located and destroyed all tapes and transcripts in their possession, as well as the equipment used in the intercepts.

Following the appointment of the Special Prosecutor, Superintendent Shepherd decided that the Technical Survey Unit would cease its interceptions immediately.

In conjunction with the Special Prosecutor's investigations, the then Commissioner of Police, Mr Abbott, initiated an investigation by a Special Task Force comprised primarily of officers from the New South Wales Police Internal Affairs Branch. The officer in charge of the NSW police team was Executive Chief Superintendent J.M. Pry. Past and present members of the Technical Survey Unit met on a number of occasions to co-ordinate their response to future investigations. Prominent in this effort was Mr Shepherd, the Superintendent in Charge of the Bureau of Criminal Intelligence. According to the Stewart Royal Commission, on one occasion:

> Shepherd addressed the meeting and suggested that the officers involved in such activity should deny any involvement when interviewed by the investigators of the Special Task Force. Those present agreed (Australia 1986a, p. 124).

Later in the year, some 50 past and present members of the Technical Survey Unit and the Bureau of Criminal Intelligence were told by Shepherd that they should deny involvement.

> According to one BCI officer who was present, Shepherd used words to the effect that telephones were not intercepted, intercepts did not exist and no person in this room knows of the existence of any material. This meeting has not occurred (Australia 1986a, p. 125).

The wall of silence was maintained, at least initially. On 29 March 1984 Shepherd wrote to the Head of the Special Task Force:

> I am not aware of any police officers or public service member in New South Wales or elsewhere in Australia who has been involved in the obtaining of illegal taped telephone conversations or in the preparation of transcriptions from illegally obtained tape recorded conversations (quoted in Australia 1986a, p. 335).

The Special Task Force failed to live up to the name of its Officer in Charge. A number of retired former members of the Bureau of Criminal Intelligence and Technical Survey Unit refused to be interviewed. Those who consented to interviews, and those currently serving police who were compelled to make statements, all denied any knowledge of telephone interceptions. The Commonwealth Director of Public Prosecutions estimated that up to forty police officers gave false evidence to the Pry inquiry (Jinks 1987, p. 15).

Superintendent Pry's convoluted response to this state of affairs reflected something less than the zeal he might be expected to show in dealing with criminal suspects outside the police force. Pry recommended that:

> in view of the insufficiency of conclusive evidence enabling a precise identification of the author of the transcriptions or creator of the tapes from which the transcripts were made or even to establish a reasonable presumption, quite apart from a conclusive presumption, of the person or persons responsible for the subject material, particularly in the absence of any admission by any person of being so involved in the making or obtaining of the tapes and/or transcriptions, no further action be taken in respect of any member of the New South Wales Police Force, or former member of the New South Wales Police Force (quoted in Australia 1986a, p. 255).

In late November 1984 a firm of solicitors acting for a number of currently serving and retired NSW police officers, advised the Stewart Royal Commission that co-operation would be forthcoming if they received formal assurances they would not be prosecuted or face internal disciplinary action. In an effort to induce police to overcome their reluctance to disclose any information about the illegal wiretapping program, Mr Justice Stewart recommended to the Attorney-General of Australia that potential witnesses be indemnified against prosecution.

At first, the Director of Public Prosecutions disagreed, and opposed granting of indemnities, but the federal government was under some pressure to authenticate those materials which made the basis for allegations of improper judicial conduct. The federal and New South Wales governments finally agreed to shield the individual officers from prosecution which could result from their evidence to the Royal Commission. The Commissioner of Police gave undertakings which contained immunities from internal disciplinary action as well. In March 1985, the Governor-General of Australia issued letters patent to Justice Stewart to inquire specifically into the alleged telephone interceptions. Complementary letters patent were issued by the Governors of Victoria and New South Wales.

The Stewart Royal Commission produced a report in two volumes, the second of which remained confidential in order not to jeopardise the ongoing investigation of various criminal matters.

The report, at least the published volume of the report, is an unusual document. It provides a fascinating account of the history and methods of illegal telephone interceptions by NSW Police. On the one hand, it condemns the criminal conduct which it so carefully described:

> Members of the NSW Police who were guilty of breaking the law over a period of years, refused to tell the truth about what they had done unless they were indemnified. Indeed not only did they refuse to co-operate with investigating authorities, but they deliberately and falsely denied knowledge of

the illegal interceptions and covered up their illegal activities . . .

Police officers are sworn, however, to uphold the law - not just laws of which they approve. There can be no justification for their having taken the law into their own hands (Australia 1986a, pp. 337-8).

That said, the Report goes to considerable length to extol the virtue of telephone interception as a technique of criminal investigation. Indeed, Mr Justice Stewart found the fruits of the illegal operation so valuable, that he recommended they be turned over to the National Crime Authority, of which he happened to be Chairman, for further analysis and investigation. He went on to recommend that powers to intercept telecommunications be extended to state and territory police forces, as well as to the National Crime Authority.

Meanwhile, allegations arose suggesting that Mr Justice Stewart was so impressed with some of the NSW police officers who gave evidence to the Royal Commission that they were offered positions with the National Crime Authority. The Chairman of the Joint Parliamentary Committee on the National Crime Authority 'recorded, on public policy grounds, the Committee's disquiet at the proposition of employing police who had received indemnities to give evidence before the Royal Commission' (Australia 1986b, p. 12).

The *Stewart Report* met with an enthusiastic reception from a number of quarters. The Attorney-General of Australia quickly introduced legislation to extend wiretap powers to state and territory police departments for all offences carrying prison terms of at least seven years. Although welcomed by state police associations generally, the idea was sufficiently controversial that the matter was referred to a Joint Select Committee of Federal Parliament. By the end of 1986, the Committee was inclined to authorise some interceptions for the purpose of state investigations, but only by agents of the federal government and under extremely strict conditions.

The Committee concluded that whilst state and territory police forces and the National Crime Authority might have a need for information gleaned through telecommunications interception, the potential for abuse would be minimised if the intercepts were made on behalf of these agencies by a telecommunications interception unit within the Australian Federal Police, working through Telecom.

Under the Committee's recommendations, a warrant, issued by a judge of the Federal Court of Australia, would be necessary before any interception could be made. Warrants would be limited to circumstances where other investigative techniques had either been exhausted, or deemed in the circumstances to have been inappropriate. In addition, warrants would only be issued on reasonable grounds for suspecting that the nominated telephone service was being used by a person suspected of committing or conspiring to commit a specified serious offence, and that the interception would materially assist in the investigation. The specified offences would be limited to murder, kidnapping and serious drug trafficking.

Applications for warrants would identify the officer seeking the warrant, and would specify the time for which an interception is sought. Under the Committee's proposal, accountability of interceptions would be enhanced by regular and independent judicial auditing. Severe penalties would be imposed on offenders engaged in illegal interception and unlawful disclosure of information obtained from legal interceptions. The possession, importation, manufacture, sale or advertising of interception devices would be made illegal.

It appeared that the criminal activities of Australian police were on the verge of being rewarded by the grant of increased powers. Whether this apparent success will tempt police to try their luck with other illegal methods remains to be seen.

Meanwhile, illegal telephone interceptions by persons unknown continue to be discovered by Telecom authorities. The Joint Select Committee reported that sixteen illegal interception devices had come to the attention of Telecom during the 1985-86 year. Seven of these were located in Queensland.

A complaint arising from the initial cover-up of the illegal interceptions was lodged with the New South Wales Ombudsman against Mr Shepherd, who had since become

Assistant Commissioner in charge of internal affairs. Under New South Wales law, the Ombudsman was precluded from conducting investigations of police complaints in the first instance. Initial investigatory responsibility lay with the Commissioner of Police. In a letter to the Ombudsman dated 21 July 1986, defending Mr Shepherd's unswerving dedication and integrity, the Commissioner urged that the Ombudsman consent to discontinuing the investigation.

In August 1987, the New South Wales Director of Public Prosecutions advised the state Attorney-General that the legally admissible evidence did not disclose an offence under state law. He did herald, however, the possibility of federal criminal charges. The following month, the federal Director of Public Prosecutions, Ian Temby, Q.C. advised that because of the indemnities granted and other evidential difficulties, he would not lay criminal charges against Assistant Commissioner Shepherd, either in respect of the illegal telephone interceptions or the subsequent misleading remarks to Executive Chief Superintendent Pry. Mr Temby took pains to register his disapproval of the alleged misconduct:

> I do not, however, consider that what was done by Mr Shepherd is in any way excusable. It is my strong view that disciplinary action should be taken against him if he in fact misled superior officers (Jinks 1987, p. 18).

The Commissioner of Police continued to seek the Ombudsman's consent to discontinue the investigation. He reaffirmed an intention stated in his July, 1986 letter:

> if the force of circumstances were to cause the preferment of charges I would, in the spirit of the undertakings and in the exercise of my discretion, decline to impose any penalties, or at least to impose the most nominal of penalties (Jinks 1987, pp. 9-10).

It thus appeared that continued litigation with the Police Commissioner would have little useful effect.

In November 1987, the Acting Ombudsman consented, with some reluctance, to the discontinuance of the investigation. In a report to Parliament he observed:

> Police officers who are the subject of Internal Affairs Branch investigations are required to answer questions truthfully. Specifically, Police Rule 11(F) casts the following duty on a member of the Police Force:
>
> > (f) he shall at all times exercise the strictest honesty and truthfulness, and in particular he shall not -
> >
> > > (i) wilfully or negligently make any false, misleading or incorrect statement;
> > >
> > > (ii) knowingly make or sign any false statement in any official document, record or book; or
> > >
> > > (iii) without good and sufficient cause, destroy or mutilate any official document, record or book, or alter or erase any entry therein.

The Rule has the force of law and makes no distinction as to rank (Jinks 1987, pp. 23-4).

In a concluding paragraph, the Acting Ombudsman referred to Assistant Commissioner Shepherd's current responsibilities:

> The Assistant Commissioner (Review) is responsible for the investigation of unethical conduct by police.
>
> The officer who holds that position should be, and be seen to be, above reproach. If that is not the

case ordinary police officers and members of the public might reasonably consider that there was a double standard. Further, the Assistant Commissioner (Review) should be expected to set a standard for officers of the Internal Affairs Branch and the Internal Security Unit. Those officers should not be left with the dangerous assumption that the end justifies the means (Jinks 1987, p. 27).

Elsewhere, other types of electronic surveillance continued, beyond the inclination of Australian governments to control. A Queensland solicitor claimed that an interview he had conducted with a client was recorded by police, transcribed, and presented to prosecuting authorities. In September 1986, a justice of the Supreme Court of Queensland described the police conduct as 'reprehensible' (Australia 1986c, p. 165).

References

Australia 1986a, *Royal Commission of Inquiry into Alleged Telephone Interceptions: Report - Volume One* (Mr Justice D.G. Stewart), Australian Government Publishing Service, Canberra.

Australia 1986b, *Parliament, Joint Committee on the National Crime Authority, Second Report*, Australian Government Publishing Service, Canberra.

Australia 1986c, *Report of the Joint Select Committee on Telecommunications Interception*, The Parliament of the Commonwealth of Australia, Canberra.

House of Representatives, *Debates*, vol. 27, 11 May 1960, p. 1423.

ibid, p. 1613.

Jinks, Brian 1987, Special Report to Parliament Under Section 31 of the *Ombudsman Act* and Under Section 32 of the *Police Regulation (Allegations of Misconduct) Act 1978.* Decision to consent to the discontinuation of an investigation of complaints concerning the conduct of Assistant Commissioner (Review) R.C. Shepherd of the New South Wales Police Force. New South Wales Ombudsman's Office, Sydney.

New South Wales 1973, *Report of the Police Department for 1972*, Government Printer, Sydney.

Senate, *Debates*, 18 May 1960, p. 1040.

Chapter 4

THE STRANGE CONFESSION OF BARRY MANNIX

In the early hours of 22 June 1984, Kevin Mannix met a horrible death. He had been bound, gagged, blindfolded and was carried from his Gold Coast unit for reasons which were not immediately clear when his body was discovered. In the course of his abduction, Mannix managed to free one hand, and to remove part of the adhesive tape covering his mouth. When he uttered a cry for help, he was thrown bodily down the flight of stairs leading from the unit, his head striking a concrete pillar. Mannix was stabbed numerous times in the chest, and his throat cut. It was a particularly brutal murder.

The nature of the crime and the background of its victim were to attract considerable attention. Mannix was the proprietor of a sex shop across the New South Wales border in Tweed Heads. He was a well-known purveyor of erotic literature, videos and assorted paraphernalia, and a producer of occasional strip-shows, who had previously been the subject of minor prosecutions on charges relating to obscene publications.

Detectives from the Broadbeach Criminal Investigation Branch, Queensland Police, began their inquiries the morning of 22 June. But the detectives had a difficult time, as the motive for the killing was not immediately apparent, and there were no obvious suspects. The days wore on without anyone having been charged. After more than ten days had passed, the inspector in charge of the Queensland Police Homicide Squad arrived from Brisbane with a senior detective to check on the progress of the investigation.

The suspicions of investigating detectives soon focused on the victim's son, Barry, who had initially notified police that he discovered his father's corpse outside the block of units. Barry had appeared remarkably composed when police had arrived at the scene of the crime. He reported having returned to his father's unit shortly after midnight on 22 June finding it unlocked with the lights on. The television set and room heater were both on as well. The father's coin collection was scattered on the floor.

Barry Mannix told police that he did not regard this situation as suspicious and he assumed that his father had gone out. Barry, who had been working at his father's sex shop, said that on returning to his father's unit, he watched television briefly, then fell asleep and discovered his father's body the next morning when he awoke and went out on the balcony of the unit to check the condition of the surf.

Barry's unusual behaviour before and after notifying the police aroused suspicion enough. Investigators also learned that Barry had arranged for the removal of a pistol belonging to his father from the crime scene shortly before police arrived. On 6 July 1984, Barry Mannix was asked to accompany detectives to the Broadbeach CIB office. He went willingly.

The techniques of interrogating a person suspected of having committed a crime have evolved considerably from ancient practices of ordeal by fire. No longer is it regarded as acceptable to use or threaten physical force to coerce a suspect to confess. The practice of 'verballing' - fabricating a confession and attributing it to a suspect - is similarly frowned upon, at least officially.

In order to maintain a psychological advantage over a suspect, interrogators do not encourage consultation with family, friends or legal counsel. They seek to convey the impression that they know more about the suspect's involvement in the alleged offence than they actually do. Interrogation over a prolonged period is designed to weaken a suspect's defences. Upon occasion, interrogators may resort to methods of deceit or guile which might not be considered appropriate in conventional social discourse. The language which they employ tends to depart from standards of polite formality.

After intermittent interrogation over the following twelve hours, during which, he later alleged, he was neither free to leave the police station nor permitted to contact his mother, Barry Mannix signed two written confessions to having murdered his father. At 1.48 a.m. he was charged with his father's murder. When his mother arrived at the station his first words to her were 'I want you to know I didn't do it'.

Barry Mannix was taken to the Southport Watchhouse for the weekend, and on Monday 9 July 1984 was moved to Her Majesty's Prison Brisbane. On 20 July 1984 he appeared before Mr O'Connell SM, in Southport Magistrate's Court and was remanded to 10 September for committal proceedings. On 15 October 1984, Mannix was committed for trial. But before the trial commenced the case took a strange turn. On 7 November 1984, another person was being questioned by police about a stolen car. Burdened with guilt, he confessed to being a party to the murder of Kevin Mannix. In doing so, he implicated three accomplices - none of whom was Barry Mannix.

Three of the suspects were arrested on 8 November, and the fourth surrendered a few days later. One had been a former employee of Kevin Mannix, and had felt that he had not received a fair share of the strip-show profits. The four had intended to abduct Mannix and to rob his home and sex shop. On 15 November, Barry Mannix lodged a complaint with the Police Complaints Tribunal of Queensland. The following day he applied for bail and was released from custody. On 6 December 1984, the Attorney-General of Queensland filed a 'No True Bill' in the Mannix case, and Barry, fearing that he might become a target for police harassment, fled to New Zealand.

In his complaint to the Tribunal, Barry Mannix alleged that he confessed only after police threatened to charge other members of the family with the murder.

Referring to one detective's questions, Barry Mannix testified:

> Then he started saying that my parents were both 'evil' and told me that if I don't give them a statement of what happened, that he would lock my mother up with me and if my grandparents knew anything about it they would be locked up as well and then my brother and sister would spend the rest of their lives in foster homes. They also said that my mother would be charged with accessory to murder and I would be charged as well if I didn't make a statement. After that they said they were going to bring in the photos of my

father's autopsy and I just kept on saying 'no, don't,
I don't want to see them.' (quoted in Queensland
1986, p. 14).

He further alleged physical abuse at the hands of police.
Referring to the conduct of one detective, he alleged.

He told me the CIB were fed up with my lying and
he started asking me how I did it and why and
when I told him that I knew nothing about it, he
slammed his fist on the table, got up and grabbed
me by the hair at the back of the head and pulled
his other hand in a clenched fist up to his side and
said: 'I ought to smash you right in the face you
shithead' (quoted in Queensland 1986, p. 13).

The Mannix case was hardly the first occasion in
Queensland in which police investigative practices had been
called into question. Indeed, disclosures by a police constable
in 1975 that a substantial portion of the evidence in one case
had been concocted by police gave rise to a wide ranging
judicial inquiry into police practices.

Anyone whose goals are thwarted by legal technicalities
is likely to become impatient. There are those police who
embrace an ideology which holds that the ends of policing
justify the means. There are others, for whom policing is
simply a way to make a living. As is the case with ordinary
citizens, the inconveniences of life often tempt one to cut
corners.

Few laypersons can appreciate the frustration which
police experience when they have identified a person whom
they are virtually certain of having committed an offence but
lack sufficient evidence to lay charges. Such frustration may be
particularly acute amongst those police who view their work
not in terms of adventure, professional advancement,
gamesmanship or intellectual challenge, but rather in terms of
a crusade against evil.

The Lucas Inquiry, as it came to be called, found
evidence of assaults on suspects, planting of evidence, forgery
of warrants and fabrication of confessions by police on a
significant scale. Its most significant recommendation called

for the routine mechanical recording of interrogations conducted by police in all cases involving indictable offences. (Queensland 1977, p. iv). The proposal met with resistance from the Queensland Police and was not implemented.

There seems little doubt that Broadbeach detectives were under some pressure to solve the Mannix murder. Given the rather lurid background of the victim, and the gruesome nature of his death, there was more than casual public interest in the case. But nearly a fortnight after the death, there was still no arrest. The presence of senior homicide detectives from Brisbane would appear to have created greater pressure on Broadbeach detectives to produce an arrest.

Various features of police performance in the case were later criticised as unsatisfactory. The Police Complaints Tribunal called attention to the extent of detail disclosed to the media shortly after police arrived at the crime scene. This included a summary of Barry Mannix' initial account of the events of the previous evening, and a description of the victim's injuries. The tribunal report criticised the degree of detail as likely to inhibit police in catching offenders or perhaps to invite false confessions by attention seekers (Queensland 1986, p. 122).

The investigation of a major crime is a very significant police operation, which can involve dozens of officers. It is, of course, important that these resources be deployed efficiently and effectively and that the efforts of all those involved be co-ordinated. Information gathered in the course of a large-scale investigation must be systematically organised and regularly assessed. Each individual investigator should conduct his or her own particular inquiries with an appreciation of the overall direction of the case. To this end, periodic conferences are held to permit a free exchange of views and suggestions.

A few years earlier the Queensland police had developed a system, termed 'The Major Incident Room Recording Structure', for organising large-scale investigations. In the Mannix case, this system appears not to have been fully implemented. Until the arrival of senior detectives from Brisbane, the local officer leading the investigation was still required to perform normal duties, and was thus unable to devote his undivided attention to the Mannix case.

The investigation was criticised as having lacked guidance and supervision, particularly in its early stages. The first forty-eight hours of a murder investigation are almost always the crucial period. In fact, one of the actual perpetrators of the murder did come to the attention of detectives early on. His name was mentioned in a statement taken from a former employee of the deceased. But through a shortcoming of the investigation, a file was not prepared in his name and this individual was not interviewed.

Police were also criticised for not placing a senior detective in charge of the investigation at the outset.

> In the MANNIX murder investigation, the Incident Room Personnel did not have sufficient rank to ensure that they were able to perform their task with total co-operation. We believe that, in future major investigations, the co-ordinator should be at the Commissioned Officer level, where his requirements are more likely to be met without any dispute of his authority (Queensland 1986, p. 124).

According to the tribunal this inadequate co-ordination made for a certain lack of enthusiasm and efficiency on the part of detectives.

> We found that many of the detectives involved in the case had little knowledge of the workings of the recording structure. Consequently, some detectives interviewed actually expressed a preference for making inquiries rather than preparing or filling out Job Logs. This attitude demonstrates the general lack of appreciation of the system and perhaps highlights the need for more support staff. We believe that every detective should have some working knowledge of the system and its importance. If any detective shows a reluctance to accept this system and fails to familiarise himself with it, he should perhaps be moved to another branch of the service (Queensland 1986, p. 124).

The officer in charge of Broadbeach CIB was also criticised for having been absent from CIB offices on the night that Barry Mannix was being interrogated 'to supervise the considerable operation that was taking place a short distance from his office involving so many detectives ostensibly under his control' (Queensland 1986, p. 123). The tribunal found fault with his managerial practices from the outset of the investigation:

> He did not check to see whether the Recording Structure was being kept up. When interviewed by us, he still did not know whether it had been kept up. Apart from several directions which he gave at the scene on 22 June, 1984 he seems to have played no part in the investigation. He claimed to us that his was a supervisory role. Since the very thing the investigations seemed to lack at the early stage was guidance and supervision, this caused us some concern (Queensland 1986, p. 123).

Further supervisory shortcomings were noted when it was observed that diaries had not been subject to regular inspection by supervising officers, if at all.

The Queensland Police Tribunal was established in 1982 in response to public dissatisfaction surrounding the objectivity of internal investigations of complaints against the Queensland Police. Its Chairman, Judge Eric Pratt of the Queensland District Court, and a former policeman himself, was a close personal friend of both Police Commissioner Lewis, and the Minister for Police, Bill Gunn.

The complaint lodged by Barry Mannix at the time of his release from prison, alleged six breaches of the Queensland Criminal Code on the part of investigating officers: conspiracy to pervert the course of justice; unlawful deprivation of liberty; assault; the use of threat to compel a confession to murder; fabrication of evidence; and perjury. The investigation by the Police Complaints Tribunal lasted fifteen months. The Tribunal examined sixty-five witnesses including the complainant Barry Mannix, who was interviewed in New Zealand over a five-day period.

The report by the Police Complaints Tribunal released in March 1986 is, to say the least, a most unusual document. Immediately following the table of contents is a full page colour photograph of the complainant taken at the time of his arrest - a 'mug shot'. Among the fifty-one other photographs in the report are those of the complainant's father's corpse, including close-ups of the wounds suffered. Others include a number of striptease performers - employees of the deceased - as well as a photograph of the deceased's mistress.

The Tribunal took an extremely narrow approach to the Mannix complaint. In the words of the Report: '[O]ur primary duty was to ascertain the existence or absence of evidence sufficient to launch and sustain prosecutions of police officers for the offences alleged, or any offence (Queensland 1986, p. 6). The basic issue addressed by the Tribunal in its report, was whether a prosecution could succeed based on the admissible evidence available. The Tribunal concluded that it could not, because of numerous inconsistencies in the testimony of the complainant.

The report offered no explanation, or even speculation, of why Barry Mannix confessed to having murdered his father. It deals only briefly with the testimony of those police who were the subject of Barry Mannix's complaints: 'All Police Officers to whom any of BARRY MANNIX'S complaints could possibly relate have been carefully examined. Each stoutly denies any knowledge of or participation in any of the behaviour alleged.' (Queensland 1986, p. 96).

The report goes to great lengths to show how the police might have been justified in suspecting Barry Mannix of culpability in his father's death. In so doing, it paints a rather unflattering picture of the complainant and his character. One entire chapter was devoted to the question of whether the complainant knew one of the men eventually implicated in the murder who, as it happened, preceded him by two years in high school.

Another entire chapter was devoted to a band named the 'Ultra Deviates', of which the complainant was a member. The chapter contained a gratuitous discussion of the band's lack of artistic achievements, noting that at one engagement at a Sydney hotel, the band was booed off the stage. The relevance of these disclosures, not to mention that of the lurid photographs scattered throughout the report, to the alleged misconduct of Queensland detectives, is unclear. One assumes that the purpose of these digressions was to demonstrate that the complainant would not have been a credible Crown witness in any proceedings against members of the Queensland Police. The report dwelled extensively on contradictions and inaccuracies in the complainant's statements, and reprinted sixty pages of transcript of Barry Mannix's testimony to the Tribunal. It concluded: 'It is clear that we have discovered a large body of convincing evidence that is available to be led by the Defence in the event that any police officer is charged with an offence arising from these allegations'. (Queensland 1986, p. 114).

The report proposed nothing in the way of remedy or compensation for Barry Mannix. Indeed, it appeared to equate his misfortune with that of the Queensland Police:

> The fact is that the system has allowed the incarceration in prison for some four months of a lad innocent of the charge on which he was being held. BARRY MANNIX has been hurt by his incarceration just as the investigating police have been hurt by the subsequent strain of having to undergo our exhaustive investigation (Queensland 1986, p. 117).

In addition to suggestions regarding the staffing and supervision of major investigations, the Tribunal's major recommendation was to introduce a 'wider system of recording that which transpires between police and suspected persons at important interviews' (Queensland, 1986, p. 117). Thus the Tribunal merely echoed recommendations of the Lucas Inquiry of some years previous regarding the sound or video recording of interrogations.

The Tribunal's report was criticised in Queensland Parliament as a whitewash, and was the subject of a critical report on the ABC's '4 Corners' program. In response to these criticisms, the Queensland Police Minister declared that he was entirely satisfied with the report of the Tribunal and that the case was closed. According to the Vice-President of the Queensland Police Union, the six detectives who had been involved in the Mannix murder investigation, were prepared to take legal action over potentially defamatory allegations in the aftermath of the report. As the Union official said: 'The detectives have been monitoring media coverage of the reaction to the report very closely' (*Telegraph*, 25 March 1986).

Two men were convicted of the murder of Kevin Mannix and sentenced to life imprisonment. Their two accomplices pleaded guilty to manslaughter and were sentenced to six years each.

Barry Mannix changed his name by deed-poll and left the Gold Coast. In a media interview his mother said 'what frightens me is that it is true what the public says - you can't win against the police'.

One wonders, in light of Barry Mannix' experience, whether other Queenslanders might be inhibited from lodging complaints against police, or whether they might choose instead to suffer in silence.

The Queensland Government continued to express its support for the Police Complaints Tribunal and its practices. The Chairman of the Police Complaints Tribunal, Judge Eric Pratt, did not seek reappointment to the Police Complaints Tribunal at the conclusion of his term. Toward the end of 1988, the Queensland Government announced that it would introduce videotaping of police questioning of suspects in due course.

References

Queensland 1977, *Report of Committee of Inquiry into the Enforcement of Criminal Law in Queensland*, (Lucas Report), Government Printers, Brisbane.

Queensland 1986, *Report by Police Complaints Tribunal: Barry James Mannix*, Police Complaints Tribunal, Brisbane.

(Brisbane) *Telegraph*, 25 March 1986.

Chapter 5

AN ABORIGINAL DEATH IN CUSTODY:
THE CASE OF JOHN PAT

The town of Roebourne, Western Australia, is hardly a major tourist attraction. Situated 1200 km north of Perth in the Pilbara Region, it lies in the traditional lands of the Ngarluma people. White settlement dates back to the arrival of pastoralists in 1864. Roebourne remained an obscure country town, with modest economic links to nearby pearling and mining industries. It was substantially effected by the mining boom of the 1960s, which saw the town of Karratha, some 40 km distant, become the regional centre. By the early 1980s Roebourne had a population of some 1200, of whom approximately two-thirds were of Aboriginal descent.

The Aboriginal community of Roebourne was afflicted by the social disorganisation which characterises many Aboriginal towns. Mining development in the Pilbara brought an influx to the area of hard-drinking single white men. In the words of one observer:

> Many Aboriginal men lost the women they had been destined to marry since birth; ancient Aboriginal laws and customs were shattered by conflict and alcohol.

> Though they proudly called themselves Aboriginal, many of the young people in Roebourne are the unacknowledged children of white mine workers (Mayman 1984).

There is little gainful employment or recreational opportunity for young people in Roebourne. The centre of the town's cultural life is the Victoria Hotel. Its two bars are traditionally segregated by race - the saloon bar for whites, the 'armpit' for blacks. It would be an understatement to characterise either place as anything less than rough; the Victoria Hotel is not the place to go for a quiet drink.

On 28 September 1983, four police officers and an Aboriginal police aide returned to Roebourne from a police union meeting at Karratha. They were off duty, and had each drunk six or seven glasses of beer at the Karratha Golf Club. Upon their return to Roebourne, they called in at the Victoria.

One local Aboriginal, Ashley James, claims he was threatened by one of the off-duty police when he sought to make a purchase at the hotel's bottle shop. A hotel barmaid later testified that police swore at James and threatened to get him when he left the hotel: "'We'll get you, you black cunt . . . " and they just started yelling and acting like idiots' (Western Australia 1984, p. 498). James himself later testified that one of the police subsequently accosted him outside on the footpath, and told him to 'get fucked'. James then claimed that he fought back, and was then attacked by the other police (Western Australia 1984, pp. 682-6). A general melee ensued, with Aborigines and police trading punches. A sixteen-year-old Aboriginal youth, John Pat, joined the fray, and according to witnesses, was struck in the face by a policeman and fell backward, striking his head hard on the roadway (Western Australia 1984, p. 883).

According to witnesses, one of the off-duty police went over to Pat and kicked him in the head. Pat was then allegedly dragged to a waiting police van, kicked in the face, and thrown in 'like a dead kangaroo' (Western Australia 1984, p. 875).

Pat and three other Aborigines were driven to the Roebourne police station. Observers across the street from the station alleged that the Aborigines were systematically beaten as they were taken from the police van. One after another, the prisoners were dragged from the van and dropped on the cement pathway. Each was picked up, punched to the ground, and kicked. According to one observer, none of the prisoners fought back or resisted (Western Australia 1984, pp. 51-7 and pp. 120-3).

One of the prisoners described his experience in response to a barrister's questions:

Who grabbed you by the arms?...... Constable Jock.

Were you still in the van or were you out of the van when you were grabbed by the arms?...... Out.

Did anything happen after Constable Jock grabbed you by the arms?...... Yeah.

What happened?...... Constable Steve started punching me in the guts.

Where was he when he did that?...... At the police station.

Where was he in relation to you? Was he side, front, back, or what?...... Back.

Who else was with you when Constable Steve started punching you in the guts?...... Constable Jock.

You told us that he had hold of you by the arms. Can you tell us, please, whether he still had hold of you by the arms when you were punched in the guts, or not?...... Yeah.

What effect did that have on you?...... Pardon?

What happened to you when you were punched in the guts?...... I fell down on the ground.

Did anything else happen after you were down on the ground?...... I just seen the boot, boots, coming up to my eyes.

You saw what?...... Boots.

Coming up to your eyes?...... Yeah.

Did you see who was wearing the boots?...... No.

You saw the boots coming up to your eyes. What happened?...... They kicked me in the eye and the guts (Western Australia 1984, pp. 192-3).

One witness from across the street said she could hear the sound of loud blows, and 'come on, fight, you bastard'. 'I thought the police had gone mad' she was later quoted as saying (Lang 1984).

One of the prisoners said he had spent a week in hospital as a result of his injuries. Another said his head had been slammed repeatedly on the concrete until he passed out. John Pat, however, was less fortunate.

He was taken to the police lockup, and a little over an hour later, when police sought to check on him, he was dead. A subsequent autopsy revealed a fractured skull, haemorrhage and swelling as well as bruising and tearing, of the brain. Pat had sustained a number of massive blows to the head. One bruise at the back of his head was the size of the palm of one's hand; another, above his right ear, was perhaps half that size. Five other bruises were visible on the right side of the head. In addition to the head injuries, he had two broken ribs and a torn aorta, the major blood vessel leading from the heart. The autopsy also showed that the dead youth had had a blood alcohol reading of .222.

The death of John Pat was but a recent chapter in the history of bad relations between police and Aborigines in Western Australia. Controlling the Aboriginal population was perhaps the central task of the Western Australian Police during the early colonial period. Indeed, enforcing the system of indentured servitude which prevailed during the mid-19th century was an important function. To this end, police were vested with wide powers of arrest without warrant (Bolton 1981).

Increasing contact between the races, and growing availability of alcohol to Aboriginal people increased white authorities' inclination to control the behaviour of natives. Today, no less than in earlier years, Aborigines, who constitute less than 3 per cent of Western Australia's population, comprise one-third of the state's prisoners. One recent census of prisoners showed that on a given day, one out of every twelve male Aborigines in Western Australia between the ages of 19 and 29 was in prison (Mukherjee & Scandia 1988).

Police are traditionally loath to discuss the specific considerations which underlie the allocation of their resources. The fact that they respond more vigorously to public drunkenness by Aborigines than to domestic violence in white society suggests something about their priorities. Roebourne, by any standard, appears to have been characterised by saturation policing. In 1983 eight officers and two police aides were stationed in the town. The nearby 'white' town of Wickham had half as many police for twice the population. Indeed, the regional centre, Karratha, with a population of over 8,000 had only fourteen officers.

Nor were Roebourne police content to sit idly by. There was an almost constant police presence in and around the Aboriginal bar at the Victoria Hotel. The power of arrest for public drunkenness was exercised freely - recent years' totals approached 2,000 annually - nearly three arrests for every Aboriginal man, woman and child in the town.

Even if such scrutiny arises from the noblest of motives (a very questionable assumption) there can be little doubt that this style of policing is counterproductive. For 150 years, police were regarded as agents of oppression. They had come to be perceived as upholding one law for whites and one for blacks. In such a setting, the overbearing presence of police can contribute to an offence where none is imminent. Relatively minor incidents may escalate as a result of police involvement.

The history of abysmal relations between police and Aborigines in Western Australia is long and bleak. Punitive expeditions involving what amounted to summary execution have been documented well into the twentieth century (Western Australia 1927). In January 1975, a group of Western Desert people en route to ceremonies sought to travel through the town of Laverton. At Skull Creek, on the outskirts of town, they were intercepted by police who arrested most if not all of the able-bodied men in the group. A Royal Commission concluded that the arrests were unjustified and that much of the evidence given by police in subsequent court proceedings had been fabricated (Western Australia 1975-76).

Discriminatory treatment in the arrest and prosecution of Aboriginal Western Australians has also been documented (Eggleston 1976). At Roebourne, in contrast to the nightly arrests at the Aboriginal bar of the Victoria Hotel, a former barmaid related that despite occasional fights involving flying jugs, tables and chairs in the saloon bar, she recalled only one arrest of a white customer.

It is hardly original to suggest that traditionally, police in Australia had been recruited more on the basis of their physical bulk than on their skills in human relations. Whatever the case in Western Australia, serious questions were raised about the adequacy of police training in Aboriginal affairs and in their relations with indigenous peoples. A formal training program began in 1975, and involved police recruits attending lectures by anthropologists, officers of the Department of Aboriginal Affairs, and senior police. When it was established, the program involved ten lectures in the course of a thirteen-week curriculum. At the time of John Pat's death, recruits received four lectures during a fifteen-week course. A survey of Roebourne police after the incident revealed that their knowledge of local history was limited (Roberts et al. 1986, p. 118).

Another difficulty which may have contributed to the hostility between Aboriginal residents and police at Roebourne concerned the suitability of those officers posted to the town. Police work in contemporary Australia has become extraordinarily diverse and often highly specialised. Whilst most police are expected to acquire a broad base of experience in the course of their career, they themselves admit that not all police are suitable for working with Aborigines. Some harbour strong prejudice against and deep dislike of Aboriginal people.

Although recruitment interviews seek to identify racist sentiments, racial prejudice is not grounds *per se* for disqualification from recruitment to the Western Australian Police. Screening of officers for posting to areas where they are likely to have significant contact with Aboriginal people also appeared to be inadequate (Roberts et al. 1986, p. 112). Compounding this were the procedures for selecting senior officers to serve in towns with significant Aboriginal populations. Seniority, rather than interpersonal skills or previous experience in Aboriginal communities, appeared to be the governing principle.

Poor leadership can transform bad police-community relations into overt hostility. Some indication as to the quality of leadership by senior police at Roebourne may be gleaned from comments attributed to a sergeant who appeared at the inquest into John Pat's death. He approved of grabbing Aborigines by the hair because 'when Aborigines get stirred up and looking for a fight, they tend to get very greasy and slippery'.

Senior police were quickly notified of John Pat's death; an inspector and detective sergeant arrived from Karratha within two hours. Two others flew from Perth the following day. One was told that the deceased had fallen heavily from the police van at the lockup.

A coroner's inquest began on 31 October 1983. The four officers and the police aide who were involved in the events leading to Pat's death drafted prepared statements denying that they had used excessive force on the night in question. Beyond this, they were disinclined to assist the coroner in his inquiry; each declined to answer questions or to give evidence. Also perhaps indicative of some lack of enthusiasm to co-operate in the investigation was the fact that the jeans and shirts worn by the arresting officers were not made available for forensic tests until one month had elapsed. By this time the clothing in question had been washed, and it was no longer possible to conduct analyses of any previous stains.

The inquest heard evidence from seventy witnesses over twenty-one hearing days. There were significant discrepancies between the evidence of Aboriginal witnesses and the official police version of events. Witnesses described Pat as having been dragged to the police van at the time of his arrest, and as having been dragged from the van to the police lockup. According to the evidence of one police officer, Pat, after having fallen from the police van, walked to the lockup and spoke coherently. A medical officer testified that a person with Pat's head injuries would be unlikely to walk or speak coherently, especially given a blood alcohol reading of .222.

A number of other inconsistencies or irregularities emerged during the inquest. Details of injuries to prisoners were not recorded at the time of their having been taken into custody. A senior government technologist testified to having found traces of human blood of the same blood group as John Pat on the boots of two of the police involved in the skirmish. There was no evidence of Pat's being assaulted by anyone other than the police.

On 6 February 1984 the five accused were committed for trial on charges of manslaughter. Consistent with police procedure they were suspended from duties without pay from the time of the committal. The police union quickly approached the Western Australian Minister for Police and persuaded him that the accused should be suspended on full pay, lest the spouses and children of those still presumed to be innocent suffer undue financial hardship.

The charges were heard in the Supreme Court at Karratha on 30 April 1984. Because of the nature of the trial, great care was taken in selecting the jury. The normal procedure for enrolling prospective jurors (door-knock visits by local police) was for obvious reasons deemed inappropriate. Instead, the Karratha Clerk of Court selected 140 names at random from the electoral rolls of Karratha, Dampier, Wickham and Roebourne. As jury service was optional for women, almost half of the 140 prospective jurors excused themselves. Of the three Aboriginals on the list, only one was called for jury service. When he disclosed that he was acquainted with one of the accused, he stood aside.

Eventually, an all-white jury of twelve men and three women was empanelled; the total included three reserve jurors, who were added because of the anticipated length of the trial.

Each of the defendants testified under oath; each maintained his innocence, as well as that of his co-defendants. The constable alleged to have dragged a prisoner by the hair denied having done so. The constable who was alleged to have provoked a fight with Ashley James denied having done so. One defendant told the court that when he had escorted Pat to the cell, he had no suspicion that Pat had been injured. Each of the accused maintained that no more force was used than was necessary. Any punches thrown by police were thrown in self-defence.

The Crown case was weakest when aggressive cross-examination of Crown witnesses reflected adversely on their credibility. Aboriginal people are often less than effective witnesses when confronted by a skilled barrister. Some Aboriginal witnesses are inherently bashful and inclined to 'yea saying'- to respond as they imagine the questioner would have them. Those not fluent in English and without an interpreter are more vulnerable than most to a crafty lawyer's semantic ambush (Foley 1984, pp. 164-9). One of the persons arrested along with John Pat testified that he saw one constable holding Pat by the hair and slam his head against the concrete footpath.

Under cross-examination, he admitted that he had not actually seen the attack: 'I didn't see it but I could hear the sounds'. The witness then conceded that he was trying to get the police into trouble.

> ... Is it fair to say that you are prepared to tell lies from what people have told you and say you saw things you didn't see simply to get the police into trouble?...... Yes (Western Australia 1984, p. 362).

The defence seized upon this admission, and sought to discredit the other Aboriginal Crown witnesses. They were destined to succeed. The trial concluded on 24 May 1986, after fifty-seven witnesses had given evidence. Upon hearing the judge's instructions, the jury retired to consider its verdict at 12.15 pm. After some deliberations, they returned and asked the judge if a police officer was on duty twenty-four hours per day. They were advised that any police officer, on or off duty, who saw a breach of the peace occurring would have an obligation to do something about it. After hours of further deliberation, the jurors requested the judge to repeat the legal definitions of manslaughter and accident. Finally, at 7.15 that evening, the jury returned with its verdict: all of the accused were not guilty.

The verdict was met with outrage on the part of Aboriginal groups. There were calls for a Royal Commission and threats to publicise the case in international forums such as the World Council of Indigenous Peoples and the United Nations. Tensions between Aborigines and police were high. Police announced their intention to proceed with charges arising from the brawl outside the Victoria Hotel against four Aborigines who had given evidence for the Crown at the trial. The state premier appealed for calm.

On 19 July 1984, charges were heard against those Aborigines who were arrested with John Pat the previous September. Ashley James, unemployed, pleaded guilty of assault and resisting arrest, and was find a total of $370 with $27 costs. Another accused was found guilty of hindering police and fined $40 with costs of $32.27.

In dismissing charges against two others, the magistrate stated that he could not accept the evidence of one of the recently acquitted police officers, choosing instead to accept the evidence of a local health officer who testified that he saw the officer walk up to the accused and punch him in the stomach. Inspired by the magistrate's findings, and in light of the government's reluctance to pursue further remedies, the Aboriginal Legal Service undertook private prosecutions, seeking to charge three of the police with assault. In the first of these cases, against Constable Young, two of the officers refused to give evidence on the grounds of potential self-incrimination, and having applied successfully for certificates under Section 11 of the *Evidence Act 1906* (WA), were thus granted immunity by the presiding magistrate. Charges against Constable Young were then dismissed by the Magistrate. With the other two police immunised against prosecution, remaining charges were withdrawn by the Aboriginal Legal Service.

In addition to the formal criminal charges of which they were acquitted, the defendants in the Pat case were liable to internal disciplinary proceedings under the *Police Act 1892-1982* (WA) and the Police Regulations 1979. The officer in charge of internal affairs at the time, Chief Superintendent Brian Bull, had sat through the entire trial. A fortnight after the acquittal it was announced that no further action would be taken against the men.

In the aftermath of the acquittals, the government sought to modify procedures for investigating complaints against police by increasing the powers of the state Ombudsman. The involvement in the investigations of alleged police misconduct of an external authority as prestigious as the Ombudsman is regarded by police generally as more than a little annoying. To propose that the Ombudsman be provided with greater powers to this end is to threaten in the extreme. Western Australian police sought to mobilise their considerable political influence to defeat the proposed legislation. The general secretary of the union organised a media campaign, involving speeches to local civic groups and contacts with sympathetic members of Parliament. The union also produced a striking television advertisement designed to elicit public opposition to the bill. The advertisement showed a brick wall with the words **WESTERN AUSTRALIAN POLICE FORCE** painted on it in crisp white letters. An ominous voice warned 'Right now, legislation that could destroy the effectiveness of your police force is before Parliament'. The camera then focused on the head of a very hefty sledgehammer with the word **OMBUDSMAN** printed across it in block letters. As the sledgehammer strikes the wall, the voice warns 'The Complaints Against Police Bill will give the Ombudsman far reaching powers. Police under investigation will be guilty until proven innocent. Young police men and women will be hesitant to take risks with their careers'. By this time, the wall is largely demolished, revealing a forlorn constable wearing a pair of handcuffs. The ominous voice concludes 'Write to your local MP today'. The police union's campaign was successful; the proposed legislation was blocked by the opposition-controlled upper house (Marr 1985).

Buoyed by this victory, the union continued its attack on the Aboriginal Legal Service. In November of 1985 police union delegates from around Australia called for a parliamentary inquiry into the alleged abuse of funds by the Aboriginal Legal Service. The following year, they called for its outright abolition.

In addition to their political victories the police union succeeded in recovering the financial costs it had incurred in supporting the legal defence of the accused officers. In July 1984 state Cabinet agreed to reimburse more than $136,000 in legal fees, including $54,000 incurred during the inquest and $82,000 incurred during the trial.

In the aftermath of the John Pat case, a number of administrative reforms were introduced which were intended to lessen the tensions between the police and the Aboriginal citizens of Western Australia. State government revived a special cabinet committee on Aboriginal/police and community relations which had been established in 1976 following the Royal Commission into the Laverton Skull Creek incident. A 'summit meeting' between senior police and Aboriginal representatives was convened.

The Minister for Police announced that greater care would be taken in selecting officers in charge of stations in country towns with significant Aboriginal populations. Criteria for selection included the ability to communicate effectively with Aborigines, and to control their officers to prevent the use of undue force in making arrests (Roberts et al. 1986, pp. 111-12).

The Western Australian Institute of Technology was invited to develop a ten-hour Aboriginal affairs module for the police recruit training curriculum. The course would address Aboriginal culture and social conditions, customary law, resources and services for Aboriginal groups, and skills for interacting with and communicating with Aboriginal people (Roberts et al. 1986, p. 114).

At Roebourne itself, a new sergeant was placed in charge of the police station in July 1985, and those police who had been acquitted in the John Pat case were transferred elsewhere. The new sergeant in charge, a veteran of twenty-six years with considerable fondness and respect for Aboriginal people, was described as 'the law enforcer with the tender touch' (Lague & Mokrzycki 1986). He sought to win the confidence of local residents by being accessible and friendly, and through such charitable gestures as providing food and firewood to local residents. A photograph showed him hand in hand with an Aboriginal child. Prisoners assisted him with various odd jobs. Within two years, however he left for another station.

By 1986 a report to state Cabinet concluded:

> Currently relations between police and Aborigines in the Pilbara are in a state of uneasy truce. That is, whilst no serious outbreaks of open hostility have occurred since the death of John Pat, the potential for serious violence exists (Roberts et al. 1986, p. 181).

There have been other Aboriginal deaths in custody since the night John Pat died. These, singly and collectively have given rise to public protests and to calls for judicial inquiries, and renewed calls for Aboriginal land rights. A Western Australian government inquiry (Seaman 1984) recommended the granting of land rights to Aborigines. The recommendations were rejected by the state government. In 1987, the federal government appointed a Royal Commission into Aboriginal deaths in custody. Brian Bull is now the Western Australian Commissioner of Police. And the police union in Western Australia continued to call for the abolition of the Aboriginal Legal Service.

References

Bolton, G.C. 1981, 'Black and White after 1897', in *A New History of Western Australia*, ed C. T. Stannage, University of Western Australia Press, Perth.

Eggleston, Elizabeth 1976, *Fear, Favour or Affection: Aborigines and the Criminal Law in Victoria, South Australia, and Western Australia*, Australian National University Press, Canberra.

Foley, Matthew 1984, 'Aborigines and the Police', in *Aborigines and the Law*, eds P. Hanks & B. Keon-Cohen, George Allen & Unwin, Sydney, pp. 160-90.

Lang, M. 1984, 'QC Tells of Brutal Attack', *The West Australian*, 1 May.

Lague, D. & Mokrzycki, J. 1986 'Roebourne's Tough Cop has a Heart of Gold', *Western Mail*, 22-23 February, 8-9.

Marr, David 1985, 'Black Death', *Four Corners*, ABC Television.

Mayman, Jan 1984, 'Back to the Dreaming', *The Age*, 25 June.

Mukherjee, Satyanshu & Scandia, Anita 1988, Crime Digest No. 88. 1, *Aboriginal Imprisonment*, Australian Institute of Criminology, Canberra.

Roberts, L., Chadbourne, R. & Murray, R., 1986, *Aboriginal - Police Relations in the Pilbara : A Study of Perceptions*, Criminology Research Council, Canberra.

Seaman, Paul, Q.C. 1984, *The Aboriginal Land Inquiry*, Government Printer, Perth.

Western Australia 1927, *Royal Commission of Inquiry into Alleged Killing and Burning of Bodies of Aborigines in East Kimberlies and into Police Methods when Effecting Arrests, Report,* (G.T. Wood, Commissioner), Government Printer, Perth.

Western Australia 1975-76, *Royal Commission Enquiring into Events at Laverton in December 1974 and January 1975 Concerning Aborigines and the Police and Other Associated Matters, Report,* (G.D. Clarkson, Chair), Government Printer, Perth.

Western Australia 1984, *The Queen Against Terrence James Holl, Steven Alan Bordes, Ian Frank Armitt, James Young and Michael Walke*r: *Proceedings,* Supreme Court of Western Australia, No. 31.

Chapter 6

THE GREAT SOCIAL SECURITY CONSPIRACY CASE*

Along with his role in the dismissal of the Whitlam government and the mysterious loss of his trousers during an overnight stay in Memphis Tennessee in 1986, former Prime Minister Malcolm Fraser will perhaps best be remembered for the quip 'Life Wasn't Meant To Be Easy'. It was a message which many Australians found neither comforting nor inspiring when, as Australia's economic decline continued in the late 1970s, increasing numbers of people became dependent on public welfare payments. The vast majority of Australian welfare recipients were both deserving and honest, but as is always the case with programs which dispense public benefits, the Social Security system was subject to abuse.

Australian governments have traditionally shown less tolerance of alleged 'dole bludgers' than of those who, often at much greater cost to the Treasury, defraud the Commonwealth in the course of evading taxes. Not long after the Fraser government came to power, it was decided to 'crack down' on abuses of the Social Security system.

Toward the end of 1976, the Sydney office of the Department of Social Security (DSS) learned of an alleged arrangement under which medical practitioners would assist members of the Greek community to obtain invalid pensions fraudulently, in return for payment. The matter was called to the attention of the Health Department and then to the Commonwealth Police (COMPOL).

In December of 1976, COMPOL were advised that DSS had been authorised to provide information to COMPOL to assist in the investigation of the alleged fraud.

The suspected fraud appeared to have been facilitated by a number of 'agents', (in Greek, *mezasons*, or intermediaries) residents of the community who were fluent in both Greek and English and who, in return for a fee, provided advice and assistance to those unable to communicate in English. It was suspected that a number of unscrupulous agents were assisting members of the Greek community to obtain sickness benefits or invalid pensions fraudulently by coaching them to contrive symptoms of psychiatric illness and to present themselves to those local medical practitioners who would, in return for a fee, accept their complaints uncritically and endorse their applications for a benefit. Consistent with the inclination in Australian law enforcement circles to regard organised crime as the root of all evil, there was even some suggestion that the alleged enterprise was controlled by a secret Greek underworld organisation known as the *Kolpo*.

On 16 September 1977 the Acting Commissioner of the Commonwealth Police wrote to the Director-General of Social Security regarding 'an ongoing fraud allegedly of great proportions which has been perpetrated against the Department of Social Security'. The allegations came from an informant, who estimated that eight medical practitioners and 'at least 500 persons of Greek extraction' were involved, at a cost to the revenue of between $2.5 million and $5 million per year.

The Acting Commissioner suggested that the co-operation of the informant could be secured for a cash reward of $30,000, and sought the advice of the Director-General regarding a proposal to:

1) compile a list of those in receipt of pensions fraudulently obtained, and of those medical practitioners involved;

2) initiate detailed procedures necessary to ensure successful penetration of the medical conspiracy by an agent; and

3) arrange for the issuance of search warrants for doctors' surgeries for records of invalid pension patients (Harper, L. pers. comm. to Secretary, Department of Social Security, 16 September 1977. Commonwealth Police Reference no. 76/7307, obtained under the *Freedom of Information Act 1982*).

The government's response to the suspected fraud was designed to be firm. It would involve the full force of the criminal law, rather than lesser administrative penalties. A high profile 'crackdown' with maximum publicity would have, it was felt, the greatest deterrent effect. Not only would those caught defrauding the government be disinclined to offend again after having their fingers burned, but members of the general public who might be tempted to try their hand at dole fraud would be disinclined to take the risk.

On 5 October 1977 a First Assistant Director-General of Social Security wrote to the Deputy Secretary of the Attorney-General's Department, and said:

> The Minister for Social Security has agreed for COMPOL to undertake investigations outlined in the Acting Commissioner's memorandum of 16 September, 1977 (Corrigan, D. 1977, pers. comm. to F. J. Mahoney, O.B.E., 5 October, [Department of Social Security Reference no. 75/16563], obtained under the Freedom of Information Act).

On the same day Corrigan wrote to the Director of the NSW Office of the Department of Social Security and requested that he 'please provide COMPOL with any assistance necessary' (Corrigan, D. 1977, pers. comm. to R. Dowell, 5 October, [Department of Social Security Reference no. 75/16563], obtained under the Freedom of Information Act).

The operation which eventuated was known as 'Don's Party', after the officer in charge of the investigation, Detective Chief Inspector Don Thomas. It involved early morning raids on some 160 homes and five doctors' surgeries by a team of over 100 officers of the Commonwealth Police. 'Don's Party' was the largest co-ordinated operation conducted to date by that agency. In order to ensure that the raids received maximum publicity, reporters from the Sydney tabloid *The Sun* were alerted in advance and invited to attend.

Initially, 181 people, virtually all of Greek ethnic background, were arrested and charged with conspiracy to defraud the Commonwealth.

On 3 April 1978, eighty-three of the accused appeared in Central Court, Sydney. On the steps of the courthouse, Chief Inspector Thomas held a news conference and jubilantly referred to his operation as 'the biggest breakthrough in the history of the police force'. Indeed, Thomas revealed that the 'party' was not yet over. He heralded the possibility of a further thousand arrests, and the extradition of a further 300 people from Greece. The publicity, as intended, was massive. Headlines blared 'Police Seek 1400 More Pay Cheats' and 'Cheats Live Luxury Life in Greece'. It was also announced that the Commonwealth Police had been stationed at all major airports to prevent others connected with the alleged fraud from leaving Australia. The Minister for Social Security was advised by the Commissioner of COMPOL that a second wave of raids would take place in Sydney the following weekend.

As it happened, these further arrests were not to eventuate. But prosecutions were begun against those arrested thus far, and a total of 669 social security recipients had their benefits withdrawn and their payments cancelled.

Unfortunately for Chief Inspector Thomas, his police colleagues, and the Department of Social Security, 'Don's Party' was something less than a smashing success. The legal costs entailed in prosecuting 180 alleged co-conspirators were massive. As the majority of the accused were people of very modest means, the cost of their legal representation was borne by the Australian government as well. The mass arrests resulted in only a handful of convictions, and outrage in the Greek community. Over the following five years, conspiracy charges were withdrawn against all but five suspects. The cost of these abortive legal proceedings reached $10 million.

But the real losers in the operation were those who were wrongly implicated in the conspiracy. Most were born in Greece, with elementary formal education, and with limited ability to speak or understand English. A number had not adjusted well to life in Australia; they tended to come from village backgrounds and coped poorly with the stresses of urban living. Many had worked for a number of years in heavy labouring jobs, and had suffered disabling physical injury from industrial accidents. A number also suffered psychiatric illness, thereby compounding these difficulties.

For a person unable to communicate in English, unfamiliar with the Australian criminal justice system, and characterised by something less than robust mental health to begin with, the experience of 'Don's Party' was traumatic.

Although the raids on doctors' premises had been conducted pursuant to search warrants, no such formalities were followed in the course of raids on patients' homes. It was generally assumed that non-English speaking migrants would be ignorant of their legal rights, or at least too frightened to invoke them. Many of the suspects experienced extreme distress as they were taken into custody in front of their families and neighbours. The suffering of spouses and children of the arrestees was no less acute. According to one authoritative account, the typical suspect

> was intimidated by the statements and conduct of the police in that they pressed him for answers to their questions and their number and physical size were overbearing. He was apprehensive that he might suffer physical violence. He believed that the police were laughing and joking about him and that they were making derogatory remarks about his Greek nationality (Australia 1986, p. 55).

When identification photographs were taken of the arrestees, a number included a sign with the word 'Greece' written on it. Many of the suspects were detained in police custody for a number of hours until friends or relatives were able to arrange bail money. The task of raising $1,000 cash on a weekend is daunting enough for an invalid pensioner. It was even more difficult for those whose bank passbooks had been confiscated. Without having been convicted of any crime, they were subjected to treatment which could only be regarded as punitive.

> The condition of the cell was disgusting. The cell was overcrowded. There was insufficient room for him to sit or lie down with any measure of comfort. The cell was putrid. It did not contain private toilet facilities nor was he given access to private toilet facilities. Some of those in the cell had the appearance of a vagrant or common drunk (Australia 1986, p. 56).

The experience of incarceration, combined with the uncertainty regarding one's future income, not to mention the outcome of the criminal process, was to take its toll. Prior to 'Don's Party', the typical suspect

> had been nervous and anxious. After his arrest his condition immediately took a turn for the worse. He was extremely frightened of anyone in authority. He was acutely and severely apprehensive for his well being and that of his family. He was stricken by grief. The change in his mental health was sufficiently grave to require treatment additional to that which he had been having at the time of his arrest.

> [H]e is a man who is insecure. He anxiously anticipates the reaction of those in authority whenever he comes into contact with them in his day-to-day affairs. Seeing a policeman reminds him of what occurred in the conspiracy proceedings (Australia 1986, pp. 59-60).

One person, who had been receiving psychiatric treatment at the time of his arrest, committed suicide. The experience of those who were not the subject of criminal charges, but whose benefit payments were suspended nonetheless, was almost as traumatic. On 1 April 1978 the Director-General of Social Security gave directions to suspend payments to those pensioners whose names appeared on a list prepared by COMPOL. The suspensions were sudden and unheralded. They were implemented without the recipients having been accorded any opportunity to defend themselves against allegations of impropriety. The administrative procedures which underlay many of these suspensions were of questionable legality. Some pensioners were left without any source of income for as long as eight months. The standard procedure of giving three months' notice of cancellation and the continuation of payments pending the outcome of an appeal, were not followed. As a result, many of those whose benefits were cancelled faced severe financial hardship, and some had to resort to scavenging in garbage cans in order to survive (Cashman 1985, pp. 228-9). Tenants were threatened with eviction, and homeowners, unable to meet mortgage payments, were forced to sell their homes. Subsequent medical examinations of those pensioners who had returned to Greece were based upon criteria more restrictive than those applying in Australia at the time. Many were unable to afford the cost of returning to Australia to avail themselves of the right of appeal.

Others no doubt recalled Chief Inspector Thomas' having heralded further arrests. Such events would be difficult enough for mainstream Australians, much less for poor migrants, unable to communicate in English, and already suffering psychiatric problems.

'Don's Party' was preceded by more than the usual police investigation, and it was far from flawlessly executed. A doctor suspected of complicity in the alleged fraud was not prepared to write the appropriate medical report for an undercover police officer of Greek ethnicity who sought to obtain a pension fraudulently. One of the persons charged in the conspiracy, a Mr Nakis, was granted an indemnity and gave evidence for the Crown as a co-conspirator during committal proceedings. Only subsequently, during defence cross-examination of Chief Inspector Thomas, did Nakis' full role in the investigation become apparent. Nakis was the person who had originally approached the Commonwealth Police in 1977, claiming that he was prepared to provide information in return for a pardon and a cash reward. After some negotiation regarding the amount, an agreement was reached some time prior to the early morning raids. Rather than a co-conspirator who chose to co-operate with police after his arrest, Nakis had been acting as a police agent in the course of the investigations.

Not only did Nakis' role as a police agent raise questions about the possible entrapment of some suspects, it cast doubt upon some of the evidence central to the Crown case. A taped conversation between Nakis and a police officer which was introduced in support of the conspiracy charges was in fact a conversation between two police agents, both acting on the instructions of Chief Inspector Thomas. Thomas introduced the tape in evidence, allowing the assumption to be made that Nakis was someone other than a police agent.

Other means employed by police to collect evidence were called into question. It was alleged that in the course of the raids, police seized personal documents, passports, bank statements and other documents without warrant. Hundreds of medical records were seized from doctors' surgeries. Chief Inspector Thomas advised that in March 1978 he received authority from Senator Withers, at the time the minister responsible for the Commonwealth Police, to install listening devices in the surgeries of two doctors suspected of complicity in the fraud. Such eavesdropping clearly constituted an intrusion on the confidentiality of communication between doctor and patient. In addition, a number of telephone conversations involving police agents and alleged conspirators were recorded without a warrant and without the knowledge of the other party to the conversation.

The police claimed to have been under the impression that such practice was within the law; the Solicitor General of Australia subsequently advised that such a practice contravened the *Telephonic Communications (Interception Act) 1960-1973* (Cwlth).

The circumstances giving rise to 'Don's Party' were varied and complex. The Commonwealth Police, a relatively new body whose future directions were the subject of consideration by the Federal government, were greatly concerned about demonstrating their competence. In light of the impending visit of Sir Robert Mark, former Commissioner of the London Metropolitan Police, for the purpose of advising the Federal government on police organisation, senior COMPOL officers saw it as imperative to put 'runs on the board'. The Department of Social Security faced growing criticism in the mid 1970s for its lack of efficiency in the administration of welfare benefit programs. The 1975-76 Report of the Commonwealth Auditor General estimated overpayments of unemployment benefits at $40 million. The report called attention to what were regarded as inadequate checks and controls for benefit eligibility. All of this was not well received by the coalition government, which was at best unenthusiastic about the welfare system and at worst antipathetic. In any event, it was much less tolerant of abuses of the welfare system than of abuses of taxation and medical benefits systems.

Patrick Lanigan, a senior public servant with a reputation for toughness, became Director General of the Department of Social Security in 1977, and made control of benefits abuses a high priority.

The strategy adopted, that of mass arrests and conspiracy prosecutions, was fundamentally misconceived. Under the most favourable evidentiary circumstances, the logistics of prosecuting 180 co-conspirators would still be daunting. In the case in question, the evidence left much to be desired.

But the police were involved in a 'trawling' operation. The plan was to charge all suspects initially with conspiracy, confer indemnity on those who were prepared to give evidence against the doctors, then withdraw conspiracy charges against the other pensioners and proceed against them with statutory charges under the *Social Security Act 1947* (Cwlth). Even by the most charitable interpretation of police strategy, the pensioners were pawns in a game.

The Department's enthusiasm to implement a highly visible 'crackdown' combined with over-zealous policing, led to a selection of suspects which proved to have been over-inclusive. Many alleged conspirators were charged simply because they were pensioners who appeared to have a name of Greek origin, and who had been treated by one or more of the doctors at the centre of the police investigation. For the purpose of laying criminal charges, the police should have exercised greater care in evaluating the evidence available.

For its part, the Department should have been more rigorous in the evaluation of evidence on the basis of which it terminated benefit payments. It could, at any time, have requested the attendance of any beneficiary for a medical review. Such internal controls were not employed. Rather, DSS relied upon a list of names provided by COMPOL, and acted in the absence of any medical or other evidence. Deference to police investigators proved as disastrous to administrative justice as it was to criminal justice.

Yet another strategic shortcoming was the focus on suspects of exclusively Greek ethnicity. Not only was it perceived as discriminatory, it provoked outrage amongst members of one of Australia's largest minority groups. The resulting political damage to the coalition government was substantial. A Greek newspaper referred to the 1979 New

Year's message of the Minister for Immigration and Ethnic Affairs as reminiscent 'of a mafia, which kills and then sends flowers to the funeral of its victims' (Kelly 1979).

The prosecution was marred by an apparent lack of planning, as well as an episode of questionable propriety. The Commonwealth Police simply did not have the staff to arrest and charge 1,000 people. Manpower limitations and the mountain of paperwork confined the operation to 181 arrests and subsequent proceedings. The prosecution stalled early on when the police were unable to provide particulars of the charges to the defence. Many months passed, during which the defendants, free on bail, were required to report regularly to local police stations.

The Department of Social Security, having become increasingly embarrassed by its involvement in the case, sought to distance itself from the prosecution, and was disinclined to proceed with any lesser charges under the Social Security Act. This locked the police into proceeding with conspiracy charges, despite the inadequacy of evidence. The prosecution case was thus dependent on the testimony of Nakis, and the deception that Nakis was in fact a co-conspirator, rather than a public agent who stood to profit from a huge reward for incriminating as many of the accused as possible.

As the defence began to focus on Nakis' precise role in the investigation, Chief Inspector Thomas was placed in a position where, under cross-examination, he would have to reveal the nature and duration of his relationship with Nakis. Taking advantage of an adjournment, Thomas requested an urgent (and most improper) conference with prosecution lawyers on 2 November 1979, during which he revealed that he had known Nakis as early as September 1977, at least six months prior to the April 1978 raids. Counsel for the Crown regarded Thomas' withholding of this information as outrageous, but nevertheless chose not to disclose it on the next day of committal proceedings (Chobocky 1987). Thomas later denied that the meeting took place. On subsequent cross-examination, Nakis refused to answer further questions on the grounds of potential self-incrimination. He flew back to Greece, first class, at the expense of the Australian tax-payer. In the words of Senator Don Grimes:

The Attorney-General's Department, through its senior officers, were involved in negotiations about paying a reward to the informant in this case. The prosecution, who were being instructed by the Attorney-General's Department, claimed that they were not informed about the reward or that there was an informant. In fact, they thought Mr Nakis was just another Crown witness until later in the case. It seems to me that the circumstances are that senior officers of the Attorney-General's Department either deliberately did not tell the prosecution of this, in which case they are likely to be guilty of a considerable breach of justice, or they didn't do so because of incompetence or inadvertence, in which case the capacity of senior people in the Attorney-General's Department who are charged with upholding justice in this country is in question. I can see no other alternative (Grimes 1987).

Nakis was not the only Crown witness who failed to live up to expectations. Anastassia Artopolou was flown in from Greece to testify, but her evidence was so discredited that the Crown had her stood down after nine days of testimony.

In late 1981, the government withdrew charges of conspiracy against 111 defendants. Four doctors were eventually committed for trial on conspiracy charges. At the conclusion of committal proceedings, the magistrate, Bruce Brown, was scathing in his criticism of police practices in the case:

I propose to bring the circumstances of these actions by Detective Chief Inspector Thomas to the notice of the relevant Attorney-General, with a view to proceedings being taken against him for conspiracy to pervert the course of justice, or for perjury, or for both . . . Turning again to the Nakis-Thomas revelation, I am of the view that the evidence has established the highest impropriety by the then Detective Chief Inspector Thomas. That he permitted Detective Theodorakis to go about his undercover duties unaware of the secret agreement between Thomas and Nakis, is nothing short of scandalous. That he contrived the second and third records of interview that he conducted with Nakis is a matter of grave concern - no doubt done for the purpose of improving the quality of the evidence (quoted in Chobocky 1987).

Federal Attorney-General Gareth Evans pre-empted further developments when he notified the Magistrate that he would not propose to take any further action against Thomas.

But the magistrate himself was accused of improper conduct. His decision to commit the doctors for trial was challenged in the Federal Court. It was alleged that he had made two telephone calls to the senior official in the Commonwealth Attorney-General's Department who was directing the prosecution case. Mr Justice Fox of the Federal Court found the magistrate's private and confidential communication of his views to the solicitor for one party constituted a denial of natural justice. The decision to commit the doctors for trial was quashed on 30 May 1985, more than seven years after 'Don's Party' had taken place.

Of 181 persons initially charged with conspiracy to defraud the Commonwealth, four were convicted on that charge. Three defendants (all patients) pleaded guilty to the charge against them. All were placed on good behaviour bonds. One defendant, a doctor, was tried and convicted on a conspiracy charge and sentenced to a term of imprisonment. He appealed successfully, but was tried and convicted a second time.

A further thirty-three alleged conspirators were convicted on substantive charges of imposition. These charges involved minor irregularities, some bordering on the trivial. Eight were fined, and the remainder placed on good behaviour bonds.

According to the official version of events, 'Don's Party' and its aftermath was almost exclusively a police operation. On 19 February 1979, Dame Margaret Guilfoyle, Minister for Social Security at the time, denied having seen the letter of 16 September 1977 outlining the COMPOL proposal for extensive investigations. Dame Margaret further maintained that the

Corrigan letter of 5 October 1977 ('The Minister for Social Security has agreed for COMPOL to undertake investigations outlined in the Acting Commissioner's memorandum of 16 September 1977') was written without her knowledge and consent.

In a minute to the Director-General of Social Security dated 11 February 1979 and entitled 'Alleged Invalid Pension Fraud' (obtained under the Freedom of Information of Act), Corrigan replied:

> I would certainly not have advised that 'The Minister for Social Security has agreed . . .' without a clear understanding of advice to me that this was the position.

In the same minute he went on to reveal another difficulty experienced by the Department:

> At the time the correspondence was handled we were concerned to prevent any leak of important minutes to the Minister and this matter was dealt with verbally because of that concern.

The government continued to be embarrassed by 'Don's Party' and its aftermath. Dame Margaret Guilfoyle, in replying to parliamentary questions, informed the Senate that none of the alleged conspirators had been photographed holding a sign on which the word 'Greek' was written, nor had any telephones been tapped. Later, she conceded that the word in question had been 'Greece' and that phone calls had been recorded by police agents without the knowledge or consent of the other party.

The extent to which federal Cabinet may have been involved in, or was at least aware of, events leading up to 'Don's Party' remains a matter for speculation. Certainly much of the business of Cabinet is trivial compared to an operation involving scores of arrests, the termination of hundreds of pensions and the targeting of members of a single ethnic group for criminal prosecution. One may have to wait thirty years, until the expiry of the standing embargo on Cabinet documents, before the question is definitively answered. But some interesting clues exist: on 19 December 1979, Patrick Lanigan, Director General of Social Security, wrote a confidential letter to Sir Geoffrey Yeend, Secretary of the Department of the Prime Minister and Cabinet. The letter was obtained under the Freedom of Information Act. In the middle of a lengthy discussion of the police operation, three blank spaces appear, each bearing the notation:

> This section has been deleted because the information is exempted under Sect. 34 of the F.O.I. Act.

Section 34 refers to the exemption of Cabinet documents, in addition to:

> a document the disclosure of which would involve the disclosure of any deliberation or decision of the Cabinet . . .

The coalition government was defeated in the elections of March 1983. On 31 January 1984, the Attorney-General of Australia, Gareth Evans, and the Minister for Social Security, Don Grimes, announced the appointment of a judicial inquiry to determine the appropriate compensation for those persons who had been wrongly prosecuted as a result of 'Don's Party'. The inquiry was headed by Dame Roma Mitchell, who was granted the powers of a royal commissioner.

In the Letters Patent issued 9 February 1984, the Australian government accepted liability, not only for any acts and omissions of its public servants, but also for those of the police and of ministers of the crown.

The government maintained that the purpose of the inquiry was restitutive, and it was declared at the outset that the inquiry would not be a witch-hunt into what went wrong nor a general review of the case. The inquiry was limited to those cases involving persons who had been the subject of criminal charges; other beneficiaries whose payments had been suspended or cancelled were left to seek redress through administrative avenues or through civil litigation of their own motion.

The Mitchell Inquiry reviewed submissions from individual claimants, as well as relevant files held by the Department of Social Security and the police. Public hearings were held in both Sydney and Athens to enable the legal representatives of claimants to make oral submissions.

The police and social security files contained material which reflected adversely upon a number of the claimants. It is interesting to note the inquiry's evaluation of these materials:

> Where Counsel Assisting considered that such evidence was relevant and of probative value it was brought to the attention of the claimant's legal representatives and an explanation was sought from the claimant in relation to it. I report that in the majority of cases satisfactory explanations were received for events and circumstances which might otherwise have reflected adversely on the veracity of the claimants (Australia 1986, p. 24).

The report of the Mitchell Inquiry was presented to the Governor-General of Australia on 30 April 1986. It recommended the payment of compensation totalling $6.1 million plus an additional sum of $1.24 million for legal costs that had thus far been borne privately by the medical practitioners who had been implicated in the alleged conspiracy.

Redress for those who managed to escape prosecution, but whose social security benefits were suspended, also proved to be a long, drawn out process. A year after the termination of benefits, a Sydney psychiatrist lodged a complaint with the Commonwealth Ombudsman on behalf of a patient. The complainant contended that the benefits had been wrongfully suspended. The Ombudsman commenced a formal investigation in December 1979. Three years later, the complainant had yet to be notified of the outcome of the investigations. In December 1982, the Public Interest Advocacy Centre (PIAC) in Sydney inquired on behalf of the complainants, and was notified that the investigation was still ongoing. Meanwhile, by early 1983 a number of complainants were still not in receipt of benefits; the more fortunate were able to rely upon the support of family and friends.

The Public Interest Advocacy Centre, which sought to proceed against the Department of Social Security, was reluctant to do so prior to completion of the Ombudsman's inquiry. Meanwhile the deadline for the commencement of action to recover damages was approaching.

In keeping with the practices of the Ombudsman's office, a draft of the report was forwarded to the Department of Social Security for its comment in March 1983. By this time, nearly five years had elapsed since the benefit payments were terminated. When the PIAC, acting for the complainants, sought to obtain details of the case from the Ombudsman's office, it was advised 'it is only on completion that the Ombudsman is in a position to give a complainant particulars of the results of his investigation' (Cashman 1985, p. 228).

As the continuing delay on the part of the Ombudsman's office was impeding the progress of legal action to recover damages, PIAC sought to obtain a copy of the draft. The Ombudsman's office refused, pursuant to the provisions of the *Ombudsman Act 1976* (Cwlth) which were interpreted as imposing strict requirements of secrecy. PIAC then lodged a formal request for the draft and related documents, under the Freedom of Information Act. This too was refused, again on the grounds that disclosure was prohibited by the Ombudsman Act. An FOI request to the Department of Social Security was refused, on the grounds of Section 16 of the FOI Act, that the subject matter of the document in question was more closely connected with the functions of another agency - the Ombudsman's office.

A request was then made of the Minister for Social Security, who, in his previous capacity as Opposition spokesman on social security matters, had expressed considerable concern for those unjustly victimised by the cancellation of pensions. The Minister advised that the Ombudsman's draft report was not in his possession. An overture to the Prime Minister, the minister responsible for the Ombudsman, was similarly unsuccessful.

An appeal to the Administrative Appeals Tribunal resulted in a decision which held that while the Ombudsman was not entirely outside the ambit of the FOI Act, the secrecy provisions of the Ombudsman Act were grounds for exemption from FOI. The implications of this decision extended well beyond the present case, given that some 200 other pieces of Commonwealth legislation contained secrecy provisions. The matter was then appealed to the Federal Court, which held that secrecy provisions of the Ombudsman Act did not in themselves preclude disclosure under FOI.

The Ombudsman's office did not take the decision lying down. Under the *Administrative Decisions (Judicial Review) Act 1977* (Cwlth) it sought to raise additional grounds of exemption from FOI such as legal professional privilege (s. 42), material obtained in confidence (s. 45), and material which might have an adverse effect on the proper and efficient conduct of an agency (s. 42(1)(d)).

These efforts by the Ombudsman inspired the following response from Mr Justice Sheppard of the Federal Court of Australia

> . . . a public official is not entitled to scratch his head every time he loses a round and say: well, I will think of something else, and put this up as a barrier. That is not the way that the thing should be allowed to go on . . . It's just not on for litigation to be conducted in this way (Cashman 1985, p. 231).

In July 1984 His Honour handed down his decision. The Ombudsman was directed to allow access to that part of the report containing truly factual material. The remainder, nearly a third of the document, was held to be a deliberative process document, and thereby exempt.

The Ombudsman's report was never published, but a copy was obtained by *The Canberra Times* and summarised in a front page article (Coyle 1984). The report was a critical condemnation of the Department of Social Security. It maintained that the decisions to suspend benefit and pension payments to clients in Greece and Australia were unreasonable and unjust. The actions of the Department were faulted for not having been based upon any formal determination of guilt, nor having accorded the beneficiaries any right of reply. The normal procedure of allowing a three-month grace period between the announcement of a decision to terminate benefits and the actual cessation of payments was not followed - nor was the practice of continuing payment pending the outcome of appeals. In addition, the Department failed to keep appellants informed of the progress of their appeals. In the words of the Ombudsman:

> There was no evidence of forethought being given to the impact of suspension before the decision was made.

> ... in any event suspension at large before proof of guilt of those affected by the suspension is a reversal of the normal concept of justice in our society.

> Justification rests on the belief of group guilt, and the action constituted a penalty in advance of assessment of all the pensioners in the light of their individual circumstances (Commonwealth Ombudsman 1984, pp. 90-2).

The Ombudsman recommended that back payments and compensation for loss of fringe benefits be made to some pensioners, and that airfares be refunded for those who had returned to Australia for the purpose of appeals.

The Department of Social Security was wounded by the Ombudsman's report. But rather than display contrition, counsel for the Department at one stage referred to it as 'one of the most prejudicial reports of any Commonwealth Officer which I have read' (Cashman 1985, p. 235).

In June of 1985 the government announced that compensation would be paid to persons whose benefits were discontinued in addition to those individuals whose circumstances were reviewed by the Mitchell Inquiry.

No disciplinary proceedings, much less criminal charges, were brought against police officers or public servants as a result of the conspiracy case.

A Welfare Rights Centre was established in Sydney in 1983 to provide a first line of defence against future infringement of the rights of welfare benefit recipients. Because of the vigilance of organisations such as this, it is unlikely that any abuses on the scale of 'Don's Party' can occur in future.

For its part, the Department of Social Security in dealing with cases of suspected fraud, now prefers to proceed with substantive charges under the Social Security Act and the *Crimes Act 1914* (Cwlth) rather than under general conspiracy charges. The establishment in 1984 of the office of Director of Public Prosecutions has provided the Department with an added awareness of evidentiary requirements in prosecution cases.

In keeping with the unfortunate Australian habit of referring to non-Anglo-Saxons in terms of their ethnic origin, 'Don's Party' and its aftermath became known as the 'Greek Conspiracy Case'. The total cost to the Australian tax-payer approached $100 million, a sum vastly in excess of that which was originally alleged to have been fraudulently acquired.

A decade after 'Don's Party', the only real winners appeared to be those members of the legal profession whose good fortune it was to have become involved in the various legal proceedings which were as lucrative as they were protracted. Political commentator Mungo MacCallum referred to the case as a *Bleak House* type picnic for the legal profession. The case culminated in what was arguably the longest and most expensive committal hearing in the history of the English-speaking world. It may not have been entirely coincidental that two of the major protagonists, Don Thomas and Patrick Lanigan, whose careers were not enhanced by the raids and their aftermath, both resigned their positions and joined the New South Wales Bar. In retrospect, Thomas concluded:

I'd certainly conduct the case in that way again, but I think that I would have the politicians put everything they said on paper before I started (Thomas 1987).

*The author gratefully acknowledges the contributions of the Public Interest Advocacy Centre, Peter Cashman and Roger West in the preparation of this chapter.

References

Australia 1986, *Commission of Inquiry into Compensation arising from Social Security Conspiracy Prosecutions: Report - Volume I,* (Dame Roma Mitchell, Commissioner), Australian Government Publishing Service, Canberra .

Cashman, Peter 1985, 'The Ombudsman - Another View', *Canberra Bulletin of Public Administration,* vol. XII, no. 4, pp. 228-39.

Chobocky, Barbara 1987, *Witch Hunt,* Documentary Films Ltd., Sydney.

Commonwealth Ombudsman 1984, *Report Pursuant to Section 15 of the Ombudsman Act 1976 on a Complaint by Dr Y. Lucire about the Actions of the Department of Social Security,* Ombudsman's Office, Canberra.

Coyle, K. 1984, 'Pensions Cut Condemned : Ombudsman Reports on Greek Social Security Case', *The Canberra Times,* 17 October, p. 1.

Grimes, Don 1987, Interview in Chobocky, B., *Witch Hunt,* Documentary Films Ltd, Sydney.

Kelly, Paul 1979, 'Conspiracy Case : A Political Powder Keg', *The National Times,* 24 November, p. 3.

Thomas, Don 1987, Interview, in Chobocky, B., *Witch Hunt,* Documentary Films, Ltd., Sydney.

Chapter 7

POLITICAL SURVEILLANCE AND THE SOUTH AUSTRALIAN POLICE

Secrecy in government is fundamentally anti-democratic, perpetuating bureaucratic errors.

William O. Douglas, 1898-1980
Justice of the Supreme
Court of the United States

To be afraid of ideas, any idea, is to be unfit for self-government.

Alexander Meiklejohn, 1872-1964
American Educator and Legal Philosopher

Citizens of South Australia have been known to take pride in the fact that theirs is the only state in the Australian federation which did not originate as a penal colony. Unlike their counterparts in the east, the people of Adelaide have a reputation for civility and tolerance. The reputation is not entirely deserved, however, as some aspects of life in the City of Churches have had more sinister overtones.

Involvement of South Australian Police in political surveillance dates to the First World War. Three officers were seconded to Military Intelligence to infiltrate the German immigrant community of Melbourne. In the immediate postwar years, detectives were assigned to monitor trade union activity in mining communities and to report on political speakers in Adelaide's Botanic Gardens (Cain 1983, p. 143 and pp. 178-82).

In 1939, following discussions with other state police forces and the Department of Defence, the South Australian Police Department set up an 'intelligence branch'. The purpose of the new branch was to identify persons of 'potential enemy nationality' or 'Members of hostile Associations who might obstruct the National War Effort.' (Huie 1967, p. 80).

The Intelligence Branch ceased to exist in 1945 when the war ended and when responsibilities for alien registration were assumed by the Australian Department of Immigration. In 1947, the Commissioner of Police established a 'Subversive Section' to collect and record information on persons engaged in or suspected of 'subversive' activities. The primary attentions of the section were devoted to members of the Communist Party of Australia.

Similar sections existed in the police departments of other states and at a 1949 conference of police commissioners, it was agreed that each be known as 'Special Branch'. The South Australian Special Branch thus began its institutional life. It was not a large organisation; in 1977 it consisted of only five officers. Special Branch officers kept a low profile in the bowels of police headquarters. Assignment to the branch was not regarded as particularly prestigious; those officers with ambitions of rising to the rank of inspector and above would have been well advised to avoid a Special Branch posting.

What Special Branch did was collect information about various individuals and groups in South Australia. Whilst their guidelines were not explicit, Special Branch officers were concerned with Communist and related organisations, and other activities which they regarded as extremist or subversive. Although it relied primarily on newspaper accounts, Special Branch also received information from police in the course of normal duties, and engaged agents who infiltrated target groups and reported back to Special Branch. Special Branch was the primary point of liaison between the South Australian Police and ASIO, the federal government's counter intelligence organisation.

By 1977, the amount of information which Special Branch had amassed was considerable. It held about 3,000 separate dossiers and over 40,000 index cards. Individual persons were the subject of some 28,500 cards. Aside from the existence and scope of such a surveillance system, its most significant characteristic was its political bias. There were extensive files on Labor Party parliamentarians including some evidence that, from time to time, they were under physical surveillance at public meetings. All but two of the state and federal Labor parliamentarians were in Special Branch files;

the proportion of Liberal parliamentarians who were the subject of files was much less than half.

Files were kept on the leaders of the trade union movement and on individual unions. There were cards on judges, magistrates, and at least one former governor of South Australia. Even religious leaders were under surveillance:

> Clergymen of the main denominations 'come under notice' and were indexed. Some have special files. Most, if not all, of the activity was peaceful and non-subversive. Even prayer meetings for peace were watched and recorded (South Australia 1977, p. 12).

The Council for Civil Liberties and its members, never among the most favoured citizens of South Australia in the eyes of the police, were all on file.

> Long before the Council was formed, the public utterances of many prominent persons who advocated any form of civil rights or liberties were indexed (South Australia 1977, p. 13).

Other causes whose exponents had aroused sufficient suspicion within Special Branch to warrant systematic attention included women's liberation, the anti-apartheid movement, and a group favouring reform of South Australia's divorce laws. Materials on conservatives and their causes, not to mention right-wing extremists, was relatively rare.

Among the most fundamental values of a liberal society are freedom of expression and freedom of association. The uninhibited exchange of ideas is a hallmark of democratic political life. Thought and discussion of public issues may be suppressed explicitly, through censorship or outright prohibitions of public assembly. But the exercise of democratic political freedom may also be inhibited more subtly. The mere possibility that one's movements and utterances are or might become the subject of police attention may suffice to discourage a person from exercising his or her rights and responsibilities as the citizen of a democratic society.

A healthy democracy requires that the expression of contending viewpoints be encouraged. But under a system of state surveillance the costs of dissenting may be such that some citizens will exclude themselves from public life. The uncertainty over whether or not one is under surveillance may erode the sense of self and sense of autonomy which are requisites of active citizenship. In a society where surveillance is undertaken on any significant scale, a climate of suspicion is created. Trust, a central element of the social fabric, is weakened.

Clandestine surveillance and records thereof pose other threats as well. Malicious accusation or merely erroneous recording practices may result in false information being kept on a person. Secret files and their keepers are not accountable; they are not accessible to their subjects for review and possible correction.

In South Australia, these risks were not merely hypothetical. In the words of the judge who first reviewed the Special Branch files:

> Material which I know to be inaccurate, and sometimes scandalously inaccurate, appears in some dossiers and on some cards. Some of this information appears to have been used in 'vetting' procedures (South Australia, 1977, p. 7). I have seen a number of cards where information, patently false to my own knowledge, has been used to the attempted disadvantage of certain persons (South Australia 1977, p. 55).

A familiar refrain of police commissioners past and present is their professed chronic shortage of personnel. Moreover, one of the more onerous aspects of the policeman's lot is paperwork.

Small irony, then, that not inconsiderable resources were devoted to political surveillance and the maintenance of records arising therefrom. The costs in question were not merely those relating to the five officers serving in Special Branch. Indeed, it appears they relied for their intelligence material on many of their brethren on patrol. A portion of the material was based on physical surveillance by informers and notes of meetings:

From 1953-1954 onwards the ordinary police (at the request of Special Branch on behalf of ASIO) gave reports on persons buying 'The Tribune' in suburbs and towns from one end of the State to the other. Police also kept watch on all meetings of communists at factory gates, at street corners and near polling booths. Police were also attending various meetings in industrial country towns where communists were expected to show up but did not. Reports on these meetings resulted in many innocent persons being watched and being clumsily and adversely reported upon (South Australia 1977, p. 55).

There seems little doubt that the difficulties involving the South Australian Special Branch arose from lack of proper supervision by senior officers in the Department. The unit was small and kept a low profile, to say the least. Organisationally, it was attached to the Criminal Investigation Branch. For those heading the CIB, faced with a regular supply of unsolved crimes to investigate, suspects to apprehend, and cases to prepare for prosecution, it was convenient to ignore Special Branch. Indeed, the senior officers of CIB traditionally left Special Branch and its affairs to the Commissioner of Police personally. In turn, Commissioners were inclined to allow the Sergeant in charge of Special Branch to manage its affairs without supervision:

> The Commissioner and Assistant Commissioner both said that they had never made a physical search of the large quantity of files and cards, that they rarely even visited Special Branch and that they relied upon information supplied by staff (South Australia 1977, p. 67).

This excessive degree of delegation was to prove more than embarrassing. Lack of supervision by senior police was one matter. Lack of accountability was another:

> Identification of the enemies of the states is one of the highest functions of responsible government and should not be delegated, without ministerial

supervision, to a police or other force (South Australia 1977, p. 61).

But ministerial supervision was not easy to achieve. As it happened, the South Australian Police concealed the extent of political surveillance in which its officers were engaged on at least three different occasions between 1970 and 1977. The circumstances were to culminate in the dismissal of a police commissioner.

Australia's constitutional arrangements placed the activities of state police special branches beyond the purview of the federal minister responsible for ASIO (the Attorney-General of Australia). At the same time, neither Special Branch officers nor the Commissioner of Police at the time considered themselves to be responsible to the state government on many matters under Special Branch purview. In the words of the then Commissioner of Police, Harold Sainsbury:

> As I see it the duty of the police is solely to the law.
> It is to the Crown and not to any politically elected
> government or to any politician or to anyone else
> for that matter (quoted in South Australia 1978,
> p. 19).

Events proved this contention to be both politically unwise and legally incorrect. Indeed, the constitutional status of the South Australian police had only recently been formalised, in the aftermath of a royal commission arising from anti-war protests in the early 1970s (Waller 1980).

The initial criteria by which individuals and activities were selected for attention by Special Branch were themselves vague. ASIO, itself an organisation with no dearth of problems (Australia, 1977) provided inadequate guidelines and training to special branches. There was no in-house training in the South Australian Special Branch beyond that flowing from day-to-day routine. As years wore on, Special Branch activities acquired a momentum of their own, as did those of the Vice Squad*, reflecting adversely on the managerial competence of successive South Australian police commissioners.

Once embarked on a course, bureaucracies, even bureaucracies as small as Special Branch, develop the impulse to perpetuate and justify their existence. Where tangible threats to national security no longer exist, less tangible threats may be perceived (or even invented). Stated another more general way, bureaucracies will find work to occupy their energies, even where none may naturally exist.

In other respects, however, the Special Branch was less adaptable. The inherent conservatism and insularity of police in general was perhaps even greater within Special Branch than in the rest of the Department. In any event, the sweeping scope of Special Branch records revealed an inability, if not an unwillingness, to distinguish between dissent and subversion. It was also suggested that the excessive zeal of Special Branch may have arisen in part from American cultural imperialism. Few Australians experienced at first hand the chilling years of the McCarthy era in the United States when careers and even lives were ruined by the mere suggestion of leftist sympathies. But then, as now, the American interpretation of reality is often embraced uncritically by Australian authorities:

> We have imported many ideas and practices from the United States, usually in a diluted form and usually late enough to avoid what have been discovered to be their worst features. Practices relating to security measures to counter subversion are no exception. I found that most of the FBI's ideas about 'subversion' security risks and information gathering have percolated down to Special Branch, no doubt through ASIO training and influence (Australia 1977, p. 38).

---

*Dr George Duncan, Adelaide University law lecturer, drowned in the River Torrens in 1973. Years later former officers of the South Australian Vice Squad were charged with manslaughter over the incident. They were eventually acquitted.

Ironically, some of the more constructive aspects of American institutions had been ignored. By the late 1970s the FBI had developed written guidelines regarding the investigation of domestic security cases:

> Under no circumstances is an investigation (to be) conducted of an individual on the basis that such individual supports unpopular causes or opposes government policies (quoted in South Australia 1977, p. 39).

Public awareness of Special Branch and its activities grew very slowly. In October 1970 the South Australian state council of the Australian Labor Party (ALP) called upon the government to state whether such a branch existed, and whether it undertook surveillance of trade unions and political parties. In a telephone inquiry to Commissioner Salisbury, the Premier, Don Dunstan, was advised that Special Branch did exist, but that it was a small operation concerned with information relating to politically motivated violence.

In mid-1975, the South Australian government was approached by Mr Justice Hope, who at the time held a Royal Commission to enquire into Australia's security and intelligence activities. On behalf of the Royal Commissioner, the South Australian Premier's Department requested an outline of Special Branch activities. An outline was provided on 30 June 1975 and was subsequently found to be inadequate by the Royal Commissioner. Additional information was requested in August and September. The Police Commissioner's response again omitted reference to surveillance of political and trade union activities.

In May 1976 the state council of the ALP and one of the party sub-branches made inquiries of the Chief Secretary (the South Australian minister responsible for police) regarding Special Branch activities in general. The Deputy Commissioner of Police replied in general terms that:

> the Special Branch specializes in subversive activities that could lead to crimes against the State (quoted in South Australia 1978, p. 79).

This vague response was then communicated to the Acting State Secretary of the ALP.

Over a year later, in September 1977, the Adelaide Bureau Chief of *The Australian* newspaper submitted a list of questions to the Premier's office regarding political surveillance and dossiers on unconvicted people. Before a response was forthcoming, the journalist, Peter Ward, who had formerly been an executive assistant to Premier Dunstan, published an article headed 'Exposed . . . the Secret Police Dossiers on Demonstrations' (Terry & Ward 1977).

The article implied that the Premier had been reluctant to act on the existence of secret police. When no response was forthcoming to Ward, he brought his article to the attention of Mr Robin Millhouse, M.P., the lone Australian Democrat member of the South Australian House of Assembly.

Millhouse placed his own questions on notice. The reply given on 1 November 1977 revealed that the police did keep records on persons who had not been charged or convicted of crime, but was otherwise vague. There followed another article in *The Australian* which criticised Dunstan's alleged failure 'to ensure that such surveillance of political dissenters and political terrorists as is necessary is conducted under the right kind of supervision, with the correct degree of care' (Ward 1977).

Such pressure from press and Parliament moved the government to act quickly. State Cabinet met in the absence of Premier Dunstan, who was overseas, and decided to hold a judicial inquiry into Special Branch.

The inquiry was conducted by Mr Acting Justice J.M. White of the South Australian Supreme Court. His terms of reference actually specified the criteria by which information should thereafter be retained on file:

> No records, or other material, shall be kept by the Police Commissioner, or any person under his control as Commissioner, with respect to any person unless:
>
> 1) That record or material, either alone or with other existing records or material, contains matters which give rise to a reasonable

suspicion that that person, or some other person, has committed an offence, or

2) That record or material, either alone or with other existing records or material, contains matters which formed the whole or part of the facts with respect to which that person has been charged with an offence in respect of which proceedings have not been dismissed or withdrawn, or

3) That record or material, either alone or with other existing records or material, contains matters which give rise to a reasonable suspicion that that person may do any act or thing which would overthrow, or tend to overthrow, by force or violence, the established Government of South Australia or of the Commonwealth of Australia, or may commit or incite the commission of acts of violence against any person or persons (quoted in South Australia 1977, p. 57).

The terms also enabled Mr Acting Justice White to require the Commissioner of Police to examine records to ensure compliance with the above criteria, and to certify formally that they were in fact in compliance. The judge was further empowered to conduct random checks to ensure the accuracy of the Commissioner's certification, and to report annually to the government on continued compliance.

The *White Report* was submitted to the Premier on 21 December 1977. As indicated by the extracts cited above, it was extremely critical of Special Branch, its activities, and its management. The Report concluded that a 'great mass of irrelevant material (often potentially harmful, sometimes actually harmful) has accumulated' (South Australia 1977, p. 71).

Moreover, the Report noted that the Commissioner of Police had failed to inform the government fully about the existence of sensitive files on matters relating to politics, trade unions and other affairs.

When Dunstan confronted Salisbury with the *White Report*, he expressed his extreme displeasure and concluded that Salisbury had misled him and that he in turn had misled the public. Salisbury conceded that some of his answers 'may have been pulled a little' (Cockburn 1979, p. 21) but maintained that the *White Report* was an over-reaction to the situation.

When Dunstan expressed the intention of publishing the Report, Salisbury expressed alarm and suggested that the effect would be 'volcanic' (Cockburn 1979, p. 21).

On 16 January 1978 Cabinet decided that the *White Report* be published immediately, that the Premier ask for the Police Commissioner's resignation, and that if this was not forthcoming the Commissioner should be dismissed from office. Salisbury refused to yield, and the notice of dismissal was delivered to him on 17 January.

The matter was far from concluded, however. Salisbury was a popular man, both within the police department and among Adelaide's conservative establishment. The Liberal Opposition questioned the rigour of the *White Report* and the legality of the dismissal. Liberal members reaffirmed their faith in Salisbury's integrity and hinted that the government had something to hide.

The Premier continued to reaffirm the principles of responsible government and argued that he had clearly been misled by the former Commissioner of Police.

The Opposition, which controlled the state's upper house, was inclined to convene a select committee of inquiry. The government acted instead, and appointed a Royal Commission on 10 February 1978. At the end of May, the Royal Commissioner, Justice Roma Mitchell of the South Australian Supreme Court, presented her report.

In firmly dismissing the former Commissioner's contention that he owed a duty to the Crown and not to any elected government, Justice Mitchell said:

> That statement . . . suggests an absence of understanding of the constitutional system of South Australia or, for that matter, of the United Kingdom (South Australia 1978, p. 19).

She concluded that the former police commissioner had indeed misled the government, that the government's decision to dismiss him was indeed justifiable in the circumstances. Justice Mitchell further concluded that the *Police Regulation Act 1952* (SA) be amended to provide for explicit grounds for a Commissioner's dismissal by the Governor. She recommended against any parliamentary involvement in a Commissioner's removal from office.

In the immediate aftermath of the dismissal of the Police Commissioner, the Dunstan government issued a set of instructions pursuant to the Police Regulation Act. These sought clearly to limit the conditions under which Special Branch could collect and retain information to those circumstances involving security, narrowly defined. Specifically, they required that the information, either alone or with other existing materials, give rise to a reasonable suspicion that an offence relevant to security has been committed, that a person might commit or incite the commission to acts of violence, or that a person might act to overthrow the federal or state government. They provided for the review of Special Branch files under the supervision of Mr Acting Justice White, and for the destruction of those materials which did not conform to the newly specified criteria. In addition, the new instructions required that approval of the responsible state minister be obtained before any Special Branch information be disclosed, and that:

> Special Branch shall cease recruiting, paying, servicing or otherwise acting as intermediary for agents of the Australian Security Intelligence Organisation or any other organisation, and shall act in all respects only as a branch of the SA Police force . . . (*South Australian Government Gazette*, 18 January 1978, pp. 287-8).

Salisbury retired to England, with the $160,000 he would have earned had he served the remainder of his term as Commissioner. Premier Dunstan resigned from Parliament on grounds of ill-health in February 1979 and by the end of the year a Liberal government was in power in South Australia for the first time in nearly a decade. In November 1980 the Tonkin government replaced the 1978 instructions with a new set which removed the express requirement for ministerial approval before information from Special Branch Files could be disclosed. In addition, it relaxed constraints on discretionary decision-making by Special Branch officers and did not specify how incorrect, obsolete, or irrelevant data might be corrected or destroyed. New procedures for independent auditing of files failed to require specifically that the actual 'hands-on' audit be performed by the independent auditor; rather, the auditing task was limited to assurance that the responsible police officers had performed certain functions (*South Australian Government Gazette*, 20 November 1980, pp. 1926-7).

Another change was necessitated by the unwillingness of the state's Chief Justice to make a member of the judiciary available for the ongoing auditing of Special Branch files. Noting that Special Branch was a part of executive government and that its activities were very much the subject of partisan political controversy, the Chief Justice maintained that principles of separation of powers and judicial independence precluded ongoing judicial oversight of its operations. As alternative, the government appointed a retired Supreme Court judge, the Honourable David Hogarth, Q.C. as auditor.

Labor returned to power in Adelaide in November 1982, and set about rectifying what were perceived to be inadequacies in the previous government's policy.

Appropriately, it chose the year 1984 in which to abolish Special Branch, replacing it with an Operations Intelligence Section. The nature of information which this new body could gather and record was defined precisely to exclude non-violent activity and peaceful dissent. The new regulations imposed strict conditions on the disclosure of information, and contained provisions to ensure that the new unit would remain accountable. The Police Commissioner is required to report to the responsible minister twice yearly regarding the unit's activities, and an auditor, independent of both the police and the public service, reports annually to the Governor. This role continued to be performed by Mr Hogarth Q.C.

Similar reorganisations had taken place following the abolition of special branches in Victoria and Western Australia. But elsewhere in Australia, governments have been reluctant to change the *modus operandi* of their security surveillance bodies. Little is known of the Queensland Special Branch. In New South Wales, however, Special Branch continues to be the subject of more scrutiny and criticism than it no doubt would prefer to receive (Molomby 1986).

References

Australia 1977, *Royal Commission on Intelligence and Security*, Reports, (Royal Commissioner, Mr Justice Hope), Australian Government Publishing Service, Canberra .

Cain, Frank 1983, *The Origins of Political Surveillance in Australia*, Angus & Robertson, Sydney.

Cockburn, Stewart 1979, *The Salisbury Affair*, Sun Books, Melbourne.

Huie, R. 1967, 'Functions of Special Branch' Internal Memorandum South Australian Police Department, Reprinted in South Australia 1977, *Special Branch Security Records* Premier's Department, Adelaide 1977, pp 78-86.

Molomby, Tom 1986, *Spies, Bombs and the Path of Bliss*, Potoroo Press, Sydney.

South Australia 1977, *Special Branch Security Records : Initial Report*, (Report of Mr Acting Justice J.M. White), Premier's Department, Adelaide.

South Australia 1978, *Royal Commission 1978 : Report on the Dismissal of Harold Hubert Salisbury*, (Royal Commissioner, Justice Roma Mitchell), Government Printer, Adelaide.

South Australian Government Gazette 18 January 1978, pp. 287-8.

ibid. 20 November 1980, pp. 1926-7.

Terry, P. & Ward, P. 1977, 'Exposed . . . The Secret Police Dossiers on Demonstrations', *The Australian*, 3 September.

Waller, Louis 1980, 'The Police, The Premier, and Parliament : Governmental Control of the Police' *Monash Law Review*, 6, 249-67.

References

Ward, Peter 1977, 'Secret Police Files a Nettle for Dunstan to Grasp', *The Australian*, 3 November.

Chapter 8

CAUGHT IN THE ACT: THE ASIS RAID

At about 8 pm on Wednesday, 30 November 1983, the Manager of the Sheraton Hotel in Melbourne was alerted by a guest to a disturbance on the 10th floor. The Manager entered a lift and upon reaching the 10th floor, he was accosted by a stranger who said 'Come with me, you're not going to get hurt, but come with me.' The Manager retreated back into the lift, the stranger followed and pressed the appropriate button to return to the lobby. The two scuffled while descending. The stranger's repeated insistence that 'nobody would be hurt' was not entirely reassuring. When the lift reached the lobby, the Manager ran out and called for his staff to ring the police. The stranger retreated to the 10th floor.

Shortly thereafter another lift reached the ground floor. A group of hotel employees were gathered near the door of the lift, and the Manager equipped himself with a nightstick - a 30 cm metal rod covered with heavy duty red tape - which was normally kept behind the reception desk. As the lift door opened, a group of men stepped out. Some were wearing masks, some were carrying weapons, ranging from Browning 9 mm automatic pistols to the formidable Heckler and Koch submachine gun. The intruders moved through the lobby into the kitchen, menacing the kitchen staff on the way, and departed in two getaway cars waiting outside a kitchen exit.

One of the cars was stopped by officers of the Victoria Police a short distance from the hotel and its occupants were taken into custody. When other police officers arrived at the hotel, they encountered a bystander, who rather strangely claimed that he could explain everything that had happened, and that he was willing to pay for any damages incurred. Hotel staff may have assumed that they were the victims of an armed robbery; in fact they were unwilling parties to an incident culminating a year of acute embarrassment for the new Hawke Labor government. The episode in question turned out to have been a resoundingly unsuccessful training exercise by officers of the super-secret Australian Secret Intelligence Service (ASIS).

ASIS, unknown to most Australians prior to its having been thrust, reluctantly, into the public spotlight, is Australia's equivalent of the United States' CIA and Britain's MI6. Although its primary function was the collection of foreign intelligence, it was also required, as a result of decisions taken by the Fraser government and continued by their successors, to maintain a 'covert action capability'. While the precise contours of this minor role remain secret, it appears that such a function involved para-military activities - for example, the rescue of hostages (Wright 1989).

To this end, a small group of part-time agents were recruited and brought together for periodic training exercises. The ill-fated visit to the Sheraton Hotel was for the purpose of rescuing a 'hostage' being held in a room by two 'foreign intelligence officers of a major power'. In an effort to make training activities as realistic as possible, it was decided to conduct the exercise in a public place, without notifying hotel staff, local police or bystanders. The trainees were equipped with weapons, albeit without live ammunition.

The episode caused considerable distress to a number of unwitting individuals. One member of the hotel staff at whom a submachine gun was pointed gave evidence to the Royal Commission that the experience was so traumatising he afterwards felt 'emotionally unstable', suffered from a 'lack of sleep' and experienced 'recurring headaches' (Australia 1984, p. 30). Moreover, the potential for physical harm to members of the public was substantial. As luck would have it, what could have resulted in tragedy came to be regarded by many members of the public as farce. In addition to the cost of their accommodation, the make-believe captors and their hostage incurred expenses of $70 for alcoholic beverages. Their hotel room door, moreover, had been smashed in with a sledgehammer.

It was apparent to Mr Justice Hope, the Royal Commissioner who was asked to inquire into the matter, that the ASIS blunder arose from serious lapses in planning and supervision of the training exercise. He fixed primary responsibility for these lapses on the ASIS officer (referred to anonymously as 'P/EM'), who was both in charge of the special operations covert action program and manager of the abortive training exercise. The most obvious deficiency was the failure to notify either the Victoria Police or the hotel manager of the exercise. The decisions were conscious ones.

In his testimony before the Royal Commission, the officer expressed concern that disclosure would compromise security of the ASIS special operations program.

> The basic reason that crossed my mind when I dismissed the possibility of informing the police was that I was probably concerned about the security of the actual operation itself, not necessarily the Exercise, and was worried that informing the police might cause them to show some interest in our activities in Melbourne at that time and perhaps even identify some of the operatives. But I must say that I dismissed the possibility of informing the police fairly early in the piece and chose myself on this occasion not to inform them (quoted in Australia 1984, p. 26).

The officer also expressed his belief that hotel management and staff would not become aware of the exercise.

> [I] didn't envisage that any of the hotel staff or any member of the public would be involved with the team and, in fact, the hotel staff would not even know the team were in the hotel (quoted in Australia 1984, p. 22).

The Royal Commissioner, noting that properly executed covert operations in the real world have contingency plans, faulted P/EM for failing to have any such plans for the Sheraton raid.

> These failures in planning effectively meant that, once the final stages of the Exercise had commenced, the trainees were out of control. Nothing short of a specific order from an ASIS officer of P/EM's seniority at least, would have stopped the trainees from completing their assignment with single-minded determination - no matter what reservations any of them may have felt

as to the propriety of their conduct (Australia 1984, p. 28).

The Royal Commissioner also called attention to what he perceived to be a lack of skills and experience appropriate to the leadership of such a raid.

I find it difficult to imagine that a real covert operation, similar in nature to the Exercise, would not require the presence of a leader with the experience, capacity and judgement which a military officer would have (Australia 1984, p. 21).

Whilst acknowledging the desirability of a certain amount of realism in training exercises, the Royal Commissioner contended that the degree of realism achieved in the Sheraton operation was excessive.

It simply was not necessary to break down a hotel door with a sledgehammer, to attempt to restrain the Hotel Manager, to carry weapons, and to display them to unwitting members of the public. The authenticity of the exercise would not have been compromised by a greater degree of simulation (Australia 1984, p. 24).

The Minister responsible for ASIS, Foreign Minister Bill Hayden, was absolved of responsibility for the agent's misconduct by the Royal Commissioner. Despite the argument by critics that security intelligence operations should be under strict ministerial control (Toohey 1983a), Mr Justice Hope concluded that Hayden had no duty to inquire into specific details of ASIS training programs, and the Acting Director General had no duty to inform him. 'Having given his general approval for the project ASIS had commenced, the Minister was entitled to believe that the Acting Director General would ensure that special operations activities were conducted legally, properly and safely' (Australia 1984, p. 18).

According to the Royal Commissioner, 'ASIS management recognised only belatedly the requirement for better supervision, closer direction and tighter control' of the covert action program (Australia 1984, p. 23). A decision was taken in early November 1983, to place the program under the control of a 'Directorate of Covert Action and Emergency Planning', scheduled to be established by 1 February 1984. In the interim, P/EM was denied the planning and administrative support which might have prevented breaches of the law arising from the Sheraton exercise.

Although P/EM bore primary responsibility for the planning and execution of the Sheraton raid, he failed to inform his immediate supervisor of the details of the operation, and to obtain his approval for the aspects which the exercise entailed. In giving brief outlines of the operation to the Acting Director General of ASIS and to the agency's Head of Emergency Planning, P/EM implied that the concealed handguns were to be carried and force was not to be used. Authorisation for the mission was granted on that basis.

The Royal Commissioner further criticised P/EM for not making it explicit to the trainees that force was not to be used in gaining entry to the hotel room, particularly as he had assured the Acting Director General that 'doors would not be bashed down' (Australia 1984, p. 37). The trainees thus assumed that the use of force, if necessary, had been authorised. P/EM moreover, was physically present when the trainees began their forced entry, and did not intervene.

P/EM failed to instruct the trainees regarding the use which they could make of the weapons which they were issued, and regarding their interaction with those members of the public with whom they might come in contact. The Royal Commissioner referred to the failure to instruct the trainees adequately as 'deplorable' (Australia 1984, p. 39).

The Acting Director General of ASIS, John Ryan, was faulted for having authorised a training operation to take place in public, in the Sheraton Hotel, involving the use of concealed weapons by trainees. The authorisation moreover, was given in ignorance of whether or not hotel management or the Victoria police were to be made aware of the exercise, or whether contingency plans had been prepared, or of what provisions for supervision had been considered.

The Acting Director General was criticised for not informing the Deputy Director General and the Assistant Director General of his interest in the exercise and of insisting that planning and implementation of the exercise occur through the normal lines of authority (Australia 1984, p. 43).

The immediate supervisor of P/EM was the Assistant Director General (Operations). He had, however, 'only the most general knowledge of the Exercise' (Australia 1984, p. 44). Whilst he apparently expected P/EM would keep him informed, he was criticised by the Royal Commissioner for taking insufficient steps to ensure that this was, in fact, the case. By virtue of the Acting Director General's passing involvement in the exercise, the Assistant Director General was less dedicated to the supervision of his subordinate than was necessary.

The Deputy Director General too came in for criticism for his lack of attentiveness to the covert action program and to the Sheraton raid. In the words of the Acting Director General, Mr Ryan:

> [W]hen you run a Branch which includes a section which is engaged in an exercise, or when you run a Division that includes a Branch, that includes a section running an exercise, in my book you're expected to know what's going on (Australia 1984, p. 46).

The Royal Commissioner was more forgiving of the ASIS trainees. The team leader was criticised for not seeking clarification of the potentially illegal aspects of the exercise, and for seeking to restrain the hotel manager. Mr Justice Hope found that the trainees were entitled to assume that they were authorised to carry weapons, but not justified in brandishing them in the presence of members of the public.

In addressing specifically the Sheraton incident, Mr Justice Hope neglected to confront more general issues of accountability of such a traditionally secret agency. However, he may have dealt with these issues in the course of a secret report. But the precise managerial dynamics of just how an agency such as ASIS is mobilised to undertake a particular task, or prevented from engaging in other activities is a vexed issue. It has, for example, been alleged that 'ASIS officers have actually murdered people in Indonesia' (Toohey 1983a).

It has, moreover, been suggested that when the Whitlam government was in office, ASIS

> was unaware of the help it was giving to the CIA by lending two officers to help in Chile at the time of the destabilisation project against the democratically elected Government of Salvadore [sic] Allende; (Toohey 1983a).

According to a previously secret document presented to the Fraser government, Mr Justice Hope himself acknowledged that espionage necessitates crime.

> We should not allow the use of any euphemisms to cloud the central issue - that ASIS exists to conduct espionage against foreign countries and that to do it successfully ASIS must probably infringe the laws of those countries and certainly be prepared to do so (Toohey 1983b).

One of the getaway cars was apprehended by the Victoria Police a short distance from the Sheraton. In the car the police found one submachine gun, a sledgehammer, a jemmy, and four plastic masks, among other equipment.

The suspects declined to identify themselves on grounds of national security.

At the time of the Sheraton raid, Australian security and intelligence agencies were already the subject of a Royal Commission. This of course, had arisen out of the Combe-Ivanov affair in mid 1983 (Marr 1984). The Commissioner was approached informally on the day following the raid by the Foreign Minister to request that the circumstances of the raid be incorporated into the inquiry.

Mr Justice Hope began collecting evidence on 2 December. Formal hearings began on 12 December and concluded on 12 January 1984. The report was published the following month. Among the requests conveyed by the Prime Minister to the Royal Commissioner was that of exploring 'whether any breach of the law was committed by anyone carrying out or authorising the exercise' (correspondence: Hawke to Hope, 7 December 1983; Australia 1984, p. 76).

The Royal Commissioner remarked that it would be 'oppressive' for him to make specific findings about individuals' possible breaches of the criminal law of Victoria, and to present such findings to the federal government which would not be responsible for prosecution. Rather, His Honour specified those statutory provisions which seemed to apply. The list was embarrassing in its length.

Firearms Act 1958

Possessing a pistol without a licence s.22(1)
Carrying a loaded firearm s.29E(1)
Possession of a machine gun s.32(3)
Possession of a silencer s.34(1)

Crimes Act 1958

Common assault s.37
Burglary s.76(1)
Aggravated burglary (firearm in possession) s.77(1)
Possession of articles for use in the course of burglary s.91(1)
Wilful damage to property s.9
Intentional destruction of another's property s.197(1)
Possession of implement with the purpose of using it to destroy
Property s.199
Aid, abet, counsel or procure the commission of an offence ss.323-4

Summary Offences Act 1966

Offensive or riotous behaviour in a public place s.17
Assault s.23
Assault in company s.24

Vagrancy Act 1966

Being found armed with an offensive weapon
s.6(1)(e)
Possessing a disguise without lawful excuse s.6(1)(f)
Possessing housebreaking implements s.7(1)(g)
Being found within a building without lawful
excuse s.7(1)(i)
Carrying a firearm with criminal intent s.8(a)

Motor Car Act 1958

Failure to provide a driver's licence or refusing to
state name and address when requested to do so by
a member of the police force s.29

Common Law

Common Assault
Affray
Conspiracy

The Royal Commissioner saw it as neither appropriate
nor as part of his Terms of Reference to make findings or
recommendations as to whether specific persons had
committed any offence or whether they should be prosecuted.

The Minister for Foreign Affairs on behalf of the
Commonwealth government submitted that as

> the persons responsible for such breaches of state
> law as may have been committed in the course of
> or in relation to the exercise neither intended to
> commit such breaches as breaches nor committed
> such breaches for their own purposes but rather in
> accordance with the directions given to them by
> persons whom they reasonably believe to be
> authorised to give such directions, no good purpose
> would be served by the prosecution of the persons
> (quoted in Australia 1984, pp. 66-7).

Nevertheless, the Premier of Victoria, upon first learning of ASIS involvement in the raid, claimed that no-one in Victoria was above the law.

Nearly one year after the Sheraton raid, the High Court of Australia dismissed the pleas by the unfortunate ASIS agents that their identities not be disclosed to the Victorian authorities. The Court held that any contract between the agents and the Commonwealth government which forbade that any individual's name be divulged were under the circumstances unenforceable. The names of the agents were duly handed to the Victoria Police. For a while, it appeared that Victorian authorities might proceed. Indeed, state parliament had even passed special legislation to suppress the names of any defendants in proceedings arising from the raid, and to provide for court hearings to be held *in camera*. To allay concerns that the criminal justice system of Victoria was returning to the ethos of the Star Chamber, the special legislation was specifically limited to the Sheraton incident, and contained a sunset clause which provided for its cessation of operation after two years. But notwithstanding previous remarks to the contrary by Premier Cain that no-one in Victoria was 'above the law', there were to be no prosecutions. Public and private requests by the Commonwealth government not to proceed prevailed in the end. Officially, the Chief Commissioner of Police, on the advice of the state Director of Public Prosecutions, announced that matters would not proceed. It was maintained that as the suspects had worn masks, it was not possible to determine who had done precisely what, and that lack of evidence precluded the laying of specific charges.

There was, however, some justice for the victims of the raid. Shortly after the incident, hotel management initiated legal action on behalf of itself and its employees against the Commonwealth government. In an out of court settlement, Victorian Holdings, a subsidiary of Brick and Pipe Industries Ltd. and manager of the hotel at the time of the raid, received $259,000 in exemplary damages from the government (*Australian Financial Review* 30 October 1984, p. 81). Employees of the hotel received additional amounts which were not disclosed. It has been reported that the total settlement amounted to approximately $300,000 (*The Age* 22 March 1984).

The mechanisms of oversight and accountability for Australian security intelligence agencies which were inherited by the Hawke government when it came to power in March 1983 soon proved to be embarrassingly inadequate. Certainly, they were relatively modest compared to those safeguards which had been adopted over the previous decade in the United States and Canada. These sister English-speaking democracies had themselves suffered embarrassing scandals in the 1970s which provided the impetus for significant reforms.

In Canada, the findings of the McDonald Commission that the Security Service of the Royal Canadian Mounted Police had engaged in warrantless entry and electronic surveillance, interceptions of mail, and other abuses led to the abolition of the RCMP security intelligence function and the creation of a new civilian security intelligence agency with a clear legislative mandate. Oversight is currently exercised by an independent Inspector General as well as by the Security Intelligence Review Committee, comprised of three privy counsellors appointed after consultation with the leader of the opposition and the leader of each party in the House of Commons (Rutan 1985).

In the United States, evidence of assassination programs overseas, of illegal entry and surveillance of American citizens at home, and of complicity in the Watergate affair on the part of the Central Intelligence Agency led to the creation of a variety of oversight mechanisms (Flanagan 1985). Both the US Senate and the House of Representatives established permanent bi-partisan intelligence oversight committees by the end of the 1970s. In addition, Congress appropriates all funds for US intelligence agencies, thereby exercising a degree of fiscal oversight.

Each US intelligence agency has its own inspector-general. Executive oversight for intelligence activities is assisted by the Office of Management and Budget, and by the Intelligence Oversight Board, a panel of private citizens charged with monitoring, through the inspectors-general of the various agencies, the legality and propriety of intelligence activities.

The final report on Australia's Security and Intelligence Agencies was presented to the Commonwealth government in 1985. While much of it remains secret, the Prime Minister did reveal a number of the report's recommendations which pertained to ASIS. These included the recommendation that ASIS no longer have an 'attack function' and that its agents henceforth be forbidden to carry out 'special political action' in any foreign countries. It was also recommended that the use of weapons by ASIS agents be discontinued, and that the agency's existing supply of weapons and explosives be disposed of. On 22 May 1985, the Prime Minister announced in Parliament that these recommendations had been accepted by the government. Ostensibly, ASIS would thereafter stick to what it did best - the collection and analysis of foreign intelligence.

A representative of the Queensland government is reputed to have recommended that Australian intelligence agents be given special indemnity from prosecution for offences which they might commit during training exercises and operations (Kitney 1985). No such policy has been adopted, however. If the Sheraton case is any precedent, future offenders will be quietly diverted from the criminal process once media attention subsides.

The Prime Minister announced additional steps to improve the oversight and accountability of ASIS and related organisations. Henceforth, the Security Committee of Cabinet would meet regularly, and would develop clear guidelines and directions for security intelligence agencies. The Committee would be assisted by a full-time Secretariat in the Department of the Prime Minister and Cabinet. In addition, the Secretaries Committee on Intelligence and Security, comprised of permanent heads of relevant government departments, would be expanded to include the Secretary of the Attorney-General's Department and of the Department of Special Minister of State.

Following a recommendation of the Hope Report, the government would also establish an Office of the Inspector-General of Intelligence and Security. The Inspector-General and a small supporting staff would perform an auditing function of security and intelligence agencies as recommended in the Australian Labor Party submission to the Hope Royal Commission. The Inspector-General would be approved to act at the request of the Attorney-General, in response to a complaint, on his or her own initiative.

The lack of strict ministerial scrutiny of ASIS activities which Mr Justice Hope found tolerable nevertheless remained troublesome to a majority of government members. While His Honour explicitly recommended *against* parliamentary oversight of security agencies by means of a bi-partisan committee, the spotty record of the agencies in question, combined with a lingering suspicion on the part of many that the agencies were insufficiently accountable under existing arrangements, carried the day. The Leader of the Opposition referred to these additional safeguards as unnecessary, attributing them to 'left wing paranoia'. The fact that it was the government, and not the opposition, which faced the risk of embarrassment from any future indiscretions was not raised in response. Whether the new oversight structures and a narrower mandate for ASIS would succeed in preventing future malpractice by Australian intelligence agents is a question which may be answered in time.

References

The Age 22 March 1984.

Australia 1984, *Royal Commission on Australia's Security and Intelligence Agencies: Report on the Sheraton Hotel Incident*, Mr Justice Hope, Royal Commissioner, Australian Government Publishing Service, Canberra.

Australian Financial Review 30 October 1984, p. 81.

The Canberra Times 14 January 1989, p. 1.

ibid. 15 January, p. 17.

ibid. 16 January, p. 1.

Flanagan, S. 1985, 'Managing the Intelligence Community' *International Security* vol. 10, no. 1, pp. 58-95.

Kitney, Geoff 1985, 'Sheraton Hotel Bungle May Cost ASIS its Covert Raiders', *The National Times* 1-7 March, p. 3.

Marr, David 1984, *The Ivanov Trail*, Nelson, Melbourne.

Rutan, G. 1985, 'The Canadian Security Intelligence Service: Squaring the Demands of National Security with Canadian Democracy', *Conflict Quarterly*, vol. 5, no. 4, pp. 17-30.

Toohey, Brian 1983a, 'Who's in Charge, Bill?', *The National Times* 2-8 December, p. 2.

------------ 1983b, 'Secret Report: Judge Content for ASIS to Break the Law', *The National Times* 9-15 December, p. 4.

Additional reading

Simpson, B. 1984, 'The Criminal Proceedings Act and the Sheraton Raid', *Legal Service Bulletin*, vol. 9, no. 4, pp. 194-6.

Chapter 9

THE DEPUTY CROWN SOLICITOR AND THE
BOTTOM OF THE HARBOUR SCHEME

The deliberate stripping of a company's assets so that it is unable to pay its debts is a time-honoured practice. It also happens to constitute a criminal fraud. During the 1970s in Australia, variations on this practice were employed by hundreds of more affluent members of the community to avoid paying taxes. This genre of tax evasion was to contribute a new term to the Australian lexicon: Bottom of the Harbour.

At the time, a company with no debts and with an annual profit of $100,000 would have a tax liability of $46,000. To avoid this liability, the owner of the company had only to sell the company to a promoter for the value of the profits, less an agreed-upon commission (for example 10 per cent). Instead of finishing the year with $54,000, the former owner of the company would walk away with $90,000. The promoter, in turn, would keep the $10,000 commission and dispose of the company by turning it over to a person of limited means, with no knowledge of the company's tax liabilities and no interest in retaining company records and books. The Australian Taxation Office and ultimately the honest taxpayers of Australia were $46,000 the poorer.

More intricate variations on this 'simple strip' may or may not have involved fraud on the revenue, depending on whether the necessary elements of dishonesty could be established. Expertise within the Australian government, indeed, within the Australian legal profession, in prosecuting such matters, was all but non-existent.

When the bottom of the harbour schemes were in full flower, the sums involved were millions of dollars, not hundreds of thousands. Indeed, the full cost of this chapter of Australian criminal history ran to thousands of millions of dollars. Some 7,000 companies were involved (Sutton forthcoming).

The proliferation of extremely artificial tax avoidance schemes in the 1970s was to a large extent encouraged by members of the legal and accounting professions. The law reports indicate the lenient attitude taken by the courts during this period. Cases such as *Curran v. The Federal Commissioner of Taxation* 74 ATC 4296 and *Slutzkin v. The Federal Commissioner of Taxation* 140 CLR 314, provide examples of the extraordinary lenience with which courts tolerated artificial tax avoidance which in many cases bordered on the fraudulent.

The medium in which these massive frauds on the revenue flourished was bureaucratic inertia. As early as 1973, Rod Todman, a senior investigations officer of the Australian Taxation Office in Perth detected one variant of the bottom of the harbour fraud involving some fifty companies. Selecting one significant case for intensive investigation, he assembled sufficient evidence to raise a taxation assessment. In mid 1974, through the Deputy Crown Solicitor in Perth, he sought an opinion from a Queen's Counsel regarding the ramifications of the case in question. The nature of the opinion was such that the Deputy Commissioner of Taxation contacted the office of the Deputy Crown Solicitor responsible for handling the legal affairs of the Australian government in Western Australia, including the prosecution of criminal charges under the *Income Tax Assessment Act 1936* (Cwlth). In a letter dated 4 September 1974, the Deputy Commissioner said:

> The recovery of company tax in this case and other cases acquired [by the promoter] raises issues which could have far-reaching implications on the collection of company tax generally (quoted in Australia 1982, p. 34).

The matter in question was delegated to a principal legal officer who was at the time second in charge of the Deputy Crown Solicitor's Office. His initial reaction was that the facts of the case 'appear to be insufficient to support a fraud claim against any of the persons involved' (Australia 1982, p. 35).

At the end of 1974, the case was referred to a senior Queen's Counsel who strongly advised that the promoter of the scheme and two other individuals should be charged under Section 86(1)(e) of the *Crimes Act 1914* (Cwlth), which then specified the offence of conspiracy to defraud the

Commonwealth. The opinion was based upon documentary evidence and upon facts which were easily proved.

After considerable delay, the case was referred to the Commonwealth Police for investigations. The police report recommended that charges be laid, and included a prepared brief for the prosecution.

In August 1975 the Commissioner of Taxation advised the Deputy Crown Solicitor in Perth that the three individuals involved in the scheme should be charged under the Crimes Act. The case had been identified as a test case, designed to determine the viability of subsequent similar actions against promoters of other bottom of the harbour schemes.

The principal legal officer who was handling the case in the Perth Deputy Crown Solicitor's Office, a Mr Abe Gleedman, took no action after he received instructions from the Tax Office in August 1975. On 25 November he advised the Tax Office that 'he intended to commence the action required to bring about the charges' (Australia 1982, p. 40). A fortnight later he admitted that 'no action . . . commenced as yet due to pressure of work.' (Australia 1982, p. 40). Despite the firm assurances from senior silk, Gleedman remained uncomfortable with what he perceived to be a lack of sufficient evidence of intent to defraud.

In March 1976, still uncertain about the strength of his case, Gleedman referred the matter to the Commonwealth Police for additional investigation. He was either under the mistaken impression that investigations might obtain additional evidence by interviewing the suspects, or sought a pretext for not proceeding forthwith to lay charges.

In November 1976 the police report recommended that prosecution of the three suspects proceed, despite the absence of any admission on their part. The police concluded, as did the Queen's Counsel some months earlier, that the documentary evidence was more than sufficient. Four more months elapsed before any further action was taken. In April 1977, Gleedman prepared draft instructions to counsel regarding the criminal charges. They were fraught with error, with regard to both fact and law. Gleedman undertook to revise them and in June 1977, before departing on sick leave, he handed the instructions to his successor for delivery to counsel. Gleedman subsequently retired because of ill health, and never returned to work.

Gleedman was succeeded by Mr Sean O'Sullivan, the son of the Deputy Crown Solicitor at the time. He approached the Tax Office investigator Mr Todman, with instructions to counsel which was not the document which had been revised by Gleedman prior to his departure on sick leave, but rather the original Gleedman instructions which were so ridden with errors.

At this point, the situation deteriorated further.

> In the following twelve months Mr O'Sullivan deliberately avoided Mr Todman. Whenever Mr Todman was able to contact him, Mr O'Sullivan stated that he was working on the matter when he was not. He made appointments to see Mr Todman which he did not keep. He made appointments for Mr Todman to come and see him on days which he was on leave. He cancelled appointments. He promised to contact Mr Todman, but failed to do so. He was deliberately seeking to avoid Mr Todman during this six month period (Australia 1982, p. 48).

Inquiries from the Taxation Office in Canberra to the Crown Solicitor in Canberra led to the latter's request for a written report from DCS Perth. The response claimed falsely that a further report was expected from the Deputy Commissioner of Taxation in Perth.

On 1 June 1978, O'Sullivan prepared a minute for the Deputy Crown Solicitor (DCS) to send to the Crown Solicitor's Office in Canberra, highlighting difficulties which were assumed to exist. The difficulties were later found to be imaginary, if not erroneous:

> (1)   He suggested that there would be 'very great difficulties encountered' by reason of the fact the Defendants were not all resident in the same state.

(2)   He suggested that there should be a further interview of one of the Defendants, without indicating that two interviews of the man had failed.

(3)   He suggested there were difficulties in obtaining the co-operation of the original shareholder and his accountant, without stating that they had been granted an indemnity from prosecution and that a subpoena would overcome the problems.

(4)   He claimed that the matter required investigation by 'a very experienced and capable Commonwealth Police Officer', without stating that such an investigation had been completed 18 months earlier.

(5)   He suggested that if the prosecution 'is considered worthwhile', it would require the services 'of an experienced investigator', without stating that the investigation had been completed 18 months earlier, that it had available to it Mr Todman, a very experienced senior Investigation Officer of the Taxation Office, and a very experienced Commonwealth Police Officer.

(6)   He suggested that one of the Defendants 'will fight with unlimited resources any prosecution', although no person in our community could be expected to match the financial resources of the Commonwealth.

(7)   He suggested that the investigation was continuing, when in fact it had been completed. He even suggested that Mr Todman was still investigating the matter, while Mr Todman's activities at this time were confined to pressing Mr O'Sullivan to get on with it.

(8)   He stated that the matter would have to be
'briefed out' but suggested that such action
'would still only involve the time of one of
my officers to an extent that cannot be
afforded'. He did not indicate that the brief
to counsel had been prepared and was ready
for delivery (Australia 1982, pp. 50-1).

Two months after the Crown Solicitor in Canberra had
been thus misinformed, Mr O'Sullivan incorrectly advised the
Deputy Crown Solicitor's Office in Sydney that the matter had
been terminated.   No such decision had been made by the
Crown Solicitor.   The suggestion that the case had been
terminated led officers of DCS Sydney to advise against
proceedings against one of the suspects, who was also facing
charges in Sydney.

By the end of 1978 the Canberra and Perth offices of the
Crown Solicitor's Office were each advising the Australian
Taxation Office that the other was handling the case. The brief
to counsel lay in the bottom drawer of Mr O'Sullivan's desk in
Perth for five years, until it was discovered in the course of
inquiries by the Costigan Royal Commission in 1982.

In 1979, the DCS Perth advised the Crown Solicitor's
Office in Canberra that evidence was insufficient to prosecute.
On 3 April 1979 the Crown Solicitor conveyed this advice
formally by letter to the Australian Taxation Office. The Tax
Office, with its traditional priorities for revenue collection over
prosecution reinforced by the permissive climate created by the
Courts, did not press the matter further.   The would-be
prosecution had lapsed. Criticism of the conduct of the case
was scathing.

The consequences of the gross negligence in the
Crown Solicitor's Office are difficult to understate.
There have been many promoters of schemes
similar to that which this case is about. With the
lack of action in the court confidence grew that the
law could be broken with impunity. The Crown
Solicitor's Office failed to discharge its primary
duty, namely, to uphold the law. By its negligence,
it permitted the law to be disregarded and brought

into contempt. The loss to the revenue is enormous (Australia 1982, p. 70).

In his defence, the then Crown Solicitor argued that conspiracy proceedings were not the most appropriate and cost-effective approach to the case at hand.

> The view I had was that conspiracy law requires very careful and costly investigation, is complex to provide and, in the result, does not get any money back. I thought that conspiracy as a criminal charge was an inadequate and ineffective remedy in this field . . . I think it is an insufficient response in the same way as I would think that the commissioning of a labourer with a wheelbarrow is an insufficient response to the task of removing Capital Hill. He may ultimately achieve the end result but it will take him a long time. The way to attack this sort of problem seemed to me . . . through new legislation which would enable the Government not only to impose criminal sanctions but also to combine with those criminal sanctions a capacity to recover tax that was unpaid (Australia, Senate Estimates Committee A, 13 September 1982, p. 287).

It is interesting to note that this lack of enthusiasm for conspiracy law did not prevent the prosecution of Social Security beneficiaries discussed in Chapter 6 above.

As it happened, further shortcomings in the operations of the office of DCS Perth were to be identified. The spouse of one of the senior legal officers operated what was euphemistically termed an escort service, and served as secretary of a number of companies which were involved in bottom of the harbour activities linked to the promoter who was the subject of Mr O'Sullivan's inattentions. The precise extent of involvement in these activities on the part of the DCS legal offices became a matter of great concern.

Although it had been alleged that the telephone number of the Perth office of the Crown Solicitor had appeared in an advertisement for the escort service, the officer in question maintained that he was not involved in his wife's commercial activities. Whatever the involvement, the association was close enough to cause profound embarrassment, not only to the Crown Solicitor, but to the entire Australian government. The casual observer could perhaps have been excused for concluding that the legal arm of the Australian government was itself involved in the very activities it was responsible for prosecuting.

Perhaps the most obvious factor contributing to the difficulties of the Crown Solicitor's Office was a lack of competence on the part of the officers handling the case. The officer initially responsible, Mr Gleedman, suffered from a chronic depressive illness which eventually led to his retirement on account of disability. Notwithstanding his disability, he was ill-equipped to handle bottom of the harbour prosecutions. He had no previous experience with the law of criminal conspiracy, and little in company law. Gleedman's inhibition to establish the intent to defraud by inference from overt acts reflected this inadequacy.

Gleedman's successor, O'Sullivan, was even less well equipped to deal with the fraud case. He had no experience in either criminal law or company law. The description of his conduct of the case in the interim report of the Costigan Royal Commission (Australia 1982, pp. 48-52) is a textbook example of a desperate search for a 'too-hard basket'. In short, O'Sullivan's tepid pursuit of bottom of the harbour schemers led him into water which was far above his head.

That the shortcomings of Gleedman and O'Sullivan were allowed to persist reflected adversely on the managerial efficacy of the Deputy Crown Solicitor in Perth, and on the Crown Solicitor in Canberra.

It was generally considered that the Australian Attorney-General's Department had not, until shortly before the revelations of the Perth debacle, taken management and management training very seriously (Australia 1983, p. 76). The Crown Solicitor's Division of the Attorney-General's Department consisted of a central office in Canberra and a Deputy Crown Solicitor's office in each of the six states and two territories of Australia. At the time of the difficulties experienced in Perth, the Perth office was not a large one, consisting of twenty-three staff of whom eleven were qualified lawyers.

Gleedman's illness and its adverse effect upon his work were no secret. As second in charge of the office, he might have been subject to greater scrutiny on the part of the Deputy Crown Solicitor himself. At the very least, on the occasion of Gleedman's retirement, it was incumbent upon the Deputy Crown Solicitor to review each of his files to determine whether or not they were in order. If such a review did occur, it was by definition ineffective.

Problems of inadequate oversight were compounded by an inordinate degree of turnover in those who served as Deputy Crown Solicitors during the period in question. At the time Gleedman was handling the case, the Deputy Crown Solicitor was Lance Odlum. Odlum was succeeded as Deputy Crown Solicitor by Mr Clem O'Sullivan at the time his son, Sean O'Sullivan, took over the bottom of the harbour case from Gleedman. In June 1978 the elder O'Sullivan retired, and was succeeded by an acting deputy crown solicitor for a period of some three months at which time a Mr Peter Massie assumed the office. Such lack of managerial continuity could not help but hinder the degree of oversight and supervision required to ensure the efficient management of active case files.

The office of the Crown Solicitor in Canberra also failed to exercise adequate supervision over the case in question. It was the conscious policy of the Canberra office to give as much autonomy as possible to each Deputy's office. Whilst there was no doubt a sound basis for delegating a certain degree of authority, the practice went so far as to contribute to a feeling on the part of DCS officers in Perth that they were neglected by central office. Indeed, the situation reached a state which was subsequently described as a breakdown in communications. Periodic reports on pending major litigation were submitted to Canberra, but rarely if ever did they elicit feedback. In 1979, an explicit request for Canberra's reaction to a report from Perth met with no reply. The Perth office stopped submitting the reports altogether (Australia 1983, p. 102).

The Taxation Office must bear its share of responsibility for the matter. Apart from the original instructions in 1974 that the case in question 'could have far-reaching implications' it neither communicated to the Crown Solicitor nor to the DCS the full dimensions of the problem, nor stated that the case was a 'test case'. Having regard to the extent of the matter and its revenue implications, the case should have been taken up by the Treasurer with the Attorney-General.

The 'forgotten' bottom of the harbour case was first called to the Crown Solicitor's attention by the Commissioner of Taxation in 1978. A request to the Perth office for a report on the matter was ignored. It allowed the Sydney and Perth offices to 'pass the buck' to each other for a period of some months. The Crown Solicitor himself visited Perth on one subsequent occasion without availing himself of the opportunity personally to enquire into the matter.

Whilst there may be good reasons for a decentralised approach to the conduct of Australian government business in the states and territories of the federation, it is obvious that a degree of central managerial oversight is necessary to achieve that purpose. Such oversight was lacking in this case.

A number of factors combined to aggravate the managerial difficulties experienced by the Crown Solicitor's Office. The economics of the legal profession in Western Australia were such that talented practitioners could often achieve greater material rewards in the private sector than in government. The situation was expressed more bluntly by the outspoken Senator from Western Australia, Reg Withers:

> When I was a law student if you were a mug you went to work for the government. If you weren't much good, you were referred to as 'real Crown Law material.' (*The National Times* 24 August-4 September 1982, p. 5).

Moreover, for those who were committed to a career in public service, salaries in the state crown law office were greater than in the service of the Australian government. The most talented lawyers in Western Australia were thus not usually attracted to employment with DCS Perth.

In addition, the late 1970s were years of growing fiscal austerity in the Australian public service. The imposition of staff ceilings often meant that overworked offices could not count on staff augmentation to alleviate their caseloads.

Indeed, at one point a decision was made actually to reduce staffing levels in the Deputy Crown Solicitor's Office.

One lesson which might be learned from the difficulties encountered by DCS Perth is that attempts to implement public policy 'on the cheap' may go astray. With historical hindsight one may surmise that a greater commitment of resources to combatting fraud on the Commonwealth revenue would have paid for itself many times over.

One additional factor was specified as having contributed to the inefficient collection of revenue by the Australian government - the secrecy provisions of the Income Tax Assessment Act. These provisions were originally incorporated in the Act in the belief that the confidentiality of taxpayer information will enhance compliance with the law. It was argued that in the absence of such protection, taxpayers would be less inclined to be completely candid in their dealings with the Tax Office.

History, it would appear, has shown that it takes more than confidentiality to ensure candour on the part of taxpayers. Meanwhile, the operation of secrecy provisions serves to inhibit proper ministerial oversight of revenue collection. In the words of the Costigan Report:

> It appears to me that the principal beneficiaries of the secrecy provisions of the Income Tax Assessment Act are the errant civil servants identified in this Report. By the imposition of secrecy, they have been able to escape detection when the normal ministerial function of supervision may have resulted in their early exposure.

> There is a real danger to the community however, by the loss of proper ministerial supervision. It is essential that the Treasurer of the Commonwealth of Australia should be able to gain full access to taxation information so that he can see the extent to which the Revenue of the Commonwealth may be affected by fiscal policy, or by the depredations of thieves and rogues (Australia 1982, pp. 25 and 95).

The difficulties experienced by the Crown Solicitor's Office lay largely unappreciated outside bureaucratic circles until an unlikely chain of events led to their disclosure. Articles in *The Bulletin* about racketeering on Melbourne's waterfront tempted the Commonwealth and Victorian governments to appoint a Royal Commission into the activities of the Federated Ship Painters and Dockers Union. Cynics were perhaps excused for suggesting that the *raison d'etre* of the Royal Commission was to discredit an unsavoury element of the trade union movement and perhaps discredit one or two notables of the Labor Party. But the Royal Commission's terms of reference were very broad, and the Commissioner, Frank Costigan Q.C. was to learn that the activities of the Painters and Dockers were quite diverse. Costigan's final report describes the moment of discovery:

> It was in the early months . . . that the extent of the tasks became apparent. Perhaps the first moment of real light occurred one morning in the Fitzroy Court. A witness was giving evidence in relation to the activities of a company said to be engaged in ship repairing. Subsequent investigations showed that not one dollar ever had been earned in that activity; nonetheless it was full of interest, involving classic racketeering and on any view right in the centre of my Terms of Enquiry. The witness had some documents, he said; not in court but back at the office. Would he mind, I politely asked him, if I adjourned for a short time while he returned to his office to collect them and bring them back into court. I offered him the assistance of one of my solicitors and a Federal policeman. He could hardly decline such an offer. The documents were provided just before lunch. I should tell you that prior to that morning I had not seen signs of money exceeding five thousand dollars or thereabouts. Imagine my surprise to find in the files a cheque for one million, five hundred thousand dollars. Two or three minutes later I found an application by an associate company to the Reserve Bank to bring into this country from

Lebanon, four million, five hundred thousand dollars. It didn't really seem to fit in with ship repairing. I decided to look more carefully at this associated company. It had a bank account in a distant suburb in another state. The bank vouchers were subpoenaed. I found that in the three months some two hundred and fifty million dollars passed through that account. It was one of a dozen such accounts throughout Australia (Australia 1984, pp. 4-5).

This paper trail, as it came to be called, led eventually to the Deputy Crown Solicitor's Office in Perth to Mr O'Sullivan's bottom drawer, and to the escort service.

The release of the interim report of the Costigan Royal Commission elicited a predictable uproar. In addition to the abuse directed against the Fraser government, there was an element of black humour. As was said at the time, the average bloke in the corner pub may have had some difficulty coming to grips with the complexities of buying and selling companies and with the neglect of prosecutorial responsibilities, but the suggestion (albeit not entirely correct) that a prostitution service was being run from the government's legal office could not fail to elicit ridicule.

A management review of the Crown Solicitor's Division had commenced in 1979 in response to an earlier request by the Crown Solicitor for increased resources. Its implementation began in 1980, but encountered delay as a result of the Review of Commonwealth Functions, otherwise known as the 'Razor Gang'.

In contrast to the stringent staff ceilings which preceded the Costigan disclosures, they were followed quickly by the appointment of seventy new lawyers to the Crown Solicitor's Office. Implementation of the management review resumed. Management systems were introduced to permit a greater level of control and supervision, both within the regional offices and from the Crown Solicitor's Office in Canberra. Particular attention was paid to the monitoring of work backlogs.

Principal legal officers were thereafter engaged for approximately 10 per cent of their time on their own cases; the remainder of their schedule was devoted to supervision and management of other matters under their purview. Procedures for improved client liaison were instituted wherein Deputy Crown Solicitors and their senior officers met regularly with their counterparts in those offices of the Australian government which were their major clientele. Management training programs were established at central office, and regular communication between Crown Solicitors and their Deputies was restored. Computer and word-processing systems were installed.

The Attorney-General, Senator Peter Durack, whose misfortune it was to receive most of the criticism in the aftermath of the Costigan disclosures, conceded responsibility for the unfortunate events but refused to resign. As a close ally of the Prime Minister, his resignation was not requested. Withering attacks from press and opposition were to take their toll however, and he suffered a heart attack within weeks.

Immediate steps taken by the government in the aftermath of the Costigan revelations included the suspension of two officers in Perth pending disciplinary proceedings under the *Public Service Act 1922* (Cwlth), and an invitation to the President of the Law Council of Australia to examine the Crown Solicitor's Office and its operations.

Major tax prosecutions were taken out of the hands of the Crown Solicitor and his Deputies with the enactment of the *Special Prosecutors Act 1982* (Cwlth) and the subsequent appointment of Special Prosecutors Gyles and Redlich. These set the stage for a total reorganisation of the conduct of criminal prosecutions by the Federal government.

Legislative activity in the area of tax avoidance had preceded the Costigan revelations; it intensified thereafter. The *Crimes (Taxation Offences) Act 1980* (Cwlth) had made it a criminal offence to enter into (or to aid or abet) an arrangement with a purpose of reducing or removing the capacity of a company or trustee to meet an income tax or sales tax liability. The *Taxation (Unpaid Company Tax) Act 1982* (Cwlth), and related legislation, provided for the recoupment of tax evaded in 'bottom of the harbour' strips.

Extensive investigations of the DCS Perth office revealed that contrary to initial speculation, legal officers were not themselves accomplices in the scheme to defraud the Commonwealth; nor was an escort service being run from offices of the Australian government. The husband of the proprietress of the escort agency was, however, just sufficiently involved in his wife's activities that he was dismissed from the Public Service.

In 1983, after a change of government, legislation was enacted creating a new Director of Public Prosecutions, whose office would thereafter conduct prosecutions on behalf of the Commonwealth.

In 1984 a Major Fraud Division was established within the DPP to take over the work of the Special Prosecutors. Investigators seconded from the Australian Federal Police and the Australian Taxation Office assisted DPP staff in the preparation of cases for prosecution. With the significant increase in the number of complex fraud cases prosecuted in the 1980s, the dearth of expertise which characterised prosecuting authorities in the previous decade became a thing of the past.

The individual who had been the Crown Solicitor during most of the period discussed in Costigan's Interim Report had become, by the time of the Report's publication, the Secretary of the Commonwealth Attorney-General's Department. After the change of government in 1983 he was made a Judge of the Federal Court of Australia.

The Tax Office, which had become the subject of unfavourable comment by the Costigan Royal Commission, the Special Prosecutors, various members of Parliament and the Auditor-General of Australia, among others (Grabosky & Braithwaite 1986, Chapter 12), began to enhance its capabilities. Increases in staff, improvements in information storage and retrieval systems and greater attention to its enforcement role, all followed.

Luck finally ran out for the two promoters of the bottom of the harbour scheme whose activities were allowed to flourish for nearly a decade. Brian Maher and Errol Faint were finally charged by the Special Prosecutor, Roger Gyles. Proceedings were long and complex. Preparatory work entailed the efforts of teams of investigators, and the committal hearing lasted for three months. Responsibility for the prosecution was eventually transferred to the new Director of Public Prosecutions. Faint pleaded guilty and received a two year prison sentence. After a five month trial, Maher was found guilty on one count of conspiracy to defraud the Commonwealth, and one count of conspiring to defraud a named company. He was sentenced to two years and nine months imprisonment on the first charge, and five years on the second, to be served concurrently. In July 1987, the High Court of Australia set aside the conviction and sentence on the second count.

References

Australia 1982, *Royal Commission on the Activities of the Federated Ship Painters and Dockers Union,* Interim Report 4, Vol. 1, (Royal Commissioner, F.X. Costigan, Q.C.), Australian Government Publishing Service, Canberra.

Australia 1983, *Report of Enquiry Concerning the Deputy Crown Solicitor's Office, Perth,* (A.F. Smith), Australian Government Publishing Service, Canberra.

Australia 1984, *Royal Commission on the Activities of the Federated Ship Painters and Dockers Union,* Final Report, Vol. I, (Royal Commissioner, F.X. Costigan, Q.C.), Australian Government Publishing Service, Canberra.

Grabosky, Peter & Braithwaite, John 1986, *Of Manners Gentle: Enforcement Strategies of Australian Business Regulatory Agencies,* Oxford University Press, Melbourne in association with the Australian Institute of Criminology, Canberra.

The National Times, 24 August-4 September 1982, p. 5.

Sutton, Adam (forthcoming), 'The Bottom of the Harbour Tax Evasion Schemes' in *Stains on a White Collar: 14 Case Studies in Corporate Crime or Corporate Harm,* eds Peter Grabosky & Adam Sutton, Federation Press and Century Hutchinson, Sydney.

Chapter 10

ELECTRICITY TRUST OF SOUTH AUSTRALIA:
FATAL ACCIDENT AT WATERFALL GULLY

In the late 1970s it became apparent that growing demand for electricity in the eastern suburbs of Adelaide would soon exceed the capacity of the existing supply system, particularly during peak summer periods. Accordingly, planners at the Electricity Trust of South Australia (ETSA) began to investigate alternative means of augmenting power supplies.

As the cost of underground cable had recently increased significantly, the Trust's options were constrained. It was decided to construct a new section of line to connect the overhead power line running from the Linden Park sub-station into the Adelaide Hills, with another existing line running south along the hills face from Magill to Panorama.

Original plans called for the new section of 66,000 volt line to cross Waterfall Gully Road, the most scenic part of Adelaide's eastern suburbs, and only a few kilometres from ETSA headquarters. However, the state Department of Environment and Planning, whose approval was required for such a project, requested significant modifications in order to preserve the existing skyline and physical environment of the Waterfall Gully area. The path eventually chosen for the new power line lay across relatively inaccessible sloping land belonging to the state Highways Department between Waterfall Gully and Mt Osmond.

Under normal circumstances, the structures built to support the new line would have been 'Stobie poles', the functional, if somewhat hazardous and less than eye-pleasing poles of steel and concrete, which line South Australia's streets and roads.

To erect Stobie poles at the site in question, however, would require the construction of access roads and site works. The resulting degradation of the hills face would have been environmentally unacceptable.

Eventually, ETSA's design office decided on three lightweight steel towers, each twenty metres tall, comprising two legs joined by a cross-arm from which the power lines would be suspended. Each leg, consisting of three tubular steel members latticed together, would be supported by steel guy-wires. In addition, the bottom of each leg would consist of a base plate with a hole in it which could fit into a vertical pin protruding from a concrete foundation set in the ground. The towers would be the first of their type to be constructed in South Australia (*see* Figure 10.1).

But the project was to be beset by problems. Opposition on aesthetic grounds was voiced by some residents of the affluent suburb of Beaumont, whose electricity supply, ironically, the new lines were intended to augment. Resistance by the Burnside Council necessitated postponement of construction for five months. A complaint was lodged with the state Ombudsman, and it was only after an on site inspection by the Ombudsman himself that clearance to proceed was granted.

The methods of construction however, were further constrained by environmental considerations. The initial inclination to use cranes was abandoned when it became apparent that extensive earthworks and bigger tracks would be required for equipment access.

ETSA authorities contemplated the use of a helicopter to transport pre-assembled towers to the hillside location. A helicopter with requisite lifting capacity was located in Queensland, but at a rental price of $3000 per hour, the cost of flying it to Adelaide and return was deemed prohibitive. Instead, a local firm which operated a smaller helicopter and which had experience in constructing oil derricks was retained. The limited lifting capacity of this aircraft necessitated that the tower components be flown separately to the hillside site and joined in place.

This means of erection would require the ETSA workers to climb a structure supported by ropes. The team recruited to construct the towers was selected from ETSA staff. Because of the novelty of the project, and the element of risk involved in climbing unsecured structures, all those concerned were volunteers. Ten experienced linesmen were chosen from the Holden Hill, Linden Park and Stirling Depots. A district foreman grade 2, who had been involved in the project during

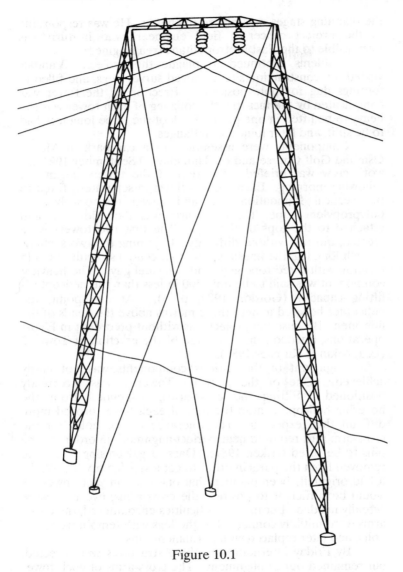

Figure 10.1

Proposed 66 kV Lightweight Guyed Structure

the planning stages, was placed in charge. He was responsible to the project officer, a field engineer, who in turn was responsible to the East Metropolitan Area Engineer.

Problems continued to plague the project. Vandals visited the construction site, removed survey pegs, and filled in footings dug for pole positions. Erection of the tower was complicated by the fact that the long leg of each tower was too heavy to be lifted in one piece. Each of the three long legs had to be split, and later joined with flanges.

Components were assembled in a car park at Mount Osmond Golf Course and on Thursday 10 September 1981 the work crew was briefed. Erection of the towers began the following morning. Each leg was flown in separately, fitted to the vertical foundation pin, and guyed temporarily with polypropylene rope. The cross arm was then flown in and attached to the tops of the legs. The first two towers were erected, but not without difficulty. In joining the two sections of each long leg, the linesmen had to ascend a structure held in position with three rope guys and two steel guys. The heaviest component was said to be only 300 lb less than the helicopter's lifting capacity (Gordon 1982, p. 3). At one point, the helicopter hovered a mere three metres above the heads of the linesmen. Because the project was without precedent in ETSA operations, a video film was made of the erection of Tower 2 (Lea, Aikin & Kutcher 1981).

Alignment of the various components was not easily achieved. One of the guys on Tower 2 was incorrectly positioned. Fitting the cross-arms, suspended from the hovering helicopter, atop the legs of each tower proved more difficult than expected. The tolerance of the holes for the cross-arm pins required near perfect alignment in order for the pins to be fitted (Aiken 1981). Dags of galvanising had to be removed from the parts in order to get a satisfactory fit. Whilst it had originally been planned that one man on each tower leg would be sufficient to position the cross-arms, two men were actually needed. Because of difficulties encountered, the cross-arms were initially connected to the legs with temporary 5/8 in bolts, and later replaced with permanent pins.

By Friday afternoon, the three structures were erected, but remained out of alignment. The cross-arms of each tower were still secured to the supporting legs with temporary bolts, pending readjustment. Work then ceased for the weekend, with the towers left in their temporary guyed state.

When work commenced the following Monday, both the project officer and the foreman were on site. Some of the men considered that alignment of the towers could only be achieved with great difficulty, involving the use of anchors and chain hoists. John Lea, the field engineer who was project officer for the tower construction, demonstrated on the first tower how minor adjustments could be made by alternately tightening and slackening the guys. The crew then made minor adjustments to the second tower, and the permanent cross-arm pins were fitted to Towers 1 and 2. The project officer left the site at 11.00 a.m., leaving the foreman in charge. The foreman left a few minutes later, having been called to an interview at ETSA headquarters. None of the senior linesmen present was instructed to take charge. The absence of supervisors was not without precedent; it had been accepted practice at ETSA that provided workers had been properly briefed, the continuous presence of a foreman or engineer at a worksite was not mandatory.

After lunch, four workers climbed Tower 3. The cross-arm remained secured to the legs with temporary bolts and rope. The incorrectly positioned guy wire on one of the tower's legs impeded proper alignment of the structure. The crew rigged an additional guy made of polypropylene rope to an adjacent point on the leg, secured it with a tarpaulin hitch, or 'truckies' knot', and released the incorrectly positioned wire guy. As the guy was being repositioned, the other leg of the tower began to move. A loud crack was heard, as a bolt connecting the cross-arm to the tower's western leg sheared. The moving tower leg stopped, but only momentarily. The entire structure then crashed to the ground. The state coroner found that the polypropylene guy rope had failed because of tensile overload, either through simple stress or through slippage of the 'truckies' knot' (Gordon 1982, p. 11).

The four workers, whose ages ranged from twenty-eight to thirty-nine, were tied to the towers by safety harnesses and crashed to the ground along with it. Three died instantly; the other, evacuated by the state rescue helicopter, was pronounced dead on arrival at Royal Adelaide Hospital. The Coroner's report reflects the violence of each of the men's deaths: cerebral lacerations due to ruptured skull; intra abdominal haemorrhage due to ruptured mesentery and lacerations to liver; cardiac temponade due to traumatic rupture of the ascending thoracic aorta; traumatic rupture of the brain stem due to fracture dislocation of the atlanto-occipital joint at the base of the skull (Gordon 1982, p. 1).

A number of defects in the planning and execution of the project contributed to the fatal accident. There had always been a degree of rivalry between departments in ETSA, and the Distribution Branch had traditionally seen itself as autonomous, requiring little or no assistance from other parts of the organisation. There appears to have been insufficient liaison between those ETSA officers who designed the towers and those who were to construct them. The Coroner's report faulted the Trust for failing to incorporate construction considerations in the design of the towers. Admittedly, the conventional 'Stobie poles' were rejected early on. But in the words of the Coroner:

> Having regard to the nature of the terrain and the comparative novelty of the towers to the officers of the Trust it is surprising that the means of erection was not given more detailed consideration before the towers were finally decided upon (Gordon 1982, p. 3).

This was not the first occasion in the history of the Trust when a serious accident had resulted from imperfect communications between design engineers and field personnel. In 1967, a linesman fell and was injured whilst changing an insulator string on a tower just south of Port Augusta. The weight of the conductor, which was supported on a chain lever hoist connected to the bottom member of the tower crossarm, caused the member to fail. Since that time, Trust engineers involved in the design of transmission structures continue regularly to emphasise the danger of loading such members in a manner which would cause failure (Sykes, L. 1987, pers. comm., 11 June).

The task force of linesmen were skilled and experienced professionals. The four deceased had worked for ETSA a combined total of 48 years. Even the least experienced of the four was a 6-year ETSA veteran. Nevertheless, certain aspects of the project were without precedent for them. Their expertise lay in maintaining towers, not in building them. None was experienced in construction operations involving a helicopter. None had worked previously on a guyed aerial structure. Although the men on the tower and ground personnel were equipped with two-way radios, the noise of the helicopter rendered the communications equipment useless.

Presumably ETSA could have contracted the project to a company experienced in aerial construction. But there was a certain pride attached to being able to do one's own work. While the men involved in the project were volunteers, there was some suggestion of pressure to ascend the towers:

> It is easy to make it look like you were volunteers, but men on the ground were told that the job had to be done. We weren't told at that time that if none of the men were prepared to do it, then the job would be called off. We felt compelled. Someone had to do it. Fair enough if that's volunteering. I volunteered . . . (South Australia 1982, p. 300).

The erection of a guyed structure entailed certain engineering principles unfamiliar to the linesmen. Alignment of the towers could be achieved by relaxing and tightening various guys. Whilst this was demonstrated on the morning of the accident, a number of workers were absent from the briefing. In addition, the different tensile strengths of rope and steel guys render them incompatible within the same structure. The rule that 'rope and wire do not mix' was either unknown to the men or went unheeded. Their use together violated the basic principle that a guyed aerial structure be steadied by equal and opposite forces. The truckie's knot, which is prone to slip if not properly secured, and which places inordinate strain on the rope, compounded this risk. The use of truckies' knots was common, if unorthodox procedure within ETSA. The linesmen, generally unaware of these engineering considerations relevant to the unusual construction task at hand, were not properly instructed. They remained ignorant of the engineering principles themselves, and of the rationales for them. Had they realised that all they needed to do to correct the eccentricity was to slacken the temporary wire guy, the accident would probably not have occurred.

One further oversight was the failure to check the positioning of the wire guys at the tops of the tower legs prior to the actual erection of the tower. In fact, the eccentricity in the tower's position which was caused by the incorrect positioning of the guy wires made it extremely difficult to fit the cross arm, and thus contributed to the circumstances giving rise to the tower's collapse (Gordon 1982, p. 7).

The Coroner was critical of what he regarded as the inadequate briefing of the linesmen:

> The situation called for something more . . . than would be usual work engaged in by linesmen. Careful and detailed explanation of the whole project, together with specific instructions as to the duties of each man, was called for.
>
> I am satisfied that instructions were given on Thursday, 10 September when the towers were being assembled in the carpark. But this was largely work which the men had not previously performed. It is unlikely that they could have assimilated and recalled all the detail required despite the discussions that took place during these briefings.
>
> Furthermore, there is considerable doubt that all or even a majority of the linesmen were present on all occasions when a matter affecting their safety did arise and explanation, advice or directions were given by the area engineer, project officer or the foreman, or that important instructions were clearly and firmly given (Gordon 1982, p. 6).

By far the most crucial factor, however, was the lapse in supervision. The foreman had been called back to ETSA headquarters to attend an interview. In his report, the coroner criticised a 'lack of communication between those responsible for the oversight of this project and other areas of the Trust's administration' (Gordon 1982, p. 12). No-one had been designated to act in a supervisory capacity in the foreman's absence. The foreman's immediate superior, the Project Officer/Field Engineer was in his office at the time of the accident, having left the site earlier unaware that the foreman was absent from the construction site. At the Coroner's inquest the foreman admitted '[t]his accident would not have happened if I had have been present' (South Australia 1982, p. 149).

In theory, ETSA was subject to the regulatory oversight of the South Australian Department of Industrial Affairs and Employment (as it then was) regarding matters of occupational health and safety. In practice, the Department deferred to ETSA's self-regulation, and made its services available on request. The Trust was, after all, a large, professional engineering organisation with a traditionally impressive safety record. With a work force of over 5,300 it was one of South Australia's largest employers. The limited resources of the state's health and safety inspectorate were thus devoted to the oversight of less reliable enterprises.

The accident triggered the standard official response to multiple fatalities. Inspectors from the Department of Industrial Affairs and Employment began an investigation. The Trust itself began an internal inquiry undertaken by senior engineering personnel. The state police accident investigation squad also became involved. The following March, the state Coroner held an inquest. The experience was a painful one for the widows of the deceased; three of them left the court during a demonstration on a model of the fatal tower for the purpose of illustrating the method of collapse (*The Adelaide Advertiser* 31 March 1982, p. 3).

Initially, there was some inclination to fix blame on the site supervisor, and to deny corporate liability. But ETSA accepted the advice of its solicitors that it was responsible. On the third day of the Coroner's inquiry, and some six months after the accident occurred, ETSA admitted full responsibility at civil law. Widows of the deceased linesmen brought actions against the Trust under the *Wrongs Act 1936-1975 (SA)*. The last of these was finalised three years later, in April 1985. In that case the plaintiff was awarded a judgment in the sum of

$254,850.40 *(Bahr   v. Electricity Trust of South Australia* 39 SASR 1983 [1985]).

On 24th August 1982 ETSA was charged with a breach of Section 29 of the *Industrial Safety, Health and Welfare Act 1972-81* (SA).   Commonly referred to as the 'general duties' provision of the Act, Section 29 requires an employer to take 'all reasonable precautions to ensure the health and safety of workers employed'. The particulars of the complaint specified that the defendant failed to provide staff to supervise the work force after 11.30 am on the day of the accident.

The matter was heard in the Adelaide Industrial Magistrates' Court on 23rd September 1982. Section 29 had been amended in 1976 to increase the maximum fine which could be imposed for an offence under the general duties provisions from $250 to $500.

Counsel for ETSA entered a plea of guilty, and the Trust was fined $250 plus $15 court costs (*Pyne v. ETSA*, Industrial Court of South Australia 82/39554-6, 29 September 1982).

The accident brought home to ETSA management the shortcomings of existing training practices. ETSA now issues detailed instructions for each engineering job, and provides each linesman with a manual which details acceptable practices and procedures. Such protocols were previously required only for high voltage and live line work. Since the accident in 1981, every project involving new or unusual procedures must be thoroughly documented, and all personnel briefed in advance of the work. There is now greater co-ordination between the different ETSA departments which are involved in the various stages of construction work and other hazardous projects. Structures under construction are now routinely inspected according to defined procedures. Supervisors are required on site whenever work is in progress. And the Trust no longer uses helicopters for structural or construction work.

References

Gordon, L. 1982, *Coroner's Report Concerning the Deaths of P.R. Stoddard, C.J. Bahr, M.H. Foale and P.D. Pike*, Coroner's Office, Adelaide.

Lea, J., Aikin, K. & Kutcher, R. 1981, *Detailed Job Briefing - Erection of Guyed Towers, Waterfall Gully*, Department of Labour, Adelaide.

South Australia 1982, *Proceedings of Coroner's Inquest Concerning the Deaths of P.R. Stoddard, C.J. Bahr, M.H. Foale and P.D. Pike*, Coroner's Office, Adelaide.

Chapter 11

THE HARASSMENT OF JANE HILL

Throughout most of its history the New South Wales Public Service would seem to have been less than hospitable to its female workforce. Traditionally, most women were in low-level, low paying positions, employed on a temporary rather than permanent basis, with limited opportunities for advancement (Deacon 1985).

The state Water Resources Commission, with headquarters in North Sydney, was one such bastion of male dominance. In the mid 1970s women comprised barely 12 per cent of over 2,000 strong staff. As recently as 1977, the Commission maintained separate male and female clerical seniority lists. Whilst men could rise through the clerical ranks to higher administrative positions, women could progress to the top of the stenographer scale and no further.

As principles of equal employment opportunity had been adopted as policy by the state Labor government, such formal barriers were soon to pass. A formal directive of Premier Wran amalgamated male and female seniority lists in 1978. Informal barriers to equal employment opportunity were to prove more durable, however.

Jane Hill had joined the Water Conservation and Irrigation Commission, as it was then known, in 1973. For five years, she served with competence and efficiency as an office assistant. With the 1978 integration of male and female seniority lists, she became an incremental clerk. Early in 1979 she was appointed as a Clerk Grade 1 in the Licensing Branch.

Ms Hill was an outgoing person who enjoyed cordial relationships with her co-workers. An active member of the Public Service Association, she was elected to a number of union committees. Eventually, she rose to become a member of the PSA Executive.

As part of the government's equal opportunity initiative, positions of 'spokeswoman' were created throughout the public service to represent women's interests in matters concerning employment and career development. Ms Hill was elected a spokeswoman as well.

Not all male employees of the Water Resources Commission were enthusiastic about their female co-workers, however. Upon her election as spokeswoman, Ms Hill received a number of snide comments. On occasion, equal opportunity circulars in her workplace were defaced. From time to time, she received telephone calls at her desk consisting of recorded messages from a venereal disease clinic.

Ms Hill nevertheless continued to succeed in her duties, impressing her superiors sufficiently to achieve further promotion. In September 1981 she became Secretary of the Tender Board in the Commercial Branch at a level of Grade 2, Clerk.

As one of the smallest branches in the Water Resources Commission, the Commercial Branch was a male bastion within a male bastion. Ms Hill's appointment as the first woman graded clerical officer in the branch met with resentment at the outset from her new colleagues.

Ms Hill's introduction to the branch can hardly be characterised as a warm welcome. When she arrived to take up her new position she was called in by the branch head, a Mr Bennett, and told that he was not looking forward to her joining the branch, as the men in the branch felt that she would not fit in. As if such a hostile reception from a new boss were not unpleasant enough, Mr Bennett had more words of discouragement. Having advised Ms Hill that the Secretary of the Tender Board normally moves into the acting Grade 3 position of Assistant Building Manager, he added that because the positions involved heavy lifting and as she was a woman, he would not be recommending her for the temporary promotions (NSW Equal Opportunity Tribunal 1985a, p. 11). A male Grade 1, clerical officer, junior to Ms Hill, was appointed to the position.

Ms Hill complained to the Commission's Equal Employment Opportunity Co-ordinator, then to the Secretary of the Commission. After six weeks and a subsequent protest from Ms Hill, the Secretary consented to her acting in the position when it again became vacant.

From her arrival in the Commercial Branch, Ms Hill was harassed by her co-workers. On two occasions when clerical staff unloaded large cartons from a delivery truck, two of the men threw the boxes at her with great force, at the same time causing them to spin. The nuisance telephone calls, which had plagued her previously, increased noticeably. Her mail was intercepted, and she received anonymous communications in the internal mail system often consisting of offensive cartoons. Additional offensive material was fixed to branch notice boards. These included advertisements for two brothels, a calendar advertising 'Rigid Tools' with a photograph of a naked woman and two boa constrictors coiled around her. Affixed to the photograph was an equal employment opportunity 'Girls Can Do Anything' sticker. From time to time Ms Hill was the target of offensive remarks and other annoying behaviour such as threats to dispose of her pet fish.

In June of 1982 when Ms Hill was acting in the Grade 4 position of Supervisor of Buyers of Mechanical Spare Parts, the previous incumbent, who was himself acting in a more senior position, refused to instruct her regarding her new duties (NSW Equal Opportunity Tribunal 1985a, p. 24). The buyers, moreover, refused to recognise her authority over them. She was told by one buyer that as she was only acting, she was not really their supervisor. All discussions were directed straight past her to the next senior officer.

The abuse from her co-workers, combined with the apparent lack of support from Commission management, began to take its toll. By the end of 1981, Ms Hill became depressed and anxious about work, and experienced a general lack of self-confidence.

Despite complaints to Commission management, the harassment increased in intensity during the first half of 1982. When Ms Hill served as Acting Assistant Building Manager, toilets were blocked, and faeces smeared on toilet walls.

The antagonism was to escalate still further. At the end of July 1982, Ms Hill was accosted by some of her workmates who subjected her to considerable verbal abuse. Shortly thereafter, Ms Hill was shifted, against her wishes, from her Grade 4 position, to a Grade 2 position in the office of the Water Resources Commission's Equal Employment Opportunity Co-ordinator.

But her difficulties were not to end with this effective demotion. In March 1983 she received through the internal mailing system and in a Commission's envelope, an anonymous threatening letter which read 'You'll get yours bitch'.

The following extract from the Equal Opportunity Tribunal's reasons for decision give some indication of the poisonous environment in which Ms Hill worked:

> At a function which took place during the Annual Conference of the Public Service Association in May 1983, there was a conversation in which Graeme Brokman told some other delegates about his dislike of Ms Hill and said 'We're going to get her' or words to that effect. When told that this was just stupid talk he persisted, saying 'No, no, we're going to put her in concrete boots'. One of the others said 'But you're talking about murder' to which Brokman is said to have replied 'That's right, murder is too good for her' (NSW Equal Opportunity Tribunal 1985a, p. 31).

Ms Hill was transferred on secondment to the Public Service Board, having been promoted to Grade 3 before leaving the Equal Employment Opportunity Branch of the Water Resources Commission.

She was under medical treatment for a stress-related condition and required counselling sessions twice weekly. Costs for her treatment were paid by the Water Resources Commission.

The intensity and duration of Ms Hill's plight arose from what can only be described as gross mismanagement endemic to the Water Resources Commission. Part of the managerial lapse at branch level may be explained by the fact that each of the three most senior officers in the Commercial branch during the period 1981-83 suffered significant health problems. Indeed, all three were to retire on grounds of ill health. Their absence for prolonged periods during the course of Ms Hill's difficulties precluded continuity of managerial oversight.

But responsibility was not confined to branch level. In the words of the Equal Opportunity Tribunal:

> Despite many complaints to Branch and upper management level about the repeated acts of

harassment either no action or no timely and effective action was taken by those in authority (NSW Equal Opportunity Tribunal 1985a, p. 4).

This apparent inaction was perceived by Ms Hill's antagonists as implicit tolerance, if not endorsement of their actions. When asked to justify his inaction, the Deputy Secretary and Director of Affirmative Action of the Water Resources Commission at the time of Ms Hill's difficulties expressed fears that he would only have made matters worse:

> I didn't want to trivialise the situation by having the Commission, or myself willy-nilly, if you like, making inquires about that and continually failing and being seen as impotent. Because it seemed to me that that would make the situation worse, make whoever was doing it even more sure of themselves (NSW Equal Opportunity Tribunal 1985b, DL 14, p. 46).

Lack of managerial initiative was suggested in further cross-examination:

> You see you know it's an offence don't you to send through the post material of an offensive nature?...... Yes.

> And it's also an offence to use the telephone system to make calls of an offensive nature?...... Correct.

> And the federal police would have been the appropriate people to investigate if the mail had been coming from outside through the post?...... Yes.

> And you've heard about fingerprinting and things like that haven't you?...... Yes.

> Those are some of the steps that you could have taken to investigate fully what was happening to

Miss Hill in the Commission weren't they?...... Yes, I could have taken those steps.

And you didn't take those steps did you?...... No I didn't.

I suppose it would also be possible wouldn't it, for you to have called in a private investigator to find out who was behind the harassment of Miss Hill?....... Yes it was possible, a private investigator never occupied my mind.

When you said that you didn't think there was anything you could successfully do about it and you thought that to be seen to try and fail was worse than to do nothing?...... Yes.

Did it enter your head that to make the presence of either the police or a private investigator known might in itself have a disciplinary effect?...... As I said I never considered a private investigator. I never though of it but it did occur to me with regard to the police, yes.

Didn't it occur to you that just the knowledge that the police were investigating those matters might have had the desired effect of itself?...... I didn't think it would.

You came to that conclusion did you?...... I came to the conclusion that there was so little that can be done that it would make it worse.

And you didn't discuss that with anybody in the police force?...... No.

(NSW Equal Opportunity Tribunal 1985b, DL 14. pp. 49-51)

The failure of management to reinforce Ms Hill's authority was made glaringly apparent in the course of further cross-examination:

> And the two different kinds of complaints were made to you on this occasion were both demonstrative of the refusal of men in the commercial branch to acknowledge the seniority of a woman?...... Yes.

> So that they were illustrations of a fundamental underlying problem in equal employment opportunity principles?...... Yes, you could put it that way, yes.

> So it wasn't just a question of an incident that had occurred and was in the past and didn't need to be worried about was it?...... As a complaint I saw it as something that was in the past and I should say I think my recollection of it was the complaint that was made about that was an incidental complaint in connection with some other complaint.

> But it was illustrative of a much more general problem wasn't it?...... Yes.

> And one for which you had particular responsibility as director of affirmative action?...... Yes.

> And you didn't do anything about it?...... No it seemed to me that it had passed by then.

> You didn't think it was a good idea to call together the men in the commercial branch and say now look here, we are an equal employment employer, you are going to adjust to the principle of equal employment opportunity and one of them is that you recognise women in senior positions?...... That's correct.

It would have been a good idea to do that wouldn't it?...... I'm not sure whether it was a good idea to do that or not.

Well you didn't think about it at the time either did you?...... No.

You've never given it a moment's thought have you?...... What before essential . . .

At any time...... No.

This is the first time you even turned your mind to it.

(NSW Equal Opportunity Tribunal 1985b, DL 14, pp. 58-9).

The Tribunal later referred to the lack of support for Ms Hill as a significant failure of management at three levels, within the Commercial Branch and the Commission as a whole.

Perhaps the ultimate illustration of managerial priorities was the transfer of Jane Hill to the Equal Employment Opportunity Section, and ultimately her secondment out of the Water Resources Commission altogether. By contrast, her antagonists, including the officer who was alleged to have spoken about murdering her, remained in the Commercial Branch.

The response of Commission management to Ms Hill's difficulties was not totally passive. On more than one occasion, the Deputy Secretary brought about the removal of offensive material from Commercial branch bulletin boards. But not until mid 1982 was any significant response forthcoming.

Following the incident in late July 1982, involving aggression and intimidation, the Water Resources Commission mobilised its disciplinary machinery. A fact finding inquiry was held, and as a result, internal disciplinary charges were laid against seven officers. Among the offences alleged were failure to provide adequate supervision, failure to prevent disruptions of work, abandoning supervisory duties when disruption was occurring, harassment, disruption of work, and insubordination.

Five officers were found guilty, reprimanded, and debited with one-half day of recreation leave. The officers appealed to the Government and Related Employees Appeals Tribunal, which held that all penalties be withdrawn with the exception of reprimands of three officers.

Recognising the managerial shortcomings in the Commercial Branch, Water Resources Commission executives transferred the entire unit, effectively making it the Purchasing Section of the Mechanical Branch, under the authority of a Principal Engineer.

Ms Hill finally made a formal complaint to the New South Wales Anti-Discrimination Board on 9th February 1983. In her complaint, she related the litany of abuses which she had suffered over the previous eighteen months, her complaints to Commission management, and the Commission's lack of response.

Ms Hill's complaint was made under the *Anti-Discrimination Act 1977* (NSW). It alleged that by being exposed to a hostile and offensive work environment, she was treated less favourably than male co-workers. The complaint further alleged that she was disadvantaged by Commission decisions regarding her transfer from the Commercial branch.

Counsel for the Water Resources Commission did not challenge Ms Hill's allegations of harassment. Rather, the defence rested on the argument that the employer was not liable under the Act for the misconduct of its employees, and that it did seek to discipline several employees as a result of the July 1982 incident. Counsel for the Commission further argued that even if Ms Hill were treated less favourably than her co-workers, it had not been shown that the treatment had been on the ground of sex.

After considering the evidence, the Tribunal concluded that the Water Resources Commission condoned the hostile work environment, and was thus in contravention of the Act. It noted that senior officers of the Commission were 'constantly made aware of the circumstances of the complainant's working environment' and that neither prompt nor adequate intervention was forthcoming to remedy these conditions.

The Tribunal concluded that Commission inaction or lack of adequate remedial action in the face of these problems served to encourage continued misconduct on the part of

Ms Hill's co-workers. Indeed, the Tribunal noted that there was a fourteen-month delay in the Commission's implementation of the Public Service Board's anti-sexual harassment policy. The Tribunal's judgment referred to 'the crucial period of inactivity' from January to July 1982. It further faulted the Commission for transferring Ms Hill out of the Commercial branch, and leaving in place the men who were accused of victimising her. The Tribunal rejected the argument that the harmful conduct in question did not constitute sex discrimination, as it would not have occurred but for the victim's gender.

On 10 May, 1985 the Tribunal found Jane Hill's complaint substantiated and ordered the Water Resources Commission to pay her \$34,872.34 in damages and \$2,888 in costs. It further enjoined employees of the Commission from discriminatory conduct towards Ms Hill while she remained an employee of the Commission.

In support of its judgment, the Tribunal cited a doctor's report dated 3rd February 1984:

> The factors which have been producing such stress have also obviously had an effect on her self confidence and ego. It is difficult to ascertain at this point how much of this present disability will continue, how much she will be able to reverse when the stress is removed.
>
> . . . it is difficult to assess at this point just how deep the scars on her psyche are and how well or completely these will heal (NSW Equal Opportunity Tribunal 1985a, p. 44).

The Water Resources Commission was not content simply to abide by the Tribunal's judgment, and sought leave to appeal in the Supreme Court of New South Wales. At this point, Premier Wran concluded that further legal resistance by the Water Resources Commission was inconsistent with government equal opportunity policy. He would not tolerate the additional expenditure of public funds for this purpose, and ordered that the appeal not proceed.

Jane Hill resigned from the New South Wales Public Service in 1985. The man who had been Deputy Secretary and Director of Affirmative Action at the Commission during the period of Ms Hill's difficulties became Secretary of the Commission in February 1984.

In addition to its less than impressive record on matters of equal employment opportunity, the Water Resources Commission had developed a reputation for being something less than successful in achieving its objectives, and somewhat extravagant in its expenditure of public moneys. For whatever reason, the New South Wales government decided in 1986 to disband the Water Resources Commission. Some of its functions and staff would be transferred to local water boards, with the remainder reconstituted as a new Department of Water Resources within the public service. The success of this new department in meeting equal opportunity goals remained to be seen.

References

Deacon, D. 1985, 'Equal Opportunity and Australian Bureaucracy, 1880-1930', *The Australian Quarterly*, Autumn/Winter, pp. 32-46.

NSW Equal Opportunity Tribunal 1985a, *Jane Hill v. Water Resources Commission*, Reasons for Decision, 31st May, N.S.W. Equal Opportunity Tribunal, Sydney. Reported in *Hill v Water Resources Commission* (1985) EOC 92-127 *Australian and New Zealand Equal Opportunity Law and Practice*.

NSW Equal Opportunity Tribunal 1985b, *Jane Hill v. Water Resources Commission*, Transcript of Proceedings, N.S.W. Equal Opportunity Tribunal, Sydney.

Chapter 12

THE ASIA DAIRY CASE

The mid 1970s were not the best years for Australian dairy farmers. In addition to problems of overproduction, the British decision to join the European Economic Community made the matter of developing new markets for Australian primary products a matter of urgency.

Despite their not infrequent protestations, Australian primary producers are often the beneficiaries of considerable government largesse. Indeed, under the Dairy Bounty Scheme which existed between 1943 and 1975, Australian dairy farmers received $795 million. As was the case with many other sectors of primary industry, Australian dairy farmers also benefited from the existence of statutory authorities created for the purpose of promoting and marketing Australian dairy produce.

Such a body was the Australian Dairy Corporation (ADC) which came into existence on 1 July 1975 as a statutory authority within the portfolio of the Australian Minister for Primary Industry. The ADC inherited subsidiaries of its predecessor body, the Australian Dairy Produce Board. Among these was a Hong Kong based company, Asia Dairy Industries (HK) which had been a wholly-owned subsidiary since 1971. Asia Dairy was a large operation indeed, with an annual turnover in the late 1970s of $120 million. Asia Dairy's primary operations consisted of marketing Australian dairy produce throughout south-east Asia.

Business practices in the Far East have long enjoyed a reputation of being somewhat rough and tumble. Asia Dairy had engaged in business practices which were to attract considerable attention. Its sales of dairy produce to Thai Dairy involved accounting arrangements structured in such a way that they resulted in the avoidance of withholding tax normally payable to the Thai government.

In 1975 Asia Dairy contracted to supply skim milk powder to a company in the Philippines, Holland Milk Products Incorporated (HOMPI). As it happened, this was a company in which Asia Dairy had a 13.33 per cent shareholding. Despite the close relationship between the two companies, and in the light of a world over-supply of skim milk powder, Asia Dairy was required to pay a $US25 per tonne rebate in order to secure the contract. The rebate was paid not to HOMPI, but to a bank account in Hong Kong controlled by two principals of the company which held a majority of HOMPI's shares. Whilst the rebate was to have been distributed to HOMPI shareholders on a pro rata basis, this did not occur. But Australian dairy farmers were thus assured a market in a highly competitive environment.

When the world price of skim milk powder fell, the contract price with the rebate taken into consideration placed Australia in violation of the 1970s skim milk powder arrangement within the General Agreement on Tariffs and Trade (GATT). The situation persisted for more than one year, from April 1976 to June 1977, when the world price of milk powder recovered. Thus, not only was the wholly-owned subsidiary of an Australian government statutory authority engaged in the evasion of taxes due to the government of Thailand, it had also placed the Australian government in violation of an agreement pursuant to an international treaty to which it was a signatory. Such conduct threatened Australia's status in the eyes of the world, and ran the risk of inviting similar behaviour on the part of Australian taxpayers and foreign companies trading in Australia. Admittedly, under-the-table concessions are not unusual in Asian commerce; but most Australian multi-nationals have stringent guidelines regarding tax compliance and inducement commissions.

The internal accounting procedures of the Australian Dairy Corporation and its subsidiaries also came into question. Reviews of Corporation accounts revealed ex gratia payments made along with retirement benefits. An overpayment of $10,000 to a former expatriate staff member was written off without any apparent evidence of attempts to affect recovery. Expenses were incurred with Corporation credit cards; their accounts were unaccompanied by supporting details, and were apparently unrelated to conventional travel expenses. Directors of Asia Dairy were hired as consultants by the Company without any record in minutes of the Company's Board meeting of any declaration of interest, and without any evidence of competitive tendering.

The Deputy Chairman of ADC, who was only a part-time board member, obtained a car for his personal use at Corporation expense which violated a number of official guidelines. It cost more than the maximum allowable value. It did not meet Australian content requirements, and it was made available for the Deputy's exclusive personal use, and not for other employees of the Corporation. In addition, the vehicle's speedometer was disconnected, and the gentleman in question claimed operating expenses from both the Australian Dairy Corporation and the United Dairy Farmers of Victoria, with which organisations he was also affiliated.

A Parliamentary committee subsequently noted

> We are not able to conclude whether Mr Pyle did in fact disconnect the speedo or whether he used this statement to attempt to explain the duplicated claims for expenses. Certainly, it makes it impossible to establish the extent of the duplication. The Committee considers that Mr Pyle's behaviour in relation to the disconnection of the speedo speaks for itself. We are not concerned to decide whether Mr Pyle's actions were, in his words, 'stupid more than dishonest' or whether they were dishonest more than stupid, they were certainly a combination of both (Australia 1981, p. 355).

Whether such indulgent practices differ significantly from those which characterise the Australian business world is an interesting question. After all, Australian farmers are renowned for their informality and their generosity. Whether such practices were in the best interests of Australian dairy farmers, might also be asked. There can be no question, however, that the travel and entertainment expenditures were inconsistent with those which were normally incurred by officers of Australian statutory authorities in the course of their official duties.

At the very least, circumstances which underlay the breach of GATT indicated significant lapse in communications. The existence of the rebate arrangement between Asia Dairy and HOMPI was not made apparent to the ADC board for more than one year, despite the fact that the Chairman of ADC was also the Chairman of ADI. Although an officer of the Australian Department of Primary Industry (DPI) sat on the ADC board, nearly five months passed before DPI notified ADC of the difficulties posed by the rebate. More than two months later, the Minister for Primary Industry requested the Chairman of ADC to cease the rebate arrangement.

The Chairman of ADC was in an uncomfortable position. To terminate the rebate arrangement and bring Australian exports into compliance with the GATT agreement would lose a valuable contract for Australian dairy farmers. In November 1976 he went to Manila, seeking to renegotiate the contract in a manner which would be consistent with Australia's treaty obligations. HOMPI executives stood their ground, and continued to receive their rebate.

The then Chairman of ADC later testified under oath that he had explicitly informed the Minister at a face to face meeting of the continuing rebate arrangement and concomitant treaty violation. Declining to testify under oath before the Senate Committee inquiring into the matter, the Minister denied that he had been so advised, and cited the only written record, a letter from the Chairman of ADC which, in referring to negotiations with HOMPI concerning the rebate, stated 'I am pleased to advise that it was possible for us to arrive at an amicable solution to our outstanding difficulties' (quoted in Australia 1981, p. 145). The Minister then sought to rationalise the apparent lack of oversight by his Department.

There were a number of companies under the umbrella of the Australian Dairy Corporation, and a number of similar statutory authorities within the portfolio of the Australian Minister for Primary Industry. As Mr Sinclair, the Minister at the time of the alleged treaty violation, was to say in a letter to Senator Peter Rae of 16 March 1981: 'it is neither physically nor administratively possible for the Minister for Primary Industry or his Department (DPI) to examine or to be familiar with all such transactions'. The Rae Committee was not entirely convinced by this excuse. Their report commented wryly that 'in the course of the inquiry the Committee was shown that Ministers were not loath to become involved in the affairs of the ADC if they felt it was necessary.' (Australia 1981, p. 266).

In any event, the vast organisational terrain of Australian primary industry appeared to exceed the oversight capabilities of the Department of Primary Industry. Despite the presence of DPI officers on the Board of the Australian Dairy Corporation, the Department was too slow in perceiving that a treaty violation had occurred, and was insufficiently attentive to whether or not the violation had ceased. The problem was compounded by the fact that many of those working for ADC did not regard themselves as public servants or as accountable to the Australian government. The *Dairy Produce Act 1975* (Cwlth) was insufficiently explicit in specifying not only the obligations and responsibilities of the ADC and its subsidiaries, but also the duties of ADC Board members.

One of the central problems which underlay the difficulties encountered by Asia Dairy, by its parent authority, and by the Minister for Primary Industry were impediments in the flow of information.

As was later observed,

> The evidence suggests that there were many occasions when the Minister was not fully informed and when the Parliament had no real idea about what was happening in the ADC, ADI (HK) Ltd., or the other subsidiaries (Australia 1981, p. 292).

information flow was selective, and imperfect:

> At the same time as attempts were made to provide information to some members of Parliament about ADI (HK) Ltd. and the other Asian operations, the minutes of the ADI (HK) Ltd. Board meeting were being withheld from the Departmental representative on the ADC (Australia 1981, p. 294).

The Department, moreover, was faulted for lack of persistence in pursuing the information. One could perhaps be forgiven for speculating that there were those who had an interest in not knowing precisely what was going on in Hong Kong and Manila.

Yet another impediment to wider knowledge about the difficulties of Asia Dairy was the secrecy attached to the special audit (Section 63p) which had been requested by the Minister. Were it not for a 'leak', parliament might not have learned of the problems at hand.

Media coverage of the Asia Dairy issue was slow to develop for two reasons. First, rural issues tend not to be of great interest to the metropolitan media. Australia's rural press, moreover, dominated as it is by country interests, was disinclined to delve too deeply into matters which might embarrass the country establishment or reflect adversely on rural interests generally. Thus, the inquisitiveness which had begun to characterise media attention to more urban issues was, in this case, initially lacking.

The excessive expenditures on travel and entertainment arose from the lack of adequate guidelines or regulations within the ADC or its subsidiaries. Decisions tended to be taken on an ad hoc, personal basis. The Chairman of the ADC issued credit cards and authorised payment of credit card accounts, including his own. Clinging tenaciously to what they perceived to be commercial autonomy, ADC officials did not look to the Commonwealth government for standards.

The Department of Primary Industry had previously expressed some reservations about Asia Dairy's relationship to the ADC and to the Australian government. A minute to the Minister in February 1975 noted that neither the government, nor the Dairy Products Board had control of Asia Dairy's operation, and recommended that the accounts and records of the company be subject to audit by the Auditor-General (Australia 1981, Appendix 1). The existence of problems within ADC first became publicly apparent in 1977. An article in the *Australian Financial Review* which called attention to the possible treaty violation (Simson 1977), came to the notice of Senator Peter Rae, Chairman of the Senate Standing Committee on Finance and Government Operations. The Committee had been concerned generally with the accountability of Australian government statutory authorities.

For reasons which were never publicised, Ian Sinclair, the then Minister for Primary Industry, asked the Australian Auditor-General to conduct a special investigation of Asia Dairy in March 1979. Word of the enquiry, which had not been publicly announced, reached the Leader of the Opposition, Mr Hayden, in August.   Mr Hayden asked a number of questions about the enquiry, but without receiving much in the way of an informative response.

The report, still secret, was presented to the Federal government in September 1979 and referred by the Minister for Primary Industry to the Management Committee of the Australian Dairy Corporation.   Peter Nixon, Ian Sinclair's successor as Minister for Primary Industry, intended to keep the report from public view.   Portions of the report however, came into the hands of the shadow Minister for Primary Industry, Senator Peter Walsh, who tabled them in the 1980 Budget session of Federal Parliament.

On 20 November 1980, Senator Rae announced a full investigation of the Dairy Corporation and its subsidiaries. Possible breaches of the law arising from inappropriate accounting practices within ADC were referred to the Commonwealth police by the Minister for Primary Industry.

A police report was presented to the government in November 1980, but rejected by the Minister for Primary Industry, who ordered that a second report be produced.   The second report, presented to the government in March 1981, was reviewed by officers of the Attorney-General's Department, and by senior counsel in Melbourne who apparently concluded that no successful prosecution could be launched against the former Chairman of the Australian Dairy Corporation.   Although Minister Nixon was keen to release this report quickly, police objections that its disclosure would jeopardise additional investigations prevailed, and the report remained secret.   Toward the end of October 1981, the police report was finally tabled in Federal Parliament.   It concluded that there was insufficient evidence available to establish beyond reasonable doubt the commission of any criminal offence by the former Chairman of ADC.

The Rae committee report recommended new expenditure control procedures for the ADC, including the requirement that the ADC Board approve all future capital expenditure over $25,000 in value.   The Committee also recommended the establishment of guidelines for expenditure on travel, accommodation and personal expenses by Board members, and corporation staff.   It recommended that procedures be devised for resolving conflict of interest by Board members. Additional recommendations called for procedures for regular reporting by subsidiary companies to the Dairy Corporation and to the Australian Parliament. A further recommendation called for financial control and auditing procedures consistent with requirements of the Australian Auditor-General.

The Rae report made a number of insightful comments on, and important recommendations about, ministerial communications. It noted that there were no satisfactory guidelines within the DPI or ADC regarding what constituted a ministerial direction, how this might differ from a ministerial request, and how each should be treated. Moreover, the Rae report was particularly critical of reliance upon oral communications:

> Serious problems arise with oral communications. Their intended force is uncertain to the recipient. The possibility of them being reported is remote. The Committee considers that communications should therefore be in writing. However, we are conscious of the apparent reluctance of some Ministers to issue written communications. The temptation to issue oral communications can be great, as they enable Ministers to have the best of both worlds i.e. to direct the affairs of the authority when so desired while maintaining the facade of the authority's independence. As stated above, we believe the Minister should have the power to direct the ADC. However these directions must be brought to the attention of the Parliament and the Public. In the absence of any ministerial direction the Parliament will assume that an authority is entirely responsible for its activities and will therefore be able to hold the authority itself accountable for its activities and decisions (Australia 1981, p. 275).

Perhaps the most sensational aspect of the Rae report was its criticism of the former Minister for Primary Industry, Ian Sinclair. The Committee, faced with the contradictory

evidence of Sinclair and the former Chairman of ADC, chose
to believe the latter.   It concluded, 'on the balance of
probabilities Sinclair was told of the terms of the compromise
which necessarily involved a continuing breach of GATT.'
(Australia 1981, p. 174).

Ian Sinclair sought to discredit the Rae report and its
conclusions concerning the credibility of his statements.   He
referred to the 'slipshod way' in which the conclusion was
reached.   Sinclair was fortunate to continue to enjoy the
support of his Prime Minister and Cabinet colleagues, who
closed ranks around him and attacked the former Chairman of
ADC.

In the aftermath of the Senate Standing Committee
Report, the government acted to rectify those managerial and
accounting procedures which had proven so embarrassing.   Not
the least important were instructions issued to the Australian
Dairy Corporation and to Asia Dairy Industries to adhere at all
times to the taxation requirements of the countries in which
they operate.   Borrowing and investment by ADI became
subject to ministerial guidelines.   In addition, guidelines were
drawn up which clearly defined the powers and authorities of
ADC and ADI management, and which specified salary rates
and conditions of service, as well as travel and entertainment
expenses for ADC and ADI management and staff.

A minor casualty of the Asia Dairy scandal was the
Deputy Chairman of ADC, who was relieved of his executive
responsibilities for the alleged abuses surrounding the vehicle
provided for his personal use.   Despite the committee's
conclusions regarding the gentleman's dishonesty and stupidity,
the government did not regard his actions as so heinous as to
warrant the extreme step of removing him from the Board of
ADC altogether.   Indeed, he remained in that capacity,
defending the interests of the dairy farmers of Victoria.   The
former chairman of ADC was requested to repay an amount of
$6,425.20 to ADI which had been claimed in connection with
travel and accommodation of family members.

In the end, the Asia Dairy scandal blew over.   Files in
ADC which might have resolved some of the questions which
had been raised, turned out to have disappeared or to have
been altered.   The government of Thailand was reimbursed,
with interest, for the $215,247 in taxes which Asia Dairy had

earlier avoided, and the discovery by American authorities of kangaroo meat in a shipment of what was labelled Australian Beef, created new headaches for the Minister for Primary Industry and his Department.

References

Australia, Senate Standing Committee on Finance and Government Operations 1981, *The Australian Dairy Corporation and Its Asian Subsidiaries*, Australian Government Publishing Service, Canberra.

Simson, S. 1977, 'Strange Philippines Dairy Deal', *Australian Financial Review*, 16 September.

Chapter 13

THE VICTORIAN LAND SCANDALS 1973-1982

It is said that every Australian dreams of owning one's own house on a quarter-acre block. The Australian dream has proven elusive for many, however; millions of Australians are unable to afford their own homes. Indeed, many are unable to afford rental accommodation on the private market. To assist such unlucky inhabitants of the lucky country, state governments provide housing for low income people through statutory authorities. Such a body was the Housing Commission of Victoria. Originally established in 1938 to oversee slum clearance in the city and inner suburbs of Melbourne, the Housing Commission presided over the construction of the Olympic Village in 1956, built houses at various locations around the state, and made its mark on the Melbourne skyline during the 1960s in the form of high-rise blocks of flats just off Lygon Street in Carlton.

It soon became apparent, however, that the aesthetics of vertical accommodation (not to mention the social and psychological consequences) left a great deal to be desired. The alternative was to provide more low density housing, at some distance from the city. As the gap between rich and poor began to widen, and the cost of accommodation on the private market became more elusive than ever, the queue for Housing Commission dwellings lengthened. By 1973, there were in excess of 14,000 pending applications for public housing in Victoria.

In the face of this demand, and in light of increasing public pressure to meet the basic needs of the state's disadvantaged citizens, the Hamer Liberal government decided to act. The pace was hastened by the aggressive housing policies of the first federal Labor government in twenty-three years, which made substantial funds available to state housing authorities. Continued failure by the Victorian government to address the housing problem would almost certainly evoke an increased federal presence in what was hitherto predominantly a state domain.

Plans for metropolitan development had previously been based on the concept of 'growth corridors' radiating outward from the city of Melbourne, and separated by 'green wedges'. In 1973, however, the government of Victoria announced that its development plans would be based on the concept of 'satellite towns'. It was with a view towards providing low density public housing in these satellite towns (and a view, no doubt, towards the forthcoming state elections), that the Housing Commission set about purchasing large tracts of land in 1973.

By the end of 1974, the Housing Commission had spent just under $11 million in purchasing a total of 3,346 acres in Pakenham, Sunbury and Melton, semi-rural areas less than 50 km from the centre of Melbourne. The real beneficiaries of this government largesse were not low income tenants, however. Nearly half of the $11 million was pocketed by speculators and developers who saw the government coming, purchased the land at low prices, and sold it to the Housing Commission at a handsome profit.

The vendors of the land at Melton realised a gross profit of $2.5 million, which represented a tax free capital gain of approximately $1.25 million in less than two years. On 24 September 1973, a finance company executed an option to buy land at Sunbury for just under $1.9 million. Later that same day it signed a contract with the Housing Commission to sell the land for over $3.4 million. Their profit, after costs and expenses, was $1,175,951. The losers in these deals were the Victorian taxpayers - whose public servants paid millions more for the land than they might have - and the clients of the Housing Commission, whose access to low cost housing remained restricted after the Commission's assets were squandered. Indeed, such land as the Commission did purchase remained undeveloped for years afterward. Some was flood prone, and other land remained subject to zoning restrictions. Land prices in general became inflated, thus contributing to the double digit inflation of the time. Private accommodation lay increasingly beyond the reach of low income Victorians, thus *adding* to the waiting list of the Housing Commission (Sandercock 1979, p. 43).

In addition to allegations of patently incompetent management, allegations of corruption were made against the

Minister for Housing, Vance Dickie, and the Minister for Planning, Alan Hunt, as well as against officers of the Commission. Indeed, as official denials of wrongdoing and mismanagement persisted over the following seven years, the legitimacy of the Victorian government was increasingly called into question.

The standard procedures by which the Housing Commission purchased land were not complex. The Commission's interest in acquiring land in a certain area was communicated to an agent, who set about locating suitable acreage. The land under consideration was then inspected by the Commission's engineer, to determine if problems of topography, drainage or other physical considerations would add prohibitively to the cost of development - for example, putting in streets, sewers, etc. The land was then subject to valuation by professional valuers, formally attached to the Valuer-General's Office but seconded to the Commission on a semi-permanent basis. A decision to make an offer for the land was reached at a meeting of the Commission, and a proposal for purchase submitted in writing by the Commission's Chairman to the Minister for endorsement, and approved by the Treasurer before a contract could be signed. Such formalities were, of course, designed to ensure that public monies would not be subject to abuse. In practice, they were totally inadequate.

Widely heralded ministerial pronouncements that the government intended to acquire large blocks of land for public housing may have been useful to the government in the run-up to an election, but it alerted speculators to the possibility of a windfall. The inflationary effect on a market which already had begun to show signs of overheating could only have worked to the disadvantage of the Housing Commission.

The use of private agents to seek out land for purchase was as dangerous as it may have been convenient. In the event, the agent on whom the Commission came to rely, one Robert Dillon, proved to be a singularly unfortunate choice. He in effect operated as a double agent, receiving commissions from vendors and their agents, and had absolutely no incentive to reduce the cost of government land acquisition.

The engineers' technical reports on land under consideration for purchase were at times grossly inadequate, and the Commission's reception of the reports insufficiently critical. The survey of the Pakenham land revealed a significant part of the area to be flood prone, and no detailed estimate was made of the cost that the necessary drainage works would entail. Moreover, an earlier report by the State Rivers and Water Supply Commission maintained that urban development should not be permitted in the area. Nevertheless the engineer concluded:

> It is doubtful whether a more centrally located area of land in the Pakenham area could be found, and accordingly, it is recommended for purchase (quoted in Victoria 1978, p. 23).

The failure of the Commission to seek further details on the economics of drainage was unwise, to say the least.

The valuation system employed by the Housing Commission, rather than serving as a safeguard against the payment of excessive prices, not only had an inflationary effect, but was also vulnerable to manipulation. The officers seconded from the Valuer-General's office were situated within the Housing Commission, and thereby exposed to the attitudes and values of their colleagues. Not only was their objectivity jeopardised by the knowledge that the Commission was firmly committed to a prospective purchase, but they were also upon occasion advised of the vendor's asking price.

In the case of the Pakenham purchase, they were not adequately appraised of the zoning and drainage problems which could affect the market price of the land, nor were they advised that the land actually consisted of two separate parcels, each with different zoning and development considerations. The valuers were also exposed to deliberate misinformation by a corrupt officer of the Commission who was receiving payments from those with land to sell to the Commission. In the Pakenham and Sunbury cases, valuers were told that other developers were keenly interested in the land, when they were not.

Another aspect of the land scandals was the tension and conflict which occurred between the Ministries of Housing and Planning. The responsibility of the Ministry of Planning, to ensure that development occurred in an orderly fashion and that sufficient open space be conserved for aesthetic and recreational purposes, stood in conflict with the desire of the Ministry of Housing to provide as much low cost accommodation as it could, as soon as possible. Indeed, a considerable amount of the land sought by the Housing Commission was not at the time zoned residential. Purchases were actually completed without any concrete assurances that the land in question would actually be re-zoned. Conflict between the two ministries actually reached Cabinet. In one instance when the Minister for Housing was opposed both by the Premier and the Minister for Planning regarding a proposed purchase, he advised them that contracts had already been signed. It was subsequently revealed that the contracts were dated later than the Cabinet meeting in question.

Public attention was first drawn to the land deals in June 1974. An article in *The Age* (Hills & Chubb 1974) disclosed the windfall profits which flowed to developers and queried the processes of acquisition which could have led to such expenditure. The Minister for Housing denied any impropriety, maintaining that the purchase was in fact, a wise one.

Shortly before, however, Geoffrey Underwood, Private Secretary to the Minister for Planning, was advised of allegations that someone in the Housing Commission was in receipt of questionable payments. Underwood notified the office of the Minister for Housing, but no action was taken.

In August 1974, renewed allegations of graft in the Housing Commission prompted the appointment of an Assistant Commissioner of Police (Crime), Bill Crowley, to inquire into the matter. The investigation could not have been intensive, having lasted all of one week. Whilst conceding that the price paid for the land in question appeared to be relatively high, the Crowley report concluded that there was no real evidence of corrupt dealings. The Assistant Commissioner appeared unusually keen to lay the matter to rest:

> Indeed, any extension of the inquiry at this stage would almost certainly extend current rumours and play into the hands of journalists and others who have recently been making further inquiries (Jost 1977b, p. 19).

The issue, however, would not go away. Continued questioning by the media and by the parliamentary opposition served to heighten suspicion among members of the public at large. The situation became untenable when, in 1977 a vote of no confidence against the government was defeated, but with two government back-benchers abstaining. The two were subsequently expelled from the Liberal Party (Sandercock 1979, p. 40).

In August 1977, continued pressure from press and opposition finally moved the government to appoint a Board of Inquiry. Sir Gregory Gowans, Q.C., a former Victorian Supreme Court Judge, presided. The Board's task was made more difficult by the time which had elapsed since the land purchases had been made. Jack Gaskin, Chairman of the Housing Commission at the time of the purchases, died late in 1974. Robert Dillon, the real estate agent who had acted for the Commission as well as for the vendors, claimed to have lost his diary. Many witnesses claimed an inability to recall details of transactions completed four years earlier. Vance Dickie, who had been shifted from the housing portfolio to that of Chief Secretary in 1976, claimed to have destroyed his personal ministerial files on the land transactions shortly after the reshuffle.

The inquiry began on 4 September, recessed for the holidays, and concluded on 25 January after hearing sixty-two days of evidence from fifty-five witnesses. The *Gowans Report* found that an officer of the Housing Commission, Neil Riach, had received a total of $31,000 from the agent Robert Dillon, and that both had given false evidence to the Commission regarding these payments. It recommended that charges be laid against both Dillon and Riach for perjury, conspiring to commit misbehaviour in a public office, and for the payment and receipt, respectively, of a valuable consideration. The day following the presentation of evidence alleging his receipt of gifts from Dillon, Riach was suspended from his public service position pending disciplinary and criminal proceedings.

A tangentially related casualty of the Gowans Inquiry was the Federal Treasurer, Phillip Lynch. In the course of the inquiry, it became apparent that a partnership which included Lynch family interests had recently realised a gross profit in excess of $74,000 from land dealings in the Mornington Peninsula. Unfortunately for Lynch, the other partner, Nandina Investments, had profited handsomely from earlier transactions with the Housing Commission. Moreover, one of its principals was a former Chairman of the Liberal Party Electoral Committee for the Federal Electorate of Flinders, and a former ministerial aide to Alan Hunt, then under scrutiny by the Gowans Inquiry. Although Lynch himself never became the subject of criminal charges, many regarded it as inappropriate that a federal treasurer be even remotely linked to questionable commercial transactions. With the 1977 federal election fast approaching, this view became even more widely held. On 18 November, Lynch tendered his resignation to the Prime Minister Malcolm Fraser, who accepted it.

Aside from the findings against Dillon and Riach, the Gowans Inquiry found that a number of individuals and firms had been in breach of the *Estate Agents Act 1958* (Vic) by receiving sums in excess of specified maximum commissions. It was noted, however, that prosecutions were barred by lapse of time.

Despite considerable speculation that one or more state ministers might be implicated in criminal activities, the *Gowans Report* failed to find such a degree of ministerial misconduct. It found no evidence of criminal activity on Dickie's part, but singled him out for trenchant criticism. Dickie's enthusiasm to acquire land for public housing contributed to a lack of oversight:

> the appropriate standards of ministerial responsibility could hardly be regarded as satisfied by an assumption by the Minister that all requirements had been met which the Housing Commission thought necessary . . . The Minister has command over the procedure to be followed in such circumstances, and it ought to have been the subject of his attention. It is considered not too high a standard to expect of a Minister that he should enquire . . . (Victoria 1978, pp. 51-2).

The publication of the *Gowans Report* did not succeed in laying the land scandals to rest. Five years after the first land

purchase, not one home had been built on the land. Part of the
Pakenham land had been re-zoned for farming only, and the
queue for public housing had reached 18,000. The Housing
Commission had even failed to charge local graziers rent or
agistment fees for use of the land (Sandercock 1979, p. 41).
Privately, government members were relieved to learn that no
minister had been recommended for prosecution. The Premier
continued to express his support for Dickie, in the face of calls
from the press, the Opposition and even the National Party for
the Chief Secretary's resignation. In a very narrow
interpretation of the criteria of ministerial responsibility,
Hamer said:

> a Minister should resign only when he loses the
> confidence of his parliamentary colleagues or
> commits a criminal act . . .

> Cabinet supports what the Minister did. He was
> carrying out Government policy and we stick by
> that policy (*The Age* 23 March 1978).

For all that Premier Hamer may have seen in him, Vance
Dickie was somewhat lacking in charisma. A number of
unfortunate remarks had been attributed to him during his
tenure as housing minister, statements not likely to have
endeared him to a cross-section of the Victorian public.
During 1974, in response to expressions of discontent on the
part of Housing Commission tenants, he is reputed to have
invited them to move out and make room for those on the
Commission waiting list. Subsequently, in response to the
disclosure of windfall profits gained by developers and
speculators, he is said to have replied:

> What's wrong with a company making a million
> dollars? That's what we Liberals are supposed to
> support. Those of us who are against that sort of
> thing are socialists (quoted in Jost 1977a, p. 3).

Soon after the release of the *Gowans Report*, Dickie, in
his capacity as Chief Secretary, departed on a two-month
overseas study tour to explore road safety policies. Upon his

return to Australia, it was apparent that criticism had not abated. A total of five months elapsed between the publication of the *Gowans Report* and Dickie's eventual resignation from parliament in August 1978, on grounds of failing health. Members of the Hamer government were reported to be privately relieved (*The Age* 16 August 1978).

Meanwhile, criminal proceedings against Dillon and Riach began to unfold, albeit slowly. On 16 June 1978, they were committed for trial on a total of twenty-one charges, including giving and receiving secret commissions, conspiracy to commit misbehaviour in a public office, and defrauding the Housing Commission. The trial was initially scheduled for November 1978, but both of the accused applied for a postponement. The application was unsuccessfully opposed by the Crown, and cynics speculated that the Hamer government wished the matter disposed of prior to the 1979 elections.

With the elections looming and the land scandals remaining high on the agenda for debate, the trial was adjourned until July 1979. Continued debate, the subsequent appointment of a Royal Commission and explicit reference to the matter by a Minister in parliament, saw proceedings postponed yet again.

The terms of reference of the 1977 Gowans Inquiry were limited to the purchases at Pakenham, Sunbury and Melton in 1973 and 1974. Not surprisingly, Housing Commission purchases since 1974 had also aroused suspicions.

In response to opposition demands, in an effort to lay the land deals to rest as an issue in the run-up to the 1979 election, the government leader in the Legislative Council and Minister for Planning at the time of the land purchases investigated by the Gowans Inquiry, Alan Hunt, declared his willingness to table files relating to purchases made over the previous five years. Two days later, Vance Dickie's successor as Minister for Housing, Geoffrey Hayes, commissioned an inquiry into additional land transactions involving Dillon and Riach. Upon completion of the inquiry in December 1978, the Minister announced that the report had revealed no irregularities, but had queried one transaction at Noble Park. Cabinet decided against pursuing further investigations.

The 1979 election campaign was a long one. On 6 February the Premier announced that the election would be held on 5 May. This timing obviously served to minimise the government's vulnerability to attack in Parliament, if not on the campaign trail. The strategy there too was one of defence. Three weeks into the campaign, Cabinet decided against releasing further files to the opposition. This unannounced policy of stonewalling, accompanied by assurances that purchasing irregularities were now history and that all dubious transactions had been investigated, endured until election day. The Hamer government survived a five per cent swing against it, and was returned with a majority of one seat.

Thus assured of another term, the government adopted a remedial approach to what had long since become the bane of its increasingly fragile existence. The announcement of the new Ministry saw the former Minister for Housing, Mr Hayes, dropped from Cabinet. Three weeks after the election, the new minister, Mr Dixon, offhandedly announced to parliament that he had referred a number of files to the Victoria Police Fraud Squad. These cases, it was noted, had been conveniently concealed from the opposition during the recent election campaign. Amidst allegations that the government had misled the parliament and the people of Victoria, the government, less than one month after the election, announced a Royal Commission.

The Royal Commission was intended to complement, rather than to overlap with, the earlier Gowans Inquiry. As such, its terms of reference confined it to purchases between 1 July 1973 and 5 December 1978 excluding the Pakenham, Sunbury and Melton purchases reviewed by Gowans. The conclusions reached by the Royal Commissioners were consistent with those of the earlier inquiry, and showed that the Pakenham, Sunbury and Melton purchases were by no means uncharacteristic of Housing Commission procedures.

> The overwhelming impression with which we are left by the evidence and from our careful observations of the principal actors over the relevant period is that the land purchasing function during the period was handled badly and with a notable lack of initiative and perspicacity on the part of many of those most directly involved in it (Victoria 1981, p. A15).

The Commissioners spoke of 'widespread ineptitude going far beyond anything which could be regarded as a normal or usual incidence of error and misjudgement' (Victoria 1981, p. A15).

Whilst they uncovered no unlawful conduct on the part of the two Ministers who had held the housing portfolio during the period in question (Dickie and Hayes) the Royal Commissioners were critical of ministerial conduct. The ministers, they concluded, were 'not as well served by the Commission as they ought to have been' (Victoria 1981, p. A20). It was implied that this was compounded by a lack of adequate ministerial oversight.

> In our view, both ministers failed to maintain a satisfactory degree of control over the Commission in its land purchasing functions ...

> On several occasions, false or misleading information was included in letters to the Treasurer to which the Minister was expected to, and did, endorse as approved by him (Victoria 1981, p. A21).

The Royal Commissioners found that ministerial communications to the Commission tended to be of an informal nature, and that there was insufficient ministerial attention to files in general, and to the procedures followed in given land acquisitions. Thus, additional broadacre purchases were made without conventional and appropriate feasibility studies. Purchases continued to be made without valuation, or based upon uncritical acceptance of those valuations which had been done. Pressure continued to be placed on valuers, and false information provided to them. In a number of cases, Housing Commission officers failed to negotiate with vendors, paying the asking price without delay or resistance. There was no serious attempt to maximise the Commission's advantage by identifying potentially suitable alternative land, and making appropriate inquiries of its owners. By failing to exploit its position as a large cash buyer, the Housing Commission wasted millions of taxpayers' dollars in addition to the sums identified by the Gowans Inquiry.

In October 1981 Riach, no longer a public servant, and Dillon, each began four-month prison terms for perjury committed during the Gowans Inquiry. Under oath, Riach had denied receiving, and Dillon had denied giving, any consideration. In March of 1982 they were convicted on the bribery, conspiracy and fraud charges. Dillon was sentenced to 5 years imprisonment; Riach to 6 years 6 months, although Riach's sentence was later reduced to 5 years on appeal.

At the time he announced the 1979 Royal Commission, Premier Hamer announced a new valuation policy designed to prevent future profligate purchases. Henceforth, the expenditure of over $100,000 would require two independent valuations, one by a representative of the Valuer-General. The expenditure of over $1 million would require three independent valuations. In addition, a new government agency, the Property and Services Department, was created to monitor every proposed purchase over $100,000 by a government department. The new department would ensure that the proposed purchase price was an appropriate one, and that the circumstances of the proposed transaction were above question.

In addition, the Hamer government restructured the Housing Ministry and the Housing Commission. Henceforth, the Director of Housing would also chair the Commission, whose members would include outside representatives.

The Hamer government was relieved once again to learn that its ministers had been absolved of criminal responsibility by the judicial inquiry. It sought to claim that the days of maladministration had passed into history, that the ministers responsible had been removed, and that at long last, housing and land would not be at issue in the forthcoming election. But eight years of less than successful efforts to sweep the issue under the rug had exhausted the tolerance of Victorians. Two ministers had resigned, and a public servant was in prison. In October 1981, the state Director of Housing resigned after the Royal Commission found that he had conducted private business, on very favourable terms, with contractors working for the Housing Commission. Hamer himself was deposed by his Liberal colleagues before the 1982 elections. Victorians sought more than a change of Liberal leadership, however. In 1982 they returned the first Labor government in twenty-seven years.

References

The Age 23 March 1978.

ibid. 16 August 1978.

Hills, B. & Chubb, P. 1974, 'Big Land Profit for Developer', *The Age* 14 June, p. 1.

Jost, John 1977a, 'Dickie "destroyed personal ministerial files" on land deals'1, *The National Times* 12-17 September, p. 3.

Jost, J. 1977b, 'Land Deals: Some More Questions for the Inquiry', *The National Times* 7-12 November, p. 18.

Milliken, Robert & Jost, John 1978, 'Land Scandals: Hamer Takes a Calculated Risk', *The National Times* 20-25 March, p. 11.

Sandercock, Leonie 1979, *The Land Racket: The Real Costs of Property Speculators,* Silverfish Books, Melbourne.

Victoria 1981, *Report of the Royal Commission into Certain Housing Commission Land Purchases and Other Matters,* S. Frost & A.J. Ellwood, Royal Commissioners, Government Printer, Melbourne.

Victoria 1978, *Report of the Board of Inquiry into Certain Land Purchases by the Housing Commission and Questions Arising Therefrom,* (G. Gowans, Board of Inquiry), Government Printer, Melbourne.

Chapter 14

THE DESECRATION OF INJALKAJANAMA (NTYALKALTYANAME)

It's like setting fire to white fellas' libraries. Or your museums and churches. There will be nothing left to show our children.

Aboriginal leader Galarrwuy Yunupingu
on the Northern Territory Government's
Aboriginal Sacred Sites Protection Act
1989

In 1788, at the beginning of European settlement in Australia, the Aboriginal population was an estimated 325,000. By the early 1930s there were only 70,000 (Australia 1984, p. 2). This trend has been reversed, but black Australians continue to experience extreme deprivation.

In the Northern Territory of Australia, Aborigines were the subject of government-condoned punitive killings as late as the 1920s (Cribbin 1984). Whilst such incidents are now part of Australia's grim history, the living conditions of contemporary Territory Aborigines are no better than those of their counterparts elsewhere in Australia. The Aboriginal infant mortality rate is three times higher than the Territory average. The life expectancy of Territory Aborigines is twenty years less than that of white Australians (Australia 1984, pp. 10-11). The threat to Aboriginal culture is further reflected in widespread diabetes, obesity, alcoholism, petrol sniffing and venereal disease. Aborigines, who constitute a quarter of the Territory's population, comprise 64 per cent of its prisoners.

With the increased mineral exploration and economic development of the Territory in the 1970s, there arose concern that the disintegration of Aboriginal society would accelerate. In the aftermath of the Gove case of 1971, which established that Aborigines had no recognisable title to land by reason of traditional tenure, the Whitlam government sought to confer land rights on Territory Aborigines. Following the dismissal of the Whitlam government in 1975, the new coalition government enacted the *Aboriginal Land Rights (Northern Territory) Act* 1976. Complementary legislation, the *Aboriginal Sacred Sites Ordinance* 1978 provided for the preservation of places which held spiritual significance to Aboriginal people (Gumbert 1984; Bell 1983).

In the thousands of years before European settlement, Aboriginal cultures developed a rich spiritual foundation. The formation of the earth and the creation of life have explanations in Aboriginal legend, as they have in Western religious mythology. Various features of the natural environment have religious significance to Aboriginal people, and serve as the basis for rituals, songs and ceremonies. More than the functional equivalent of a place of worship for Europeans, certain sites are regarded as places where important religious events had actually taken place. Many Aboriginals believe that desecration of some sites would bring severe consequences, including sickness or even death. Desecration is perceived as a threat to social order and an adverse reflection on the custodians of the site (Bell 1983, p. 282).

The unwillingness or inability of many white Australians to appreciate Aboriginal culture, combined with the economic imperatives of Western culture, rendered Aboriginal sacred places particularly vulnerable to desecration, whether through nonchalance or intent.

It was to reduce the threat to places of traditional significance to Aboriginal Australians that the Aboriginal Sacred Sites Ordinance was enacted by the Northern Territory government. Responsibility for funding the Aboriginal Sacred Sites Authority (which the legislation created) was undertaken by the federal government until 1 July 1981 when financial responsibility for the Authority was transferred to the Territory government.

The responsibility of the Sacred Sites Authority is to examine and to evaluate all claims by Aboriginal people regarding the significance of sites in question, and to establish and maintain a register of sacred sites in the Northern Territory including details of their spiritual significance. The Authority also assists custodians of registered sites in consulting with developers, mining companies, and other governmental authorities regarding matters of access. Given the mood and temper of many white Territorians, conflict with the Authority was perhaps inevitable.

The city of Alice Springs, close to the geographic centre of Australia, is one of the more rapidly developing parts of the Territory. Established in the 19th century as the site of a remote telegraph station, it now boasts of a casino, and it has become an increasingly popular tourist attraction for Australians and foreigners alike. The secret United States intelligence facility at Pine Gap is located only 22 km away.

By the early 1980s Alice Springs was prospering, but the town and its environs had a rich cultural heritage, a fact which began to cause some anxiety on the part of the Territory government. In 1981, the Minister for Lands was quoted as saying:

> The town of Alice Springs had been 'ring barked' with land claims and claims of sacred sites . . . We can't build the planned light industrial sub-division on the east side because of some supposed more sacred sites . . . The town is sick of the strategy by the Aboriginal organizations - and so am I . . . The Government will not buckle (quoted in Bell 1983, p. 288).

A new residential subdivision had been approved for development next to the golf course, across the Todd River from the centre of town. Following consultation with local Aboriginal representatives, the company which designed the new development had revised its plans in several locations to avoid disturbing sites in the area which local Aboriginal people regarded as sacred. Likewise, in a conscious act of co-operation and conciliation, Aboriginal custodians had accepted compromises in the delineation of those traditional sites. Similarly satisfactory agreements were reached with the Northern Territory government over the siting of sewerage facilities and a gas pipeline. Nevertheless, one sacred site, the soakage Ilpeye Ilpeye, was bulldozed in March 1981 (Bell 1983, p. 290).

The road between the new development and the East bank of the Todd River, known as Barrett Drive, was earmarked for upgrading by the Territory Department of

Transport and Works. Between the road and the river bank
was a rocky formation known as Injalkajanama
(Ntyalkaltyaname). This, together with a stand of eucalypts
across the road were part of the Caterpillar Dreaming Track,
and constituted a site of some significance to local Aboriginal
people. The trees in question were some of the largest trees in
Alice Springs.

A consultant to the Aboriginal Sacred Sites Authority
informed the Department of Transport and Works, which was
to oversee the development, that discussions with the
traditional owners had yet to be held. The Department replied
that the design for the work was already 90 per cent completed.
Tenders were called in May 1982, and it appeared that the
government sought to expedite the project.

Concerned that the urban development of Alice Springs
might jeopardise the Injalka sites, the local custodians sought
to register them with the Sacred Sites Authority. The rocky
outcrop was first registered on 13 May 1982, the stand of trees
some two months later on 28 July. Signs were posted indicating
the significance of the sites and stating that unauthorised entry
on the sites was a violation of Territory law.

As the time approached for works to commence on the
upgrading of Barrett Drive, the government began negotiations
with the Rice, Stevens and Golders families, the traditional
custodians of the Injalka sites. Original plans called for the
road to run straight through the outcrop. Several alternative
options were under consideration, including minor diversion of
the road or the construction of a bridge over the outcrop. In
proposing the slight curve in the road, the custodians indicated
that they were prepared to sacrifice some of the trees which
comprised the site. The Department of Lands regarded any
deviation of the road as unacceptable.

Negotiations proceeded slowly, and the government grew
increasingly impatient about the delay in development.
Nevertheless, the Roads Division of the Territory Department
of Transport and Works reassured the Aboriginal Sacred Sites
Authority that

> This department will not proceed with the
> reconstruction until the Department of Lands has
> resolved the sacred sites issue (correspondence,

Department of Transport and Works to Aboriginal
Sacred Sites Authority, 9 September 1982).

Earlier, the Department had advised the Sacred Sites
Authority that until there was a clearance from traditional
owners, the Department would not let contracts for the project.
In September, the Chief Minister advised a local member of
the Territory parliament that there were outstanding
clearances relating to sacred sites that had to be made before
contracts were proceeded with. The reassurances proved to be
unwarranted. In early December 1982 the Injalka outcrop was
blasted by a company in receivership and levelled by bulldozers
of Dussin Constructions Pty. Ltd. of Alice Springs, under
contract to the Territory government. Days later, the stand of
eucalypts was also destroyed.

According to a senior official of the Department of
Transport and Works, the destruction of the Injalka site was
authorised by the Territory's Minister for Lands, Marshall
Perron. Claiming an obligation to complete the road
improvements as a matter of urgency, the Minister was quoted
as saying:

> I was fully aware that negotiations with an
> Aboriginal group which claims that there is a
> sacred site in the area had broken down completely
> as far as alternative courses of action were
> concerned, and the Government had no option at
> all but to fulfil its obligation and build the road as
> originally planned (quoted in *The Centralian
> Advocate* 4 February 1983, p. 3).

Whether the negotiations had broken down completely,
as the Minister had been led to believe, is open to question.
The Sacred Sites Authority understood the issue to be still
amenable to a compromise agreement.

A wider motive was suggested for the government's
course of action, however. A senior official of the Department
of Transport and Works alleged that the government had
ordered the sites destroyed in order to challenge the validity of
the sacred sites legislation (Ellis 1983).

Whatever factors underlay the destruction of the Injalka site, one imagines that it did little to reinforce the legitimacy of white man's law in the eyes of black Territorians. In the words of one non-Aboriginal member of the Sacred Sites Authority, his Aboriginal colleagues

> have conveyed to me their disappointment that a contractor employed by a government department should have desecrated a registered site without warning or ultimatum and at a time when negotiations were ongoing. These men, and those they represent, had been led to believe that they could rely on the Government's law for the protection of their sacred places. Their acceptance of the law was an act of faith in the Government, since most could not read the details of the Act and understand it. The importance of these places is demonstrated by the severity of the Aboriginal law which would exact the extreme penalty for such desecration.

> The result of this action, which has implicated the Government in breaking its own law, has been to leave this group confused, and concerned to question whether those responsible believe in the rule of law. As a non-Aborigine who can read the Act, I am personally appalled (Ford, K. 1983, pers. comm. to R. W. Ellis, 10 June).

The economic viability of the Northern Territory has always been fragile. For years, it was dependent upon the massive infusion of subsidies from the federal government, and upon the spending power of Commonwealth public servants. Nevertheless, Territorians (the vast majority of whom have recently arrived in the Territory from southern states) have tended to regard themselves as rugged frontiersmen, and have deeply resented their dependence on the distant Federal capital. With the advent of Territory self government in 1978, those in power realised that true independence from Canberra could only be achieved through economic development. The discovery of rich mineral resources inspired a tempting vision of the economic promised land; anything which might conceivably impede the exploitation of these riches was anathema.

Resentment of Canberra's concern with the environmental impact of mining was one matter. Through its power to grant or refuse export licences and its power to regulate activities in world heritage areas such as Kakadu National Park, the federal government still exercises considerable power over the mining industry in the Territory. In addition, the virulent racism which characterised 19th and early 20th century Australia is by no means a thing of the past. Many Territorians hold Aborigines in contempt and are deeply resentful of Canberra's concern for Aboriginal Australians.

From the perspective of the Territory government, therefore, not only does the existence of federally inspired land rights and sacred sites protection legislation constitute an unwarranted federal intrusion on Territory autonomy, it also impedes the Territory's economic development.

In addition to the inevitable tensions of federalism, certain aspects of the legislation governing sacred sites protection were regarded as imperfect, and may thereby have invited the government's defiance. Under the Act, the Sacred Sites Protection Authority may, in addition to registering a sacred site, recommend a site to the Administrator of the Territory, the Queen's representative and equivalent of a state governor, for declaration as a sacred site. Both the Northern Territory Aboriginal Lands Commissioner, Mr Justice Maurice, and the full bench of the Federal Court of Australia have held that the law extends as much protection to a registered site as it does to one which has been declared. In the event of desecration, declaration does assist in prosecution by providing prima facie evidence that the area is a sacred site. But a Cabinet so possessed with the imperative of economic development would be disinclined to recommend formal declaration to the Administrator.

Governments should be aware that many details of spiritually significant places in the Northern Territory have long been identified to white Australians (Spencer & Gillen 1899; 1904). Nevertheless, traditional custodians of sacred sites in Central Australia are normally reluctant to disclose the existence of a site and to publicise its spiritual significance.

217

Such disclosure tends to occur only when a direct threat to a site is perceived; details tend to be limited to only as much information as thought necessary to impress the outside with the significance of the site. Governments and developers therefore often gain the cynical impression that only when a site acquires economic significance to white Australians does it take on spiritual significance to Aboriginal people.

The procedures involved in declaring a sacred site, moreover, require the disclosure of details of the site's spiritual significance, details which may be of utmost secrecy under customary law. Despite the willingness of custodians in some areas to present documentation to the government if they could be assured personally by the Chief Minister that improper release of secret/sacred information would not occur, such undertakings have never been given. In view of the lack of respect with which Aboriginals and their culture are regarded by many Territorians, the threat of sacred secrets coming into ridicule are sufficient to discourage most from proceeding with the formalities of declaration. On the other hand, as happened in the Injalka case, this lack of formal declaration may be seized upon by antagonistic Territorians as detracting from the legitimacy of a claim despite its earlier acknowledgment in preliminary negotiations.

Following the destruction of the Injalka sites, the Aboriginal custodians protested to the Sacred Sites Authority. At a meeting with the Authority on 22 April 1983, the thirty-six Aboriginal custodians of the Injalka site unanimously recommended that those who desecrated the site be prosecuted. At the request of the custodians, the Authority formally instructed the Director of the Authority to lay a complaint under the Northern Territory Sacred Sites Act.

On 31 May 1983 a summons was issued in Darwin alleging that Dussin Constructions committed three offences under the Act including entering and remaining on a site (31(1)), carrying out works on a site without written permission (31(4)), and knowingly desecrating a site (31(3)). An additional summons was issued against Marshall Perron, the Minister responsible, alleging that he aided and abetted the construction company in the commission of the alleged offences. Each charge carried a maximum penalty of a $2,000 fine, or imprisonment for twelve months, or both.

The problems faced by the Authority in assembling evidence were substantial. On several previous occasions it had sought the assistance of the Northern Territory Police in obtaining evidence through enquiries and interviews. In one case, it provided police with copies of materials assembled, together with an exposed film regarded as illustrative of the matters in question. The evidence was lost by police, who later advised that they did not consider the matter worthy of follow-up.

Among the evidentiary burdens confronting the Authority in its prosecution was proof that the area in question was indeed a sacred site, since it had not been formally declared as such. This would involve having to obtain detailed statements from local Aboriginal custodians, supported by anthropological evidence. This was difficult, not because such information was not available but because the site in question had different levels of significance, some of which could only be discussed in particular situations and with particular people present. Full disclosure of the significance of the site could not occur in open court.

In addition, successful prosecution of the company would require either eye-witness testimony, or admissions made by the company and its employees that they engaged in the acts alleged. It was also incumbent upon the prosecution to rebut the defence that the contractor was unaware of the significance of the site. (A sign identifying the site had been removed by government employees days before the contractor was to begin work). Successful prosecution of the Minister would require evidence that he personally aided and abetted the offences in question by directly communicating instructions to the contractors or explicitly to the contractors through members of his Department.

The Minister in question did not deny his role in the destruction without warning of the Injalka site. In a statement on 8 November 1984, he stated:

> I considered it the responsibility of the Government to proceed with the works.
>
> I appreciate that my decision may have caused anguish to some, which of course is regrettable.

However, I am of the view that there was no practicable alternate route for the road and therefore that my decision was the proper one in the circumstances (Perron 1984).

He gave an undertaking that in future, if he decided that works were to be carried out which could cause damage to a registered sacred site, he would give the Sacred Sites Authority reasonable prior notice of the activity.

On 14 November 1984 the Authority sought leave in the Alice Springs Magistrates Court to withdraw all charges against both Perron and Dussin Constructions. The Authority's legal advisers had discovered a technicality which meant that the government was not bound by the Sacred Sites legislation. Thus, it was unlikely that Dussin, as agent for the Department of Transport and Works, and Perron, as responsible minister, could be found guilty of the offences charged. For similar reasons, the Authority announced that it would not proceed against the Department for damage done to sacred sites at Billy Goat Hill and Dunlop Corner during construction on the Stuart Highway.

The Authority's decision was as much political as it was based on legal grounds. Under the Everingham government, antipathy to Aboriginal interests was so great that all available legal avenues were used to thwart Aboriginal land claims including, in one case, expanding Darwin town boundaries to four times the size of Greater London in order to pre-empt the Kenbi Land Claim (Mowbray 1986, p. 41). With the departure of former Chief Minister Paul Everingham for federal politics, hopes arose that more co-operative relations could be established with the new Chief Minister Ian Tuxworth and the new Minister for Lands and Sacred Sites (Mr S. Hatton). Indeed, partly as a consequence, custodians were granted a residential lease for a town camp as a sign of government goodwill. Successful sacred sites clearance of the Northern Territory gas pipeline in 1985 was another encouraging development.

But optimism in the new Chief Minister proved to have been misplaced. The new Chief Minister announced the government's intention to establish a toxic waste dump at a location subject to a land claim by local Aboriginals (*The*

Centralian Advocate 1 March 1985). At the end of 1985, he refused to attend a ceremony at Uluru (Ayers Rock) at which title to the Rock was returned to its Aboriginal custodians. He likewise instructed civil servants, including staff of the Authority, that they too should boycott the ceremony. Tuxworth, who was soon forced to leave office following disclosures of irregularities relating to his travel allowance, was succeeded as Chief Minister by Steve Hatton, who proved to be no more sympathetic to Territory Aboriginals, but somewhat more pragmatic in his dealings with them.

Under Ian Tuxworth the government had amended the Sacred Sites Act to enable the Minister for Lands to dismiss the Director of the Sacred Sites Authority. In November 1985, after criticising a decision of the Land Commissioner, Mr Justice Maurice, the Director, Bob Ellis, was given a week's notice by Mr Hatton to show cause why he should not be sacked. Ellis sought and obtained an injunction in the Northern Territory Supreme Court to prevent his dismissal. The Chief Justice of the Northern Territory subsequently ruled that the Amendment to the Sacred Sites Act could not be retrospective - that is Ellis' employment could only be terminated under the conditions of his original contract, which specified that he could only be dismissed by the Authority, not the minister.

The Territory government would not relent. Officials of BHP and members of the Jarwon community had, with Authority assistance, begun negotiations over access to potentially rich gold and platinum deposits at Coronation Hill in the Alligator Rivers region. When negotiations became protracted and the Murdoch press in Darwin began an anti-land rights campaign based upon no negotiations, the government grew impatient and announced a review of the Sacred Sites Authority and its operations. Those appointed to conduct the review included the Territory Solicitor General (who had earlier been involved in the suspension of the Authority Director), the Secretary of the Lands Department, and a senior official from the Chief Minister's Department (himself a ministerial appointee to the Sacred Sites Authority).

With the Hawke government's repudiation of ALP policy on Aboriginal land rights, the issue had become distinctly unfashionable in Canberra. The future of Sacred Sites protection in the Northern Territory did not appear favourable. Toward the end of 1986 the Opposition in the Territory Legislative Assembly introduced an amendment to the Sacred Sites Authority Act which would bind the crown. The Bill was defeated on party lines. Marshall Perron referred to many sacred sites as imaginary.

In the Territory, hostility toward Aboriginals remained intense. The Hatton government was returned by a comfortable majority in the March 1987 elections. Media (particularly newspaper) coverage of land rights and sacred sites was cynical and patronising. With 60 per cent of Australia's newspapers under the control of Rupert Murdoch, there seemed little likelihood that portrayals of Aborigines and their threatened culture would be any more sensitive than that depicted on the front page of Murdoch's Australian flagship, *The Australian* in April 1985. A cartoon showed an accumulating pile of empty beer cans next to a sign which read 'No Entry to Whites: Aboriginal Sacred Site Being Erected on This Spot' (*The Australian* 6 April 1985, p. 1).

Ironically, at about this time, Dussin Constructions employees were damaging a further site in central Australia. But prosecutions were again unsuccessful. Charges against a bulldozer driver were dismissed on the grounds that doubt existed whether the accused had been instructed by his employer to avoid the site. A subsequent prosecution against the company failed when the magistrate found that the company had adequately instructed the bulldozer driver. Aboriginal people could perhaps be forgiven for being confused about the operation of Northern Territory law.

As Australia approached the 200th Anniversary of its settlement by Europeans, there was understandably little inclination by its Aboriginal citizens to join in the celebrations.

Postscript

In May 1989 the government led by Chief Minister Marshall Perron passed legislation which abolished the position of Director of the Sacred Sites Authority, and provided for ministerial responsibility for sacred sites registration.

References

Australia 1984, Department of Aboriginal Affairs, *Aboriginal Social Indicators*, Australian Government Publishing Service, Canberra.

The Australian 6 April 1985.

Bell, Diane 1983, 'Sacred Sites: The Politics of Protection', in *Aborigines, Land and Land Rights*, eds. Nicholas Peterson & Marcia Langton, Australian Institute of Aboriginal Studies, Canberra, pp. 278-93.

The Centralian Advocate 4 February 1983, p. 3.

ibid. 1 March 1985.

Cribbin, John 1984, *The Killing Times*, Fontana Collins, Sydney.

Ellis, J. 1983, 'Sites Go For Roads', *Northern Territory News* 31 January, p. 1.

Gumbert, M. 1984, *Neither Justice nor Reason : A Legal and Anthropological Analysis of Aboriginal Land Rights*, University of Queensland Press, St. Lucia.

Mowbray, Martin 1986, *Black and White Councils: Aborigines and Local Government in the NT*, School of Social Work, University of NSW, Kensington.

Perron, Marshall 1984, Ministerial Statement, 8 November.

Spencer, B. & Gillen, F. 1899, *The Native Tribes of Central Australia*, Macmillan, London.

------------ 1904, *The Northern Tribes of Central Australia*, Macmillan, London.

Chapter 15

WATER POLLUTION AND THE YASS SHIRE COUNCIL

The town of Yass, located 60 km from Canberra, is familiar to many who have driven between Sydney and Melbourne. Situated amidst rolling hills in rich grazing country, Yass is heralded as the 'Fine Wool Centre of the World'. It is a typical New South Wales country town with a broad main street, Comur Street, which is in fact the Hume Highway. The shire of Yass has about 7,000 residents, of whom 4,500 live in the township. American media baron Rupert Murdoch owns a property nearby which he visits occasionally in the course of his infrequent visits to Australia. Ironically, in light of the difficulties described in this chapter, the name Yass is derived from an Aboriginal word meaning 'running water'. The Yass River, a tributary of the Murrumbidgee, flows through the town.

The 1970s were good years in Yass, but not without their unpleasant aspects. The infrastructure of the town was under stress. Despite the fact it had been augmented as recently as 1978, the sewage treatment works needed modification when the State Pollution Control Commission (SPCC) required changes in the means of effluent disposal. The town's garbage tip had also become saturated. Nature, too, was becoming uncharitable, as a drought had set in.

By the late 1970s residents living along the Yass River, downstream from the town, had noticed unpleasant changes in the river. There was considerable growth of algae, some of which tended to rot and give off an offensive smell. The river had become enriched; excessive nutrients had flowed into the river in the treated effluent from the sewage treatment plant, and had leached into the river from the town's rubbish tip. The problem was not without precedent in the Yass region; in the early 1970s, Burrinjuck Dam on the Murrumbidgee, had become polluted as a result of effluent from the Australian Capital Territory. Indeed, pollution had been a problem *upstream* of the town, apparently as a result of superphosphates leaching from areas undergoing intensive pasture improvement. This process of eutrophication, as environmental scientists would term it, accelerated during periods of low flow, with severe ecological consequences. With the river choked by vegetation, there was a fall in population of fish and other aquatic species. Recreational use of the river had become curtailed. Its usefulness for swimming, boating, fishing and even as a source of potable water, were limited. At a meeting of the newly constituted Yass Shire Council in January 1980, the Council health surveyor reported the findings of an inspection which he had conducted with an officer of the State Water Resources Commission. They reported an algal bloom extending approximately four km. Whilst isolated patches of algae characterised the first three km, the composition of algae growth changed from a coarse mat to a slimy gelatinous mass further down stream (*Yass Post* 30 January 1980, p. 10). As the drought of the 1980s became worse, so too did the condition of the river. Downstream residents complained to the Shire Council, then to the SPCC, and finally to the state Ombudsman.

Among the many functions performed by local government agencies in Australia is the control of noxious weeds. For many years, one of the substances used by the Yass Shire Council for this purpose was 245T, a highly toxic chemical containing dioxin. Dioxin, it will be remembered, was used extensively as a defoliant in Vietnam under the name of 'Agent Orange'. The Council's Inspector of Noxious Weeds, a Mr Bush, advised the Council that he used over 2,000 litres of the substance over the previous year (*Yass Post* 5 March 1980, p. 23).

In July 1982 it was disclosed that council workers had been using a mixture of diesel oil and 245T to spray stumps along the banks of the Yass River, and that an estimated two gallons had found its way into the river. The ecological impact of this herbicide was not great; tests carried out by the NSW Health Department indicated insignificant levels of pesticide in the water. Nevertheless, the resulting oil slick further offended the sensibilities of residents already uneasy about water quality; the Secretary of the Yass Acclimitisation Society expressed his concern to state government authorities (*Yass Post* 7 July 1982, p. 1).

The Yass Shire Council also encountered public dissatisfaction over the condition of the town's rubbish tip. A front page article in the *Yass Post* (12 March 1980) headlined 'RESIDENTS ANGRY OVER TIP', claimed that the *Post* offices had been 'inundated with complaints' about the 'shocking conditions existing at the tip'. It commented on the tip's 'perennial saturation' and resulting 'shocking odours' and suggested that a new tip be found. Such a task proved to be easier said than done; the Council, which had been endeavouring to locate a new site since 1976, was to be plagued by problems of waste disposal and public indignation for the following six years.

The issue of eutrophication was regarded by Council officers as a temporary problem, caused by runoff of superphosphate fertiliser and animal wastes from grazing properties upstream, and one which had been aggravated by the prolonged drought. It was assumed that the inevitable breaking of the drought would see the river flow clean again. There was thus no need for hasty and expensive engineering intervention; the sewage treatment works had been upgraded as recently as 1978, and the Council's modest fiscal base could scarcely support another large project.

The difficulties encountered by the Yass Shire Council appear to have arisen from the rather cumbersome manner in which local government in New South Wales is organised and from the time-honoured bureaucratic inclination to avoid decisions when confronted with conflicting pressures from constituents. Prior to 1980, Yass township was governed by a Yass Municipal Council, while the surrounding area was governed by the Goodradigbee Shire Council. In April 1967 the Yass Municipal Council sought to extend its rubbish tip to land owned by the Pastures Protection Board. In late 1975, the Yass Municipal Council sought to extend the tip on to land owned by the Goodradigbee Shire Council. To this end, it began negotiations with the Pastures Protection Board, the Department of Lands and the State Health Commission. In October 1976 the Goodradigbee Shire Council refused to cede the land and objected to any extension of the tip; so too did the State Electricity Commission, which claimed to have had easements over part of the area under consideration.

In August 1977, the Yass Municipal Council and the Goodradigbee Shire Council established a Joint Committee to consider future rubbish disposal. Seven months were to expire before the Committee met for the first time. Eventually the Goodradigbee Shire Council offered to grant land for a small extension of the existing tip if the Yass Municipal Council undertook to look for an alternative site entirely. In April 1978, the Yass Municipal Council contacted the local member of State Parliament, who referred the matter to the Ministers for Local Government, Environment and Planning, Lands and Health. In 1978 the State Health Commission, which had already agreed to an extension of the old tip site, pressured the Municipal Council to re-locate the rubbish depot. The Council sought unsuccessfully, once again, to negotiate with the Goodradigbee Shire Council.

A request to the State Lands Department for permission to dump rubbish in a quarry was refused in December of 1978. The following month, January 1979, the Council asked the Lands Department if any Crown land was available in the vicinity. In response, the Lands Department noted that the only possible land available was under the control of the Pastures Protection Board, the body that was contacted originally, twelve years before, in 1967.

Meanwhile, the Municipal Council came under pressure from the SPCC in 1979 for violations of the *Clean Air Act 1970* (NSW) arising from the burning of rubbish at the, by then, saturated rubbish tip. By this time, it had been decided by state government to amalgamate the Yass Municipal Council and the Goodradigbee Shire Council. With this amalgamation pending, the Municipal Council wrote to its local member of Parliament requesting that further action be postponed. In 1980 the new Yass Shire Council referred the matter of the tip to another committee. In June of that year, Council arranged an inspection of nine alternative tip sites with inspectors from the State Health Commission. Correspondence with the Health Commission and SPCC ensued, and by late November of 1980 the Yass Shire Council announced its choice of a preferred site along Yellow Creek Road.

It is perhaps not surprising that this choice met with some disapproval from the owners of the land in question, and from their neighbours. In the face of strenuous objections, the

Council reconsidered its choice. In March 1981, the Council health surveyor proposed that as an alternative to a new site, the existing tip be extended. This met with objections from the State Health Commission and SPCC.

In late 1981, the SPCC became impatient with inaction on Council's part and began sending letters by certified mail. By October 1981, the Yass Shire Council had narrowed its choice to two sites. Negotiations with the land owners took place over the first six months of 1982.

After protests by parties affected, and consideration of additional reports, Council resolved to choose one of the sites for its new rubbish tip. It then rescinded its decision and reverted to the previous choice. In October 1982, the Yass Shire Council had its preferred site subject to valuation, and had resumption documents drafted. At that point the land owners complained to the state Ombudsman and to the New South Wales National Parks and Wildlife Service that the site in question contained Aboriginal graves. An archaeologist from the National Parks and Wildlife Service stated that this was indeed possible. The project was thus postponed again.

Meanwhile, the Yass Shire Council continued to dispute the contention that the sewage treatment plant was in fact the source of pollution of the Yass River. It argued that the sewage plant was effective, and that effluent did not contain bacteria or organic residues. It argued that whatever pollution existed, could as easily have been caused by agricultural chemicals and other substances leaching from surrounding agricultural properties. Moreover, it argued that similar problems existed *upstream* of the town and the treatment works. Knowledgeable environmental scientists however, would observe that algae growths such as that which gave rise to the downstream residents' complaints, would quite likely have arisen from the concentration of nutrients flowing from the sewage treatment facility.

With so many arms of state government involved in the affairs of Yass Council, some difference of opinion was inevitable. Council's disinclination to proceed with haste was reinforced by encouragement it received from some quarters. As recently as 1978, the state Department of Public Works had designed and built a new Pasveer treatment plant in consultation with the Department of Health and the SPCC. In

1980 the State Water Resources Commission had advised that the algal bloom then evident resulted from natural runoff, and was not directly related to a point source discharge (Kaub 1986, p. 3). In 1982, the Department of Public Works investigated eutrophication complaints, and after consulting with SPCC, concluded that no further works were required. This judgment was reaffirmed two years later (Brereton, L. 1984, pers. comm. to T. Sheahan, 9 March). Whilst the state Ombudsman concluded that the Council was playing one state agency off against another, Council found enough justification for its decision to proceed slowly.

In December 1982, the SPCC issued orders under the *Clean Waters Act 1970* (NSW) for the Council to install a water spray irrigation system within ninety days. On 2 March 1983, the Yass Shire Clerk requested an extension, pleading, 'it is very difficult to make quick decisions in this matter, as the procedure to direct treated sewage effluent away from discharge into the Yass River cannot be achieved overnight' (quoted in New South Wales Ombudsman 1985, p. 169).

Downstream residents' frustration with poor water quality and with what was perceived as inaction on the part of responsible public authorities gave rise to a complaint to the New South Wales Ombudsman in 1981. Soon thereafter, the problem of eutrophication was called to the attention of the state Minister for Environment and Planning. At this point, the Ombudsman's inquiry was postponed for a number of months in deference to ministerial involvement, then resumed when it became apparent that matters remained essentially unchanged. The investigation culminated in a report presented to the Council and to the complainants toward the end of 1983 more than two years after the initial complaint.

The report was strongly critical of the Council for its delay in rectifying waste disposal problems. The Ombudsman's Office had become as impatient as the aggrieved residents of Yass. The language of the report was not delicate:

> The garbage tip is a disgrace to any community, and to the representatives and officials who are responsible for that community's welfare. Within sight of the Hume Highway, the tip spreads sheets of paper and dirty plastic bags over the

surrounding countryside and dangles them from the crooked fences that surround it. Garbage is now being buried in older garbage, since there is no more earth left. Cartons and papers are burned, in order to reduce bulk, so that there is often a column of smoke over the tip. In holes in the garbage into which yet more garbage is to be thrown, there are pools of repulsive fluid, which seeps through the patches of weeds below the tip and then enters the creek and the Yass River (NSW Ombudsman 1983, p. 15).

The report urged that Council obtain a new site for a rubbish tip and begin operations there within six months; that it immediately begin spray irrigation of land adjoining the sewage treatment works; and that it cease discharging treated effluent into Bango Creek and the Yass River. The Ombudsman further requested compliance reports from Yass Shire Council on 31 October 1983, 31 January, 30 April and 31 July 1984. The report urged that these recommendations be implemented 'before Yass becomes known not as the fine wool hub of the world, but as the pollution centre of the south.' (NSW Ombudsman 1983, p. 21).

The SPCC issued licences to the Yass Shire Council in 1983, and again in 1984 permitting the Council to continue to discharge its treated effluent into the Yass River. The licences were subject to two conditions - the submission of quarterly analysis reports and the eventual installation of equipment to monitor daily flow of effluent.

But the patience of SPCC authorities had become exhausted. In December 1983, SPCC issued a summons to the Council. By this time, the Member for Burrinjuck, the state electorate in which Yass is situated, had become state Minister for Planning and the Environment. For a time it was hoped that he might be prevailed upon to intervene to have the prosecution withdrawn. Whether because of media attention drawn to a previous act of similar largesse on behalf of another constituent (Bacon 1984) or the persuasive powers of SPCC staff, the case went ahead. In late 1984, nearly two years after its spray irrigation order, the SPCC prosecuted the Yass Shire Council for failure to comply with the notices in the prescribed ninety day period. It was the first shire council to be subject to prosecution by SPCC.

On 12 November 1984, charges were heard by Smith SM, in Yass Petty Sessions for breaches of the Clean Waters Act. The maximum fine which could be imposed was $4,000. An SPCC industrial chemist testified that a recent inspection had shown severe deposits of black rotting matter on the river bed, and the photographs taken by one land owner showed the river to have been 'effectively mutilated' and of no real recreational use.

The Council's evidence in mitigation rested on the argument that as its sewage treatment works had been designed and constructed by one government agency and licensed each year by another, it had become 'the meat in the bureaucratic sandwich'. The Council thus sought to fix responsibility for the delay on the Department of Public Works. The defence endeavoured further to argue that it was inconsistent for SPCC to continue to license effluent after ordering its control. Moreover, with the breaking of the drought, the eutrophication of the river had significantly abated.

The magistrate found the Yass Shire Council guilty of the offence, but pursuant to s.556a of the *Crimes Act 1970* (NSW) did not record a conviction or impose a fine. He did, however, award costs of $1,000 against the Council. The magistrate explained his lenient decision in part, by suggesting that any penalty imposed would ultimately be borne by ratepayers. He also observed that the Council had faced considerable difficulties in acquiring suitable land for a new rubbish tip and that it had in fact been obliged to consult with seven different departments of state government. The magistrate found that Council had taken all reasonable steps to ensure that work on the spray irrigation system proceeded, and he did not see how the Council could have complied with the SPCC notice within the ninety day period.

The Council, through its Shire Clerk, gave an undertaking to the Court that it would have the required works completed by February 1985. It then engaged the NSW Department of Public Works to design and install an effluent spray disposal system. In December 1984, SPCC advised of new conditions attached to Yass Council's licence to discharge sewage effluent. From 1 June 1985 treated effluent was to be directed to disposal by spray irrigation at all times, except when the river flow exceeded fifty megalitres per day. But again, the Yass Shire Council found that it could move no faster than those other branches of the NSW government on which it depended. Technical problems delayed completion of the project; however, in this instance, the SPCC did not seek to enforce the conditions of the Council's licence, instead choosing to negotiate with the Public Works Department.

The new plant finally began operating in June 1986. It is designed to operate continuously when the level of the river flow falls below the threshold specified by the SPCC. The total cost of the system was $430,000, half of which was provided by the state, and half borne by the ratepayers of Yass.

Meanwhile, Council had yet to locate a suitable site for a new rubbish tip, or at least a suitable site which would not arouse the wrath of its prospective neighbours. The challenge will be a daunting one, as long as ratepayers continue to regard a rubbish tip as a place where one is free to dump indiscriminately, and with total disregard for other users of the area. At the existing tip, the problems with saturation which had been the source of so much concern appear to have been alleviated to a large extent by more attentive management. Burning of bulk materials is now undertaken with greater care, and burial of appropriate matter is now done more frequently. The tip no longer causes visual affront to users or passers-by. Abundant rainfall and a free flowing river have soothed public indignation over leachate. But Council officials remain indignant over what they perceived as insensitive treatment by bureaucrats in Sydney.

References

Bacon, Wendy 1984, 'Charges Dropped Over Sale of Protected Birds', *National Times* 3-9 May, p. 14.

Kaub, W.B. 1986, 'Yass Wastewater Treatment Plant and Associated Effluent Spray Disposal System', paper to NSW Recycled Water Co-ordination Committee, 13-14 November.

NSW Ombudsman 1983, *Yass Shire Council Report*, NSW Ombudsman, Sydney.

NSW Ombudsman 1985, *Annual Report for the Year Ended 30th June 1984*, Government Printer, Sydney.

Yass Post 30 January 1980, p. 10.

ibid. 5 March 1980, p. 23.

ibid. 12 March 1980, p. 1.

ibid. 7 July 1982, p. 1.

Chapter 16

A TOXIC LEGACY: BRITISH NUCLEAR
WEAPONS TESTING IN AUSTRALIA

The destruction of Hiroshima and Nagasaki by nuclear weapons in 1945 marked the beginning of a new era in warfare.

At the end of World War II only the United States commanded the resources and the expertise required to produce a nuclear weapon. This nuclear monopoly was to be short-lived, however. The Soviet Union detonated its first atomic device in 1948. France and Britain, each presiding over shrinking empires and anxious to arrest the decline of their prominence in world politics, sought eagerly to join the nuclear club.

Britain's decision to build an atomic weapon was taken in 1947. Although she remained a close ally of the United States, collaboration with United States weapons development programs was precluded by American legislation which prohibited the transfer of nuclear weapons technology to other nations, no matter how friendly. Thus, the British founded the Atomic Weapons Research Establishment at Aldermaston, United Kingdom, and began to develop atomic weapons of their own.

The development of such high technology weaponry, of course, required periodic testing, ideally (for reasons of security as well as public health) in an uninhabited or sparsely populated area. It was originally hoped that United States nuclear weapons testing facilities either in Nevada or in the Pacific might be made available for British weapons tests. But United States willingness to form even such a limited nuclear partnership was inhibited by the escalation of the Cold War. The Soviets had begun to develop a nuclear weapons program of their own, assisted in part by secret information conveyed to them by British subjects Alan Nunn May and Klaus Fuchs.

Thus the British, keen to begin their testing program and lacking the complete confidence of the United States, began to explore other venues for testing their new weaponry. The remoteness and sparse population of Australia made it an attractive alternative; sites considered by the British in the course of an initial geographic perusal included Groote Eylandt in the Gulf of Carpentaria, and an island in the Bass Strait off Tasmania. In 1950, Labor Prime Minister Clement Atlee sent a top secret personal message to Australian Prime Minister Menzies asking if the Australian government might agree to the testing of a British nuclear weapon at the Monte Bello Islands off Western Australia. Menzies agreed in principle, immediately; there is no record of his having consulted any of his Cabinet colleagues on the matter. A preliminary assessment of the suitability of the proposed test site was conducted in October-November 1950.

The Monte Bello site was deemed suitable by British authorities, and in a message to Menzies dated 26 March 1951 Atlee sought formal agreement to conduct the test. Atlee's letter did not discuss the nature of the proposed test in minute detail. He did, however, see fit to mention the risk of radiation hazards:

> 6.   There is one further aspect which I should mention. The effect of exploding an atomic weapon in the Monte Bello Islands will be to contaminate with radio activity the north-east group and this contamination may spread to others of the islands. The area is not likely to be entirely free from contamination for about three years and we would hope for continuing Australian help in investigating the decay of contamination. During this time the area will be unsafe for human occupation or even for visits by e.g. pearl fishermen who, we understand, at present go there from time to time and suitable measures will need to be taken to keep them away. We should not like the Australian Government to take a decision on the matter without having this aspect of it in their minds (quoted in Australia 1985, p. 13).

Menzies was only too pleased to assist the 'motherland', but deferred a response until after the 1951 federal elections. With the return of his government, preparations for the test, code-named 'Hurricane', proceeded. Yet it was not until

19 February 1952 that the Australian public was informed that atomic weapons were to be tested on Australian soil. On 3 October 1952 the British successfully detonated a nuclear device of about 25 kilotons in the Monte Bello Islands.

The newest member of the nuclear club was by no means content to rest on the laurels of one successful test, however. Indeed, even before the Monte Bello detonation, British officials had visited sites in a remote area of South Australia with an eye to conducting future tests.

In December 1952, the new British Prime Minister, Churchill, asked Menzies for agreement in principle to a series of tests at Emu Field, some 1,200 km northwest of Adelaide in the Great Victoria Desert. Menzies replied promptly, in the affirmative. On 15 October 1953, Totem 1, a device with a yield of approximately 10 kilotons was detonated; two days later, Totem II was exploded with an approximate yield of 8 kilotons.

By this time, the British government had become firmly committed to a continuing nuclear weapons program. Three days after the conclusion of the Totem trials, the Australian government was formally advised of British desires to establish a permanent testing site in Australia. In August 1954, the Australian Cabinet agreed to the establishment of a permanent testing ground at a site that became named Maralinga, north of the transcontinental railway line in southwestern South Australia.

Following the 'Mosaic' tests in mid-1956, which involved the detonation of two weapons at the Monte Bello site, the British testing program in Australia was confined to the mainland. Four 'Buffalo' tests were conducted at Maralinga in September and October 1956, and three 'Antler' explosions were detonated there the following year.

Each of these explosions generated considerable radioactivity, by means of the initial nuclear reaction and the through dispersion of radioactive particulate colloquially known as 'fallout'. In addition to British scientific and military personnel, thousands of Australians were exposed to radiation produced by the tests. These included not only those involved in supporting the British testing program, but also Aboriginal people living downwind of the test sites, and other Australians more distant who came into contact with airborne radioactivity.

A series of British hydrogen bomb tests was conducted in the Pacific Ocean during 1957 and 1958 without Australian involvement. In addition to the major weapons testing programs, the British undertook a number of minor trials at Emu and at Maralinga during the period 1953-1963. The 'Kittens', 'Tims' and 'Rats' series of experiments tested individual components or sub-assemblies of nuclear devices. Subsequent series, called 'Vixen A' and 'Vixen B' sought to investigate the effects of accidental fires and explosions on nuclear weapons.

While less spectacular than the major detonations, the minor trials were more numerous. They also contributed to the lasting contamination of the Maralinga area. As a result of the nearly 600 minor trials, some 830 tons of debris contaminated by about 20 kg of plutonium were deposited in pits which graced the South Australian landscape. An additional 2 kg of plutonium was dispersed over the area. Such an outcome was unfortunate indeed, as plutonium is one of the most toxic substances known; it dissipates more slowly than most radioactive elements. The half-life of plutonium is 24,000 years. At this rate of decay, the Maralinga lands would be contaminated for the next half-million years.

Thus, Australia's hospitality, largesse and loyalty to Britain were not without their costs. Moreover, the sacrifices made by Australians on behalf of the 'motherland' were not equally borne. Whilst low population density and remoteness from major population centres were among the criteria for the selection of the testing sites, the Emu and Maralinga sites in particular were not uninhabited. Indeed, they had been familiar to generations of Aboriginal Australians for thousands of years and had a great spiritual significance for the Pitjantjatjara and Yankunytjatjara people.

In the interests of the testing program, it was decided to curtail the movements of those Aboriginal people traversing the Maralinga area. In addition, a number were taken to a reserve which had recently been established at Yalata, some distance to the south, across the transcontinental railway line. The removal of Aboriginal people from their traditional homelands was more than an inconvenience. The Maralinga lands contained mythological sites of spiritual significance for their inhabitants, a significance which was at best only vaguely appreciated by white officials. Indeed, this lack of sensitivity was illustrated by the consideration given by authorities to identifying sacred objects and 'removing' them to areas of resettlement (Australia 1985, pp. 300-1). During the 1950s, hundreds of former inhabitants of the Maralinga lands sought to reaffirm their threatened culture by travelling considerable distances from the Yalata area in order to attend ceremonial functions and to visit other Aboriginal groups. These movements extended as far west as Cundalee, Western Australia, and as far east as Coober Pedy and Mabel Creek.

Some Aboriginal people were even less fortunate. Security patrols in and around the Maralinga area were intermittently effective, and from time to time some Aboriginal people were evicted from the area. Years later, Aboriginal people from Western Australia would recall how they were directed away from Maralinga along a road which diverged from their standard water hole routes, and how some of their party died from lack of access to water.

For those who survived, there seems little doubt that for the Western Desert (Maralinga) people the alien settlement of Yalata and lack of access to their desert homelands contributed significantly to the social disintegration which characterises the community to this day. Petrol sniffing, juvenile crime, alcoholism and chronic friction between residents and the South Australian police have become facts of life (Brady & Morice 1982).

The security measures taken to restrict access to the testing site were not without flaws. One morning in May 1957, four Aboriginal people, the Milpuddie family, were found by range authorities near the crater formed by the 'Buffalo 2' explosion the previous October. The man, woman, two children and two dogs had set out on foot from the Everard Ranges in the northwest of South Australia, and were unaware that the Aboriginal inhabitants of the Maralinga area had been removed. When authorities discovered them, the family was immediately taken to a decontamination centre at the site, and were required to shower. After this experience, which must have been frightening enough, the family was driven to Yalata.

As one of the site personnel described the experience:

It was a shocking trip down as they had never ridden in a vehicle before and vomited everywhere (Australia 1985, p. 320).

On instructions from the Secretary of the Commonwealth Department of Supply, the dogs were shot. The woman was pregnant at the time the family was taken into custody; subsequently, her baby was born dead. Australian authorities went to great lengths to keep the incident secret, but they appear to have been less concerned with the family's subsequent health. Commenting upon the fact that no-one appears to have taken the time to explain the experience to which the hapless Aborigines were subjected, a team of anthropologists was to comment:

[T]he three remaining members of the family have been subjected to a high degree of stress and unhappiness about the events of twenty-eight years ago (Australia 1985, p. 323).

Knowledge of the hazards of radioactivity has accumulated only gradually over the past century. Some of the dangers posed by radiation become apparent soon after the discovery of X-rays in 1895. It was recognised early on that exposure to sufficient doses of radiation could cause injuries to internal organs, as well as to the skin and the eyes. Only after a number of years did scientists become aware of the risk of genetic damage, and of carcinogenic effects as well, at low levels of exposure. Degrees of exposure regarded as tolerable in the 1950s are now internationally recognised as unsafe.

The amount of radioactivity generated by a nuclear explosion can vary considerably depending upon a number of factors. These include the size of the weapon, and the location of the burst - an explosion at ground level may be expected to generate more dust and other radioactive particulate matters than an air burst. The dispersion of radioactive material is also dependent upon weather conditions.

The heritable and carcinogenic effects of radiation often do not manifest themselves for considerable periods. Moreover, both effects may result from other causes, unrelated to radiation, or may even occur spontaneously. Thus, any determination of the health consequences of nuclear weapons testing in Australia would require very detailed records identifying those citizens who were exposed to radiation, and the degree of radiation to which they were exposed.

Although most of the British and Australian personnel involved in the testing program were equipped with film badges and dosimeters to record the extent of their exposure to radiation, some did not. Moreover, those measuring devices which were provided did not record exposure with perfect accuracy.

Nor could the risk to the general public be assessed with any real rigour. Despite the fact that airborne radiation from the Monte Bello tests was detected as far away as Townsville and Rockhampton, official fallout measurements were not compiled, and available data was insufficient to estimate collective exposure. Whilst it is probable that some cases of cancer and genetic damage were caused by radiation generated by the nuclear tests, a realistic estimate of their extent is not possible.

A variety of factors underlay the harm to public health, Aboriginal culture and the natural environment which the British tests entailed. Perhaps most significant was the secrecy surrounding the testing program. The decision to make the Monte Bello Islands available to the British for their first nuclear test appears to have been made by the Prime Minister alone, without reference to Cabinet, much less Parliament or the Australian public. During the entire course of the testing program, public debate on the costs and risks borne by the Australian public was discouraged through official secrecy, censorship, misinformation, and attempts to denigrate critics.

Admittedly, in the 1950s knowledge of radiation hazards was not as advanced as it is today. At the time it was not generally recognised that small doses of low level radiation might increase the risk of cancer years later. But even in the light of knowledge of the time, the information on which Menzies based his decisions was seriously deficient.

There seems little doubt that the secrecy in which the entire testing program was cloaked served British rather than Australian interests. From the outset, the British were under pressure to demonstrate to the Americans that they were able to keep secrets at all. Full disclosure of the hazards and potential costs to Australia entailed in the testing program were out of the question. Information passed to Australian officials was kept to the minimum necessary to facilitate their assistance in the conduct of the testing program. The use of plutonium in the minor trials was not disclosed.

Australian tolerance of the British and their obsessive secrecy may be explained by the deference and loyalty to the 'motherland'. Prime Minister Menzies identified so strongly with Britain that he considered British national interest as Australia's national interest. Although he was later to seek assurances that hazards inherent in the testing program would be minimal and that appropriate safeguards would protect the Australian public, his enduring faith in the British was to blunt his critical faculties.

It is perhaps illustrative that on the occasions chosen by Australian authorities to assert themselves on matters of policy, the issues of concern were purely symbolic. The Antler series of tests was renamed, after Australians objected to the proposed name 'Volcano' (Milliken 1986, p. 226). On another occasion, a detonation scheduled for a Sunday was postponed in deference to Australian sensibilities (Australia 1985, p. 287).

Another factor which underlay Australian deference during the course of the testing program was the role of Sir Ernest Titterton. A British physicist, Titterton had worked in the United States on the Manhattan Project, which developed the first nuclear weapon.

After the war, he held a position at the British Atomic Energy Research Establishment, and in 1950 he was appointed to the Chair of Nuclear Physics at the Australian National University. Among Titterton's earliest tasks in Australia was that of an adviser to the British scientific team at the first Monte Bello tests. In 1956, the Australian government established an Atomic Weapons Tests Safety Committee (AWTSC) responsible for monitoring the British testing program to ensure that the safety of the Australian environment and population were not jeopardised. To this end, it was to review British test proposals, provide expert advice to the Australian government, and to monitor the outcome of tests. Titterton was a foundation member of the Committee and later, its Chairman.

While Menzies had envisaged that the Committee would act as an independent, objective body, evidence suggests that it was more sensitive to the needs of the British testing program than to its Australian constituents.

Members tended to be drawn from the nuclear weapons fraternity, as was Titterton; from the Defence establishment, from the Commonwealth Department of Supply, from the Commonwealth X-Ray and Radium Laboratory, and from the Australian Atomic Energy Commission. Although the expertise of these individuals is beyond dispute, one wonders if they may have been too closely identified with the 'atomic establishment' to provide independent critical advice. The nuclear weapons fraternity have often been criticised as a rather cavalier lot; no less a person than General Leslie Groves, who headed the Manhattan Project which developed the first atomic bomb, has been quoted as having said 'Radiation death is a very pleasant way to die' (Ball 1986, p. 8). In retrospect, the Australian safety committee suffered from the absence of biologists and environmental scientists in its ranks.

The plight of Aborigines in the vicinity of the prohibited zone was in many respects a reflection of their status in Australia at the time. In a revealing statement to the Royal Commission, Sir Ernest Titterton was quoted as having said that if Aboriginal people objected to the tests they could vote the government out (Australia 1985, p. 121). It is naive to suggest that such a small disadvantaged minority might wield electoral influence; doubly so since Aboriginal people were denied full voting rights at the time of the tests, and indeed, were even excluded from census enumeration until 1967. There is no dearth of evidence of the low regard in which Aborigines were held at the time. The chief scientist of the Department of Supply, a British expatriate, criticised an officer whom he regarded as overly concerned with Aboriginal welfare for 'placing the affairs of a handful of natives above those of the British Commonwealth of Nations' (Australia 1985, p. 309).

Because of their unique lifestyle, and often their lack of clothing, footwear and permanent shelter, Aboriginal residents in remote parts of Australia were particularly vulnerable to radiation. Although this was recognised and acted upon later in the testing program, the AWTSC was initially ignorant of or unconcerned with these risks.

Disinformation, whether deliberate or unintentional, was all too common during the testing programs. In order to provide accurate meteorological data for the weapons tests, a small weather station was constructed across the Western Australian border from Maralinga. The Australian Minister of Supply at the time, Howard Beale, quite falsely claimed that it was sited very carefully away from Aboriginal watering places (Australia 1985, p. 373). In fact, the site was chosen without seeking the advice of the native patrol officer. Moreover, the roads which were built to provide access to the weather station contradicted the assurances made by the government in 1947 that no roads would encroach upon the Aboriginal reserve.

In the aftermath of the second Monte Bello tests in 1956, the AWTSC filed a reassuring report which failed to refer to complications with the tests and to levels of fallout on the mainland which were higher than expected (Australia 1985, pp. 257-9).

In 1960, the British advised the AWTSC that 'long lived fissile elements' and 'a toxic material' would be used in the 'Vixen B' tests. Titterton requested that the materials be named, and later announced 'They have answered everything we asked.' The substances in question were not disclosed (Australia 1985, p. 414). In recommending that the Australian government agree to the tests, he appears to have been either insufficiently informed of the hazards at hand, or to have failed to communicate those hazards to the Safety Committee, and through it, to the Australian government. Earlier, before the Totem tests, he had reassured the Australian Prime Minister that

> the time of firing will be chosen so that any risk to health due to radioactive contamination in our cities, or in fact to any human beings, is impossible. . . . [N]o habitations or living beings will suffer injury to health from the effects of the atomic explosions proposed for the trials (quoted in Australia 1985, p. 467).

There were other examples of Titterton's role in filtering information to the Australian authorities, a role which has been described as 'pivotal' (Australia 1985, p. 513). He proposed that he be advised informally of certain details of proposed experiments. In one instance, he advised the British that 'It would perhaps be wise to make it quite clear that the fission yield in all cases is zero', knowing that this would be a misrepresentation of fact (Australia 1985, p. 519). Years later, the Royal Commission suggested that Titterton may have been more a de facto member of the British Atomic Weapons Research Establishment than a custodian of the Australian public interest.

The Royal Commission's indictment of Titterton would be damning:

> Titterton played a political as well as a safety role in the testing program, especially in the minor trials. He was prepared to conceal information from the Australian Government and his fellow Committee members if he believed to do so would suit the interests of the United Kingdom Government and the testing program (Australia 1985, p. 526).

British secretiveness and imperfect review of test proposals and consequences by Australian officials notwithstanding, the degree to which Australian authorities went in limiting debate and discussion of the testing program and its effects cannot be ignored.

Such media coverage of the tests as was permitted by British and Australian authorities tended to be trivial and generally celebratory (Woodward 1984). Restrictions were onerous, in some occasions to the point of absurdity. D-notices were applied in such a manner that Australian journalists were forbidden from reporting items which had already been published freely in the United Kingdom.

Dissent or criticism by Australian personnel involved in the testing program was not tolerated. One patrol officer who objected that the development of testing sites was proceeding without due regard for the protection and welfare of local Aborigines was 'reminded of his obligations as a

Commonwealth Officer' (Australia 1985, p. 304), and warned against speaking to the press.

Occasionally, when Aborigines were sighted in restricted areas, reports of these sightings were disbelieved, or less than subtly discouraged. One officer who reported sighting Aborigines in the prohibited zone was asked if he realised 'what sort of damage [he] would be doing by finding Aboriginals where Aboriginals could not be' (Australia 1985, p. 319).

After the Milpuddie family was found in the restricted area at Maralinga, the Range Commander invoked the *Defence (Special Undertakings) Act 1952* (Cwlth) to prevent disclosure of the incident by any personnel on the scene.

The flow of information within government departments was at times impeded, with adverse consequences. According to one account, incomplete information about plutonium contaminations at Maralinga was given to Vic Garland, a Minister in the McMahon government, causing him to mislead Parliament in 1972 (Toohey 1978).

The full legal and political implications of the testing program would take decades to emerge. The secrecy which surrounded the British testing program and the remoteness of the tests from major population centres meant that public opposition to the tests and awareness of the risks involved grew very slowly.

But as the ban-the-bomb movement gathered momentum in Western societies throughout the 1950s, so too did opposition to the British tests in Australia. An opinion poll taken in 1957 showed 49 per cent of the Australian public opposed to the tests and only 39 per cent in favour.

Evatt and Calwell, Leader and Deputy Leader of the Federal Opposition, called for an end to the tests. Following the conclusion of the Antler series in October 1957, the British conducted their large thermonuclear tests at Christmas Island in the Pacific Ocean; only the so-called 'minor' trials continued at Maralinga.

By the early 1960s, the United States, the Soviet Union and Great Britain signed an agreement to cease atmospheric nuclear tests. The British, having finally gained the confidence of the United States, were invited to conduct underground tests at United States facilities in Nevada. It was thus decided to close the Maralinga facility.

In 1967, the British undertook an operation to decontaminate the Maralinga range. 'Operation Brumby' as it was called, involved burying a variety of radioactive debris, including plutonium, in pits which were covered with concrete. Radioactive fragments scattered over the terrain were ploughed into the earth or covered with topsoil to reduce the likelihood of dispersion and subsequent inhalation or ingestion. A top secret report on the operation was prepared, submitted to the Australian government, filed, and soon forgotten. In September 1968, the British and Australian governments signed an agreement which released the British from all legal liabilities or further responsibilities arising from the testing program.

The issue lay dormant for almost another decade. In 1974, the Commonwealth government made a compensation payment of $8,600 to the widow of a warrant officer who had died of leukemia six years previously. The officer had been exposed to a relatively high dose of radiation while repairing a tank at the Maralinga test site. In December 1976 an Opposition frontbencher, Tom Uren, queried whether the minor trials had been in breach of international agreements in force at the time, and whether radioactive wastes were buried at Maralinga. He was reassured by the Minister of Defence that rumours and allegations to that effect were unfounded. Despite Uren's call for a Royal Commission, the media failed to develop the story (Milliken 1986, p. 263).

Later in 1977 The Australian Ionising Radiation Advisory Council (AIRAC) began a review of waste at Maralinga. But before it was completed, the leak of a Cabinet document shed further light on the matter. An article in the *Australian Financial Review* (Toohey 1978) revealed that the Minister of Defence had warned Cabinet that the quantity of weapons-grade plutonium buried at Maralinga was vulnerable to theft by potential terrorists, and that Australia might thereby be in breach of international safeguard arrangements.

The Fraser government, anxious to minimise embarrassment in general and to minimise any political threats to the burgeoning Australian uranium industry in particular, quickly asked the British government to remove that plutonium which existed in recoverable form. The British were agreeable, subject to further conditions, including that they would bear no further responsibility for removal of additional waste.

Not long after this operation was completed, the Fraser government released a 'sanitised' version of the previously top secret report, but by this time, the issue was to remain on the agenda for public debate. A team of investigative reporters from *The Adelaide Advertiser* published a series of articles raising questions about the incidence of cancer among Australian ex-servicemen and civilians who worked at the site. They further suggested that fallout from one test reached as far as Adelaide, and that local Aborigines had been contaminated by radioactivity (English & DeIonno 1980a; 1980b; 1980c).

These articles generated interest throughout Australia. Ex-servicemen who had worked at Maralinga formed organisations to press for enquiries into the health consequences of their service. Aborigines who had lived north-east of Maralinga at the time of the tests came forward with allegations that on one occasion, they had encountered a 'Black Mist' which left a number of people ill. An article in *The National Times* (Toohey 1984) raised questions about continued plutonium contamination at Maralinga. Rumours began to circulate in the British press that intellectually handicapped civilians were used as 'human guinea pigs' in the tests (Watts & Brock 1984). Although strenuously denied by British authorities, such rumours persisted, as did uncertainties surrounding the health of ex-servicemen. The South Australian government, desirous of granting additional land rights to the Pitjantjatjara people, expressed concern about the habitability of the former test area and surrounding lands.

A study commissioned by the Federal Minister for Resources and Energy, Senator Walsh, criticised the previous (AIRAC) report and recommended a public enquiry into the British testing program and its aftermath. The Hawke government announced a Royal Commission in July 1984.

The Royal Commission faced a daunting challenge - its terms of reference were broad, but it had no power to compel the disclosure of British government documents, many of which remained classified top secret. Most of those who had been personally involved in the testing program were not young; the difficulty of recalling events which had taken place three decades earlier is sufficient challenge for anyone.

The President of the Royal Commission was Justice James McClelland, Chief Judge of the New South Wales Land and Environment Court. Other Commissioners included Jill Fitch, a health physicist, and Dr William Jonas, a geographer of Aboriginal descent.

The official opening of Commission hearings was held in Sydney on 22 August 1984. The following fifteen months were to see the Commission sit for a total of 118 days in ten different locations as diverse as London and Marla Bore, South Australia. Hundreds of witnesses were examined; transcript of proceedings ran to 10,424 pages. In addition, Commission staff waded through literally tonnes of documents.

The Royal Commission's report, presented in November 1985, constituted a scathing indictment of British and Australian governments. It faulted the British for failing to disclose sufficient information to permit the Australian government to make informed decisions about the testing program, particularly the early Monte Bello tests and the minor trials. Indeed, the Royal Commission observed that the first series of 'Kittens' trials, conducted in 1953, was carried out without formal Australian government approval and without advice being provided to the Australian government by either British or Australian scientists (Australia 1985, p. 524).

The Australian government was criticised for entering commitments without adequate discussion of the issues by Cabinet, much less Parliament or the public. The oversight machinery established to provide the Australian government with technical advice also came in for strong criticism. The Royal Commission described the atmosphere of mutual trust between the 'watchers and the watched' as 'altogether unsatisfactory and dangerous.' The AWTSC was criticised as 'deceitful' and having allowed unsafe firing to occur (Australia 1985, p. 525).

Treatment of Aborigines during the testing program attracted some of the strongest condemnation. Organisation, management and resources allocated to ensuring the safety of Aborigines were described as inadequate. Responsible officials demonstrated 'ignorance, incompetence and cynicism' (Australia 1985, p. 323).

The Commission made seven recommendations regarding decontamination of test sites and compensation of those harmed as a result of the testing program. It maintained that the Australian government should compensate the Aboriginal people who were displaced from their traditional lands, by providing technology and services necessary to re-establish traditional relationships with the land.

The Commission further recommended that decontamination and clean up of the former testing sites take place, and that the costs be borne by the United Kingdom government. Regarding compensation of those who may have been injured as a result of exposure to radiation produced by the tests, the Commission recommended significant changes to existing procedures.

The Compensation (Commonwealth Government Employees) Act 1971 already permitted ex-service personnel to recover compensation if they were able to prove, on the balance of probabilities, that their disability resulted from exposure to radiation from the tests. The Commission recommended that eligibility be extended to civilians at the test sites and to Aborigines and others exposed to the 'Black Mist', and that the onus of proof be shifted to the government - in other words, that claimants be entitled to compensation unless the government were able to prove on the balance of probabilities that the disability *did not* result from radiation produced by the tests.

Despite the findings of the Royal Commission, the British government continued to deny both legal liability or moral responsibility for the consequences of its tests in Australia. The British insisted that they had made sufficient information available to Australian authorities to permit informed decisions, and that the agreement of 1968 and 1979 absolved them of further responsibility for decontamination or compensation.

In 1986 the British and Australian governments decided to defer further discussions of liability, and jointly to engage in an assessment of alternatives for the decontamination of the sites at Monte Bello, Emu, and Maralinga. The British agreed to participate in these evaluations on the basis that their involvement constituted no admission of responsibility or liability.

By 1986, the economic and financial constraints which the Federal Labor government faced had begun to shape its response to the Royal Commission report. Committed to the continued mining and export of uranium, Australian officials were disinclined to dwell extensively on the mistakes of the past, or to highlight the risks posed by radioactive substances. Concerned about reducing government expenditure, they sought to minimise outlays for compensation. The generosity which led previous Australian governments to spend millions of dollars to host the British tests had become a thing of the past.

In 1986 the government announced a payment of $500,000 compensation to Aboriginal groups for land contaminated during the course of the British testing program. The announcement was made shortly after publication of the 1986 Federal budget, which announced resumption of uranium sales to France. The savings to result from this change in policy were estimated to reach $60 million per year.

The Federal government's response to compensation claims by nuclear veterans and civilian support personnel was even less charitable. There exist two basic avenues of redress for those who claim to have been injured as a result of the testing program. Under the Compensation (Commonwealth Employees) Act a claimant may obtain benefits by demonstrating that an illness was probably caused by exposure to radiation.

It is not necessary to prove that the exposure resulted from any negligence on the part of the government. The decision rests with an administrative body, the Commissioner for Employees Compensation. The Federal government accepted the Royal Commission's recommendation that eligibility for compensation under this Act be extended to Aborigines and other civilians who may have been affected by the tests.

To obtain common law damages, on the other hand, an injured party must demonstrate in a court of law that his or her illness was probably caused by exposure to radiation, *and* that the exposure resulted from negligence on the part of the government.

The major obstacle faced by claimants in either jurisdiction is the formidable task of proving that their disability resulted from exposure to radiation produced by the tests. The task is compounded by the fact that in these cases, the ex-service claimants are totally dependent upon their former employer for the evidence necessary to present their case.

Cancer has many causes, and to demonstrate conclusively that a particular case was caused by Maralinga exposure and not by smoking, diet, exposure to X-rays, or some inherited predisposition is extremely difficult. The Royal Commission's recommendation that the onus of proof be borne by the government was not accepted. For this reason, most claims have thus far been unsuccessful.

By October 1986, a total of 272 claims arising from the testing program had been registered. The Commonwealth government, concerned over the possibility of having to defend common law actions alleging negligence in its involvement in the testing program, vigorously contested each claim. Of the 126 cases in which determinations had been made, claims were denied in 116 cases, and liability was found in only 10, two of which related to causes other than radiation exposure. Common law damages were sought by a few claimants, but the likelihood of success seemed low. Public assurances that the nuclear veterans were being well looked after did not appear to be borne out in the courts and hearing rooms of Australia.

In 1984, the South Australian Parliament passed the *Maralinga Tjarutja Land Rights Act* conferring freehold title to the Maralinga lands upon their traditional owners. But Aboriginal control over their land was not absolute. Mineral rights remained vested in the Crown, and the Act did not confer a right of veto on the Aboriginal owners. Rather, in the event of a dispute over whether the lands could be explored or mined, an Arbitrator would weigh the interests of the traditional owners against the economic significance of the proposed operations to the state and to Australia.

One wonders if the interests of a 'handful of natives' might on some future occasion again be deemed subordinate to those of the dominant culture.

References

Australia 1985, *The Report of the Royal Commission into British Nuclear Tests in Australia,* (Royal Commissioner, Mr Justice McClelland), 2 vols., Australian Government Publishing Service, Canberra.

Ball, H. 1986, *Justice Downwind: America's Atomic Testing Program in the 1950s,* Oxford University Press, New York.

Brady, Maggie & Morice, Rodney 1982, *Aboriginal Adolescent Offending Behaviour: A Study of a Remote Community,* School of Medicine, Flinders University of South Australia, Adelaide; Criminology Research Council, Canberra.

English, David & DeIonno, Peter 1980a, 'SA Atom Tests: Was Cost Too High?', *The Advertiser* 16 April, pp. 8-9.

English, D. & DeIonno, P. 1980b, 'New Claims of A-test Link With Cancer', *The Advertiser* 17 April, pp. 1 and 11.

English, D. & DeIonno, P. 1980c, 'Fall-out Blankets a Sleeping City', *The Advertiser* 17 April, pp. 10-11.

Milliken, Robert 1986, *No Conceivable Injury,* Penguin Books, Melbourne.

Toohey, Brian 1978, 'Maralinga Issue Raises Defence Dept. Question', *Australian Financial Review* 13 October, p. 7.

Toohey, Brian 1984, 'The Terrible Legacy of Maralinga', *The National Times* 4-10 May, p. 3.

Watts, D. & Brock, G. 1984, 'A-tests: The Human Guinea Pig Question', *The Australian* 25 June, p. 4.

Woodward, L. 1984, 'Buffalo Bill and the Maralingerers', *New Journalist,* vol. 43, pp. 18-24.

Chapter 17

VANDALISM OF THE LEA TREE

Of the many unique features of Tasmania, one of the most celebrated is the Huon Pine. *Dacrydium Franklinii*, as it is known to botanists, exists only in the rain forests and river valleys of south-west Tasmania, and is the only member of the genus *Dacrydium* native to Australia. Since the early 19th century, its timber has been prized for its beautiful texture, and for the ease with which it can be worked; unlike most timbers, it can be turned on end grain. Rich in aromatic oil, the wood is exceptionally resistant to decay. Trees which fell centuries before, and had been submerged or buried for years, still yielded remarkably well preserved timber. During the first century of Tasmania's European history, Huon Pine was regarded as ideal for boat building.

Because of its valued properties, the Huon Pine was energetically exploited during the colonial period. The decimation of the Huon Pine began shortly after the establishment of the notorious Sarah Island Penal Settlement in Macquarie Harbour in 1822. Pining became an important industry in Southwest Tasmania, and by the turn of the century, mature Huon Pine were rare in the Lower Gordon (Long 1983). A Parliamentary select committee was appointed in 1879 to enquire into the preservation of the species; it recommended that further felling of Huon Pine be prohibited. In 1882 the issuance of licences to cut Huon Pine was suspended (Millington 1982). The government sought to designate for protection a strip on either side of the Gordon for 16 miles upriver from Macquarie Harbour.

These conservation efforts were not entirely successful. In the 1960s, the rarity of the wood, combined with the technological advantages of helicopter transport and chain saws, saw renewed exploitation of the resource. Development was to take an even greater toll. The construction of the Gordon River Dam in the mid 1970s flooded extensive stands of Huon Pine. Before the waters rose, much of the timber was salvaged - over 3,000 m^3 in all. Further stands were threatened by the proposed Gordon below Franklin project in the early 1980s.

The reason behind concern for the Huon Pine is its exceptionally slow growth rate. Most Huon Pine is not millable until it has been growing for half a millenium. Indeed, a tree merely 20 cm in diameter could be as much as 500 years old. One of the oldest Huon pines on record, felled prior to the flooding of Lakes Gordon and Pedder, was found to be at least 2,183 years old. Mature Huon Pine are therefore the oldest living things in Australia.

The existence of another ancient Huon Pine in the area designated to be flooded by the Gordon below Franklin Dam was not disclosed at the time by the Tasmanian government, lest the case against the Dam be strengthened. Its age was subsequently estimated at 3,452 years, making it the second oldest living thing in the world (Woolley 1987).

The Huon Pine, those who would exploit it, and those who would preserve it, in a sense symbolise Tasmania and its divisions. The conflict between advocates of conservation and those of development, a recurring theme over the past century of Tasmanian history, began to heighten in the 1970s. On the one hand, there were those who sought to preserve one of the world's last great wilderness areas - that of Southwest Tasmania. On the other there were those who sought to harness the state's resources to develop its fragile economy. The first major confrontation arose over the proposal to dam the Gordon River for a hydro-electric project and thereby flood Lake Pedder, the only glacial outwash lake in Australia, and the centrepiece of Tasmania's Southwest (Southwell 1983). The project went ahead in the mid 1970s, despite the fact that it encroached upon a national park and was thereby illegal under the *National Parks and Wildlife Act 1971* (Tas). A group of citizens tried to challenge the project on these grounds. To sue the government required the permission of government, however, and this was denied. Government quickly enacted the *Hydro-Electric Commission (Doubts Removal) Act 1972* (Tas) which gave retrospective authority to the project where it might have come into conflict with the law. The lake was then flooded.

In the late 1970s a proposal to construct a dam on the Gordon below Franklin gave rise to one of the more divisive episodes in Australian history. Strongly embraced by the Hydro-Electric Commission (HEC) and those who saw Tasmania's economic future inextricably linked with hydro-electric power generation, it was tenaciously opposed by those who sought to preserve one of the world's last great wilderness areas.

The public debate over the Gordon below Franklin plan was intense. Supporters and opponents of the proposal took to the streets of Hobart in their thousands. The state Labor premier resigned when his party split on the issue. Non-violent protests by opponents of the dam resulted in over 1,500 arrests.

Interest in the conflict heightened throughout Australia and around the world. In 1983 the federal government intervened on the grounds that its international treaty obligations gave it the constitutional power to protect what had been designated a world heritage area. Many Tasmanians resented what they regarded as the will of a majority of Tasmanians regarding the management of their economy being overridden by distant politicians and bureaucrats in Canberra. Commonwealth-state conflict reached the High Court of Australia. Tensions were further heightened when it became apparent that aircraft from the Royal Australian Air Force had been engaged in photo-reconnaissance over the dam site.

On 1 July 1983 the High Court handed down its decision in the case of Commonwealth of Australia v. Tasmania. Construction of the dam would not proceed. Reaction on the part of pro-dam interests ranged from sadness to rage. Anonymous threats were made to a number of federal Labor senators from Tasmania. Both conservationists and HEC workers were warned by police to avoid physical conflict. Concerned about their economic future, some residents of the south-west were more resentful than ever of the conservationists:

> People down here, we want to work. We want our jobs, we don't want to bludge like the Wilderness Society (*The Examiner* 3 July 1983, p. 3).

Some HEC workers expressed defiance, giving notice that they would continue working despite the High Court ruling:

We're going back upriver on Monday and Bob the
Slob can send his F111's over, but we'll stay put
mate, just like the greenies did (*The Examiner* 2
July 1983, p. 1).

It's more than just a job. We take a lot of bloody
pride in our work. A number of blokes are
prepared to work on without pay to register their
protest at what has happened (*The Examiner* 4 July
1983, p. 1).

On 4 July some 50 to 80 HEC workers boarded a boat at
Strahan Wharf. Mainland television crews in attendance were
the targets of verbal insults. HEC supporters brandished
placards reading

Bob You Slob
We Will Finish This Job
(*The Examiner* 5 July 1983, p. 3)

At the wharf, as the proprietress of the Strahan
Wilderness Shop sought to photograph the protest, she was
attacked by several women who had turned out to cheer the
HEC workers. Two police officers intervened, but not before
she sustained a cut over the right eye. The workers returned to
Strahan Wharf without proceeding to the HEC camp at
Warner's Landing. But officials were still concerned that the
rainforest area at Warner's Landing might be vandalised in
protest against the High Court decision.

These concerns proved to be well founded. Near
Warner's Landing stood a Huon Pine tree some 9 feet in
diameter. It was a sufficiently prominent landmark to have
acquired a name - the Lea Tree. Three men, all over six feet
tall, found that they were unable to link arms around the trunk.
The tree was so old that it had been left by the convict cutters
of the 1820s as of no use for boat building. Given its size, it
was quite likely more than 2,000 years old. On the night of
5 July, the tree was chainsawed, holes were drilled in it, oil was
poured in the holes, and the tree was set alight. The fire
continued for at least twenty-four hours.

Whilst it has been suggested by some that the tree was burned by conservationists to attract publicity, a more plausible explanation is that the tree was vandalised by pro-dam interests as an act of reprisal. Allegations that HEC personnel were responsible for the incident are supported by photographs of HEC workers holding placards bearing various anti-conservationist messages in front of the charred tree. One photograph shows three workers posed next to the smouldering trunk, on which the words '[Expletive] You Green [Expletive]' were painted (*Wilderness News* April 1987).

Founded in 1914, the Hydro-Electric Commission has long been one of the most powerful interests in Tasmania. Given the island state's distance from the mainland of Australia, its small population, and its remoteness from raw materials and markets, the challenge of developing and maintaining a viable economy has always been daunting. With the inherent limitations of primary production and the eventual depletion of Tasmania's mineral resources looming, another basis for economic development was sought.

The HEC is an engineering organisation of considerable size and substantial expertise. Conflict with conservationists was inevitable, for the very raison d'etre of engineering is to conquer and to exploit nature, not to preserve it or submit to it. Reinforcing this fundamental philosophical division are two bureaucratic imperatives: those who manage organisations like them to grow, or at the very least, not to shrink. In addition they seek to maintain the organisation's autonomy - freedom from constraint whether political or economic.

The HEC enjoyed considerable freedom indeed. It was constituted as an autonomous statutory body, not responsible to any minister. More often than not it was the provider rather than the recipient of policy guidance, an economic planning agency in its own right. It forged a coalition of industrialists and trade unionists which made it a formidable political force in Tasmania.

By virtue of its status as one of the state's largest employers, the HEC wielded additional power. Thousands of Tasmanians were dependent upon the Hydro for their livelihood, whether directly - as employees or contractors and their families - or indirectly - as those in line to benefit from the spending power of those on the HEC payroll.

259

Indeed, the HEC has not been loath to remind its employees of their interests. During state elections in 1972-73 at the height of the Lake Pedder controversy, electoral notices were placed in employees' pay packets warning them that they could lose their jobs if candidates opposing the Gordon River Dam were successful in the forthcoming elections.

HEC officials are often outspokenly critical of environmentalists. At one point the Commissioner of the HEC was quoted as referring to opponents of the organisation as 'communists or subversives' (quoted in Southwell 1983, p. 18).

A number of Tasmania's political leaders from both sides of politics, have spoken contemptuously of the natural environment. Former Labor Premier, Eric Reece, an ex-trade union leader whose enthusiasm for hydro-industrialisation earned him the name 'Electric Eric', was quoted as having said of the Tasmanian Tiger, that the state would be better off

> if it was extinct and joins such departed species as dinosaurs, moa-birds, and Kiwis (quoted in Southwell 1983, p. 14).

Electric Eric could perhaps be excused for failing to note that the Kiwi is alive and thriving in New Zealand.

More recently, Liberal Premier Robin Gray sought to minimise the environmental significance of the Franklin River by referring to it as 'a brown ditch, leech-ridden, unattractive to the majority of people'. His public appearance while wearing boxing gloves contributed to the defiance of pro-dam supporters.

It is thus easy to understand how workers who perceived themselves to be economically dependent upon an organisation which exists to conquer nature, might respond, when thwarted, with an act of vandalism against a mere tree. They no doubt regarded the burning as a fairly mild act of protest.

The burning of the Lea Tree was not reported in the public media, in part because security procedures then in place excluded non-HEC personnel from the area. The HEC refused a television crew permission to land a helicopter at Warner's Landing, and announced that access to the area would remain restricted until it reverted back to a national park by act of parliament. State Police announced that they would continue to arrest trespassers at their discretion. No criminal charges arose from the burning of the Lea Tree, however.

The matter became the subject of jokes by government members in state parliament. The tree's burning was described by the Attorney-General of Tasmania as 'a set-up by the "greenies" to discredit the Hydro workers' (Tasmania, House of Assembly 1983, pp. 1415 and 1417).

The Premier of Tasmania said in Parliament that 'quite frankly the Hydro-Electric Commission and the police have better things to do with their time . . .' (Tasmania, House of Assembly 1983, p. 1418). Nearly four years later, when the photograph described above was sent to the Premier, he replied:

> Apart from showing three unidentified men in front of a tree trunk doubed with graffiti, the photograph proves little of substance. If you have sustainable evidence of any breaches of the law, it could be examined by the appropriate authorities (Gray, R. 1987, pers. comm. to Dr R. Brown, MHA, 27 May).

Life in Tasmania goes on. Before the High Court decision, the Commonwealth government had assured the Tasmanian government that were the project not to proceed, a compensation package would be negotiated to ensure that no jobs would be lost, and alternative construction schemes introduced to provide continuity of employment.

Another area of natural beauty in Tasmania, the Lemonthyme Forest, soon became the focus of conflict. Here tensions between conservationists and the timber industry were reinforced by the traditional struggle between federal and state governments.

Back in Southwest Tasmania, the Huon Pine which still stand continue their slow growth. They remain under threat from future dam construction, from pollution by mine tailings, and from fire, to which they and their rainforest ecosystem are extremely vulnerable. Indeed, the risk of fire has been heightened by the increased accessibility of rainforest areas. Todays' seedlings, should they survive predatory man, will reach maturity around the time of the 700th anniversary of European settlement of Australia. Meanwhile, tourists who ply the lower Gordon in large sightseeing boats can view what is left of the tree, and afterwards buy a small effigy of the state of Tasmania, or perhaps an ashtray, carved from Huon Pine.

References

The Examiner 2 July 1983, p. 3.

ibid. 3 July 1983, p. 1.

ibid. 4 July 1983, p. 1.

ibid. 5 July 1983, p. 3.

Long, C. 1983, 'Tasmania's Wild Western Rivers', *This Australia* vol. 2, no. 4, pp. 33-40.

Millington, Robert J. 1982, 'Woodman, Spare that Tree' *Geo : Australia's Geographic Magazine*, vol. 4 (June/Aug), pp. 124-31.

Southwell, L. 1983, *The Mountains of Paradise: The Wilderness of South-West Tasmania*, Les Southwell Pty Ltd, Camberwell, Vic.

Tasmania, House of Assembly 1983, *Debates*, 6 Sept., pp. 1415, 1417 and 1418.

Wilderness News 1987, vol. 8, no. 3, April.

Woolley, B. 1987, 'The Huon Pine', *Sunday*, Nine Network, 26 April.

Chapter 18

MACHINE POLITICS, CORRUPTION AND
THE RICHMOND CITY COUNCIL

Richmond, an inner suburb of Melbourne, was constituted as a municipality in 1855. From the outset, its politics were characterised by something less than genteel civility. At the first municipal election, one of the returning officers was himself elected, along with six non-residents of the district, including the British Secretary of State. In the aftermath of the election, angry residents petitioned the Governor of Victoria to disallow the returns, alleging that many electors were debased with drink, and that supporters of both sides in the contest had impersonated voters (Barrett 1979).

During the 19th century, Richmond became a classic working-class Australian suburb, known colloquially as Irish Town. It remained a close-knit community for the best part of 100 years. Even after the postwar influx of southern and eastern European migrants, Richmond still retained much of its character. It remained a Labor stronghold, surviving the split of 1955. Richmond politics, and power in the city council, became synonymous with the O'Connell family. O'Connells and their relatives through marriage held seats on the city council and numerous positions of employment with council.

The Richmond City Council was described as a 'feudal feifdom' (Victoria 1982, p. 78). Indeed, it embodied many of the characteristics of the 'political machines' which grew up in American cities during the 19th and early 20th Centuries - extreme social conservatism and a strong element of reciprocity, where political favours were dispensed in return for continued electoral support.

The Richmond dynasty was to pass, but only after a prolonged and bitter struggle.

The O'Connell machine was able to adapt to the influx of European and later, Vietnamese migrants; these groups were very much working class, politically quiescent, and took little interest in local politics. The real challenge to machine politics came with a development familiar throughout urban Australia;

the 'gentrification' of working class inner suburbs. Middle-class 'trendies', as they were contemptuously described, constituted more than a symbolic affront to the traditional values of old Richmond - they were a real threat. Many of the new arrivals took what the rulers of Richmond regarded as an unhealthy interest in local politics. They began to question the ways in which the Council had gone about its business, and it was not long before independent candidates began to contest Council elections.

In doing so, they posed an explicit threat to the only source of power, prestige and in some cases, economic well-being which was available to the rulers of Richmond and their followers. The latter, in turn, responded with the only resources available to them.

It has been said of Richmond that it is the only place in Australia where dead men voted. In 1975 an employee of the Council was fined $1,500 after having been found guilty of having voted twice under another person's name. The case merely confirmed the general suspicions which surrounded Richmond elections. No less a person than a former Deputy Prime Minister of Australia, Dr Jim Cairns, remarked that old-timers in Richmond did not regard multiple voting as criminal, but rather as a kind of game (Victoria 1982, p. 65).

The first independent was elected to Richmond City Council in 1978. By 1981 the Council comprised five independents and ten members of what was termed 'the ruling group'.

Electoral fraud in Richmond took two basic forms. The first was good old-fashioned multiple voting. This involved the impersonation of individuals whose names were on the electoral rolls, but who for various reasons, such as the fact that they had died or had moved away from the municipality some years before, were disinclined to vote.

The second type of fraud involved tampering with ballots. On two occasions, there was evidence of seals having been broken on bags containing ballots. In both of these elections non-labor candidates who appeared to have won, lost their seats after a recount.

The time-honoured practice of ballot box stuffing was also common in Richmond. This involved the insertion of false ballot papers into the ballot box, and the removal of a sufficient quantity of valid papers to reconcile the numbers. On occasion, those engaged in this practice demonstrated some lack of finesse. In 1981 the presiding officer in the East Ward reported having counted eleven more ballots than he had issued (Victoria 1982, p. 97).

Tampering with postal votes was yet another form of electoral malpractice. Here, envelopes containing postal votes were opened, and false ballot papers substituted for the votes actually cast. To this end, one of the major electoral strategies of the Richmond ruling group was to encourage postal voting.

It was also common for candidates and their supporters actually to fill out ballot papers for voters, in violation of the law. Indeed, a board of inquiry was later to conclude that

> **the Mayor, his wife, another councillor, and a Council officer were ready to admit to the wholesale commission of criminal offences as a means of providing a defence to the more serious charge of ballot forgery and substitution** (Victoria 1982, p. 115, emphasis in original).

Such practices in fact were against the law. Regulation 4(c) of the Postal Voting (Elections of Municipal Councillors) Regulations 1980 states

> No person shall persuade or induce or associate himself with any person in persuading or inducing a person to make application for a postal ballot paper.

The penalty for contravention was a fine of up to $200 or imprisonment for a term of up to three months.

In addition to direct interference with ballots, supporters of the Richmond ruling group engaged in a variety of unorthodox campaign techniques. In August 1981 motor cars belonging to two independent councillors were firebombed. A prominent supporter of independent candidates received a pamphlet stained with human blood. Three men were attacked and beaten while delivering how-to-vote cards for independent candidates. One was struck in the face and sustained a broken jaw. Another was beaten unconscious. Local newspapers containing unfavourable editorial comment about the sitting Council were stolen from letter boxes. A brick was thrown through the window of a house whose occupants displayed a poster supporting an independent candidate.

Rowdyism and bullying outside polling places was not uncommon. Supporters of independent candidates were subject to pushing, insults and menacing remarks. How-to-vote cards were snatched away and occasionally burned. Activities on the occasion of an extraordinary election in April 1981 were such that a board of inquiry later remarked:

> The scene outside the polling booth on the day of this election might be thought to be more appropriate to a menagerie (Victoria 1982, p. 217).

Resuming the classic understatement which is typical of the legal profession in Victoria, he said, in reference to supporters of the Richmond machine:

> I do not regard the persons associated with this particular group as being capable of great subtlety in their approach to political problems (Victoria 1982, p. 252).

In addition to the above electoral irregularities, Richmond Council experienced difficulties of a financial nature. In addition to the traditional local government concerns of 'rates, roads, and rubbish', the municipality of Richmond owned an abattoir. In 1961, Richmond Council entered into a leasing arrangement with a company, Protean Enterprises Pty. Ltd., to operate the abattoir under terms which could only be regarded as a windfall for the lessee. They involved, among many other things, the leasing of land at a very low fixed rent, based on 1961 values, for a period expiring in 1991.

Subsequent variations to the lease increased the advantage to the lessees still further. The annual rent was low to begin with, and the Council undertook to make costly improvements for which it borrowed funds. On one occasion, it committed an additional $100,000 in return for a rental increase of $5,000 per year. The 5 per cent return on borrowed capital was considerably less than the interest which the Council was paying for the loan.

In August 1967 the Council agreed to spend an additional $400,000 on the abattoir in return for a rental increase of $11,675 per year, commencing three years after completion of the improvements. This represented nil return to the Council while the improvements were being undertaken (or for three years thereafter), then 3 per cent on capital for the next seventeen years, then nothing. It was hardly an astute business arrangement from the Council's point of view. Indeed, in 1979 counsel for the City of Richmond were to describe the situation brought about by these variations to the original Protean lease as **'wholly oppressive to the Council if not scandalous'** (quoted in Victoria 1982, p. 591, emphasis in the original).

It was not unusual for local governments in Victoria to own and to lease abattoirs. What was unusual was the extent to which the ratepayers of Richmond were subsidising private enterprise. It was estimated that during the course of the arrangements with Protean, an estimated $4.2 million in revenue was lost. At the same time, Richmond Council was faulted for providing inadequate or inefficient services to the poor and elderly residents of the municipality.

The difficulties which beset the municipality of Richmond arose from a number of factors. Perhaps most striking was the tribalism which characterised municipal administration. No less than two brothers, two sons, two nephews, one niece, one sister-in-law and one cousin of the mayor were employed by the Council; several other Council employees were themselves former councillors. Nepotism and the Richmond Council were synonymous. The close family relationships between Council employees and elected officials led to a situation where perpetuation of the political status quo was seen by Council staff as in their best interests.

Despite widespread allegations of electoral misconduct, Council officials themselves undertook no investigations. Indeed, the pattern of behaviour seemed to indicate that the misconduct was condoned, if not encouraged, by the ruling group.

In 1975 one Council employee was charged and convicted of voting more than once and voting under another persons's name. Members of Council were something less than indignant about the criminal acts. The person in question retained his position with the Council and the fine was paid after colleagues at the Council passed the hat. By contrast, an Assistant Town Clerk who informed police of a case of multiple voting was excluded from further Council electoral duties and was ostracised by Council officers.

The person responsible for the overall administration of municipal government in Richmond was the Town Clerk. Charles Eyres served as Assistant Town Clerk for ten years, before becoming Town Clerk in 1958. He was to hold the position for twenty-two years. A member of his local branch of the Australian Labor Party (ALP), Eyres was closely allied with the ruling group in Richmond City Council. Eyres went about his duties with a certain lack of integrity and competence.

Charles Eyres' partisan inclinations were reflected in the manner in which he administered the electoral process in Richmond. As Returning Officer he was vested with significant power under the *Local Government Act 1958* (Vic) to take action against rowdyism and bullying by supporters of the Richmond machine. He never did.

Eyres had a statutory duty to post out notices to those on the electoral rolls who had not voted in any given election. He failed to do so. Inclined to ignore complaints from non ALP sources, he was quick to respond to complaints about independent candidates and to forward these to the state Department of Local Government. Eyres appointed a traffic officer, whom he knew to be corrupt, to be the Council officer in charge of postal voting. The administration of postal voting in general was exercised with an almost total lack of security precautions. Keys to rooms containing voting material were readily accessible; the postal voting room in any event, was often left unlocked.

In keeping with the tradition of nepotism which characterised personnel management at Richmond Council, Eyres' son Carl was appointed rate collector in 1970. Among his responsibilities was that of keeper of the electoral rolls. Carl Eyres was less than impressive in the discharge of his duties:

It is difficult to imagine Mr Eyres being appointed to any responsible office in any organisation and were he not the son of Mr Charles Eyres I doubt that he would even have been employed at Richmond. He appears to have demonstrated a degree of incompetence, both as a rate collector and as the keeper of the electoral rolls . . . My own observation of him leads me to doubt whether he would have the capacity to detect the most obvious type of electoral malpractice if it was to occur in front of him, in the unlikely event that he had the inclination to do so. For the purposes of those engaged in electoral fraud, he no doubt was and is an ideal person to be holding a responsible electoral position (Victoria 1982, p. 54).

Under the guiding hands of Charles and Carl Eyres, the system of electoral administration in Richmond left much to be desired. The electoral rolls were poorly maintained, and badly out of date. A considerable number of persons left on the rolls had died or had long since moved out of Richmond. If it did not constitute an open invitation to voter impersonation, the state of the electoral rolls certainly facilitated the practice.

Under normal democratic criteria the operations of government are accessible to the public. Not so with the Richmond Council. Indeed, throughout the 1960s and 1970s it was common practice to conceal council business from the public deliberately. No notice papers or agendas were available to enable members of the public to follow council meetings. It was not uncommon for meetings to be adjourned immediately after they commenced, to enable Labor councillors to caucus privately, thus excluding both the general public and independent councillors from their basic deliberations. Minutes of council meetings were not even circulated to councillors. The government of Richmond was government by men in the back room.

The financial affairs of Richmond Council were in no less a state of disarray than were the electoral rolls. There was a history of non-compliance with municipal accounting regulations and members of the Council were routinely denied elementary financial information. The terms of agreements which the Council entered into with Protean were never fully disclosed. Documents relating to the transactions remained under lock and key, and were not made available to councillors outside the abattoir committee. No proper records were kept of how Council funds were spent on the abattoir.

In theory, the activities of local government are subject to oversight by the state minister, through the Department of Local Government. In practice, state government oversight was ineffective. Traditionally, the government of Victoria regarded municipalities with a degree of deference, as independent organs of government. State authorities were content that electoral accountability would be realised through the democratic process. This avoidance of paternalism on the part of state government was reflected in the size and operating style of the inspectorate of municipal administration within the Department of Local Government. There were some five inspectors to oversee some 211 local governments, all of whom conducted elections at the same time each year.

The inspectorial style was one of considerable tolerance. Perhaps understandably, given their lack of resources, inspectors did not usually initiate investigations of their own motion but rather responded to complaints from aggrieved members of the public. They approached their investigative tasks with strict legalism but with something less than messianic zeal. Inspectors would confront Council officials with allegations of misconduct, which the officials would promptly deny. The inspectors would then find that there was insufficient evidence to substantiate the allegation and advise the complainant accordingly.

In part, the task of inspectors was made more difficult by the ethic of silence which characterised the Richmond community. It was quite simply unthinkable to divulge incriminating information to the authorities. One gentleman, who had been assaulted with a broken beer bottle by the brother of the then Mayor, and who as a result required thirty stitches to his face, made no complaint to police. In the words of the former state member for Richmond and later Federal Minister for Aboriginal Affairs, Clyde Holding:

> . . . you can't give people up. I mean between 1955 and '65 in Richmond, if I walked into a hotel and

someone from the DLP said 'There's Holding', and he had a few beers in him and landed one on me, the one thing I couldn't do would be to report it to the police (Victoria 1982, p. 59).

But it seemed that there was on the part of the inspectorate a reluctance to pursue allegations or indeed, to enforce the law. It was alleged in one case of suspected voter impersonation, an inspector '**suggested off the record that it was very difficult to get prosecutions in these cases, and that his advice would be to press the matter no further and to not give the names**' (Victoria 1982, p. 123, emphasis in the original).

On another occasion, following allegations of multiple voting and complaints about the operation of tickboards and access by messengers to a polling booth, a departmental inspector reported:

It is generally accepted at municipal elections that provided there is no interference to voters or threat to the orderly conduct of the poll, returning officers and presiding officers cannot prevent the compilation of such lists by scrutineers and do not prevent the passing of such listings to other persons (Victoria 1982, p. 86).

Explicit breaches of the Local Government Act were thus condoned.

In 1978, following a complaint by an independent councillor that Council employees were delivering postal ballots to voters by hand, an inspector

was apparently satisfied with the assurances he received at the Town Hall and did not, in fact, conduct personal interviews with these voters.

This episode highlights a difficulty relating to a number of the Local Government investigations in that Local Government Officers are no doubt used to dealing with officials who are basically honest, and thus in the case of Richmond were, perhaps, over ready to accept assurances given (Victoria 1982, p. 104).

Deference to the decisions of elected local governments also characterised ministerial oversight. Sir Murray Porter, the Minister for Local Government, may have regarded the signing of a 24-year fixed rental lease with Protean as something less than an astute business arrangement. It nevertheless satisfied departmental statutory regulations. The policy of the Local Government Department continued to rest on the principle of not interfering with the commercial judgment of councils.

Financial oversight of Council business by state government authorities was also ineffective. Despite annual audits and directions by the Local Government Department to reduce the deficit, financial irregularities persisted. State authorities did not follow-up to ensure that anomalies were rectified. As far back as 1966 inspectors of the Local Government Department recommended that the Council maintain a record of capital improvements to the abattoir and costs incurred by Protean and the Council respectively, to ensure compliance with the term of the lease. Council failed to heed the advice.

On two occasions during the 1970s inspectors from the Department recommended that a special audit of Council finances be conducted. The special audit provisions of the Local Government Act were regarded as too cumbersome, requiring evidence of either wilful or culpable negligence or misapplication of monies by councillors. The conduct of such audits would entail considerable work and expense to the municipality. The recommendations were rejected by the Minister.

The windfall for Protean and corresponding financial disaster for the ratepayers of Richmond did not result from either generosity or carelessness on the part of municipal administrators. Charles Eyres acquired considerable wealth during the 1960s. To his eventual embarassment, Eyres did not offer the time-honoured explanation of uncanny success at the races. Indeed, he failed to provide an explanation to the satisfaction of the authorities. The conclusion reached was that he was the beneficiary of considerable largesse on the part of the company - in the form of bribes.

In the entire history of local government in Victoria, state intervention in local matters was extremely rare. Keilor Council was dismissed in 1975 after intractable divisions. It was replaced by a state appointed commissioner. Following a petition by ratepayers and the report of a public inquiry which identified breaches of the Local Government Act, Sunshine Council was dismissed in 1976. Melbourne City Council was dismissed in May 1981.

In light of these precedents, it is perhaps surprising that the government of Victoria did not intervene earlier into the affairs of Richmond Council. A government backbencher, Morris Williams, had conducted a lengthy crusade against the Council, and had for many years been critical of the comfortable arrangements between the Council and Protean. At one point he presented a petition to Parliament calling for an inquiry. In 1978, the Attorney-General, Haddon Storey, requested that the Victoria Police investigate allegations of bribery. Detectives reported that they had been unable to obtain evidence sufficient to substantiate the allegations.

As the gentrification of Richmond continued into the 1980s, the council machine had to work that much harder to maintain its control over Town Hall. Independent candidates observed that Labor councillors, who usually received between 48 and 52 per cent of the primary vote, were winning in excess of 90 per cent of the postal vote. The contrast was too great not to compound the chronic suspicions surrounding Richmond electoral politics. Following a by-election in April 1981, independent councillor Andrew Alexander sought out voters who had cast postal ballots. He obtained statutory declarations from fourteen people who had voted for an independent candidate - the same candidate who received but five postal votes according to the official tally.

Alexander enclosed the statutory declarations in a letter to the Secretary of the Local Government Department. The state Liberal government, having recently completed a quarter century in power, remained under relentless criticism from the Opposition for alleged irregularities in the acquisition of land for public housing. With an election looming the following year, the opportunity thus presented itself to discredit the ALP. The government was thus moved to abandon its traditional posture of tolerance toward the shortcomings of municipal government. The Minister for Local Government requested that the Victoria police conduct forensic tests on postal ballot papers to determine if they had been interfered with. Indeed, analyses revealed that the envelopes in which postal ballots were enclosed had been opened and resealed with a glue different from that used in their manufacture. On 21 July 1981 the government appointed Alastair Nicholson, Q.C. to conduct an inquiry into electoral irregularities in Richmond. His terms of reference extended to postal voting in Richmond since 1970.

Only a matter of days after the inquiry was established, political tensions in Richmond heightened in the run-up to the annual Council elections. In the aftermath of the firebombings and assaults noted above, the Nicholson terms of reference were widened to include the outbreak of violence preceding the 1981 Council elections. Not long after commencing the inquiry Nicholson began to explore the relationship between the Council and Protean. Arguing that its affairs were outside the inquiry's terms of reference, the company unsuccessfully sought an injunction to stop the hearing of evidence relating to its affairs. Corruption, maladministration and electoral irregularities were in the eyes of many, inextricably linked.

An interim report was tabled in Parliament on 15 December 1981. The report noted that the 1980 annual election and April 1981 by-elections were marked by serious electoral frauds, and concluded that a number of ALP councillors might not have been elected had the poll been conducted honestly. Hearings continued into 1982 and more than 250 witnesses eventually appeared before the inquiry, which sat for nearly a year.

On 29 June 1982 the new Labor government tabled the three-volume, 900 page *Nicholson Report* and introduced legislation to dismiss the Richmond City Council. On 5 July, the Council had its last meeting. At the conclusion, the outgoing councillors who had been members of the ruling group were presented with certificates which specified their services to the municipality. With the dismissal of Richmond Council, the Cain government installed as Administrator a person with accounting qualifications and with wide experience in local goverment.

The Local Government Act 1958 provided that no penalties could be imposed for offences under the Act unless prosecutions commenced within one year of the commission of the offence. By the time the *Nicholson Report* was tabled, the time available for prosecutions under the Local Government Act had passed. Another of the Report's recommendation was that the time specified be extended from twelve months to four years.

Few prosecutions were brought under the *Crimes Act 1958* (Vic). Charles Eyres, a key figure in the alleged irregularities, had fallen ill by the time the *Nicholson Report* was published, and died soon thereafter. The forensic evidence relating to the alleged forgery of ballot papers, while sufficient to meet the civil standard of proof applied by the Board of Inquiry, was regarded as insufficient to support a criminal prosecution in all but one case. Vasilios Sevastopolous pleaded guilty in the County Court at Melbourne on 31 May 1985 to 32 counts of forgery and 32 counts of uttering relating to postal ballots for the 1978 election in the North Ward of Richmond. He was sentenced to a total of 64 weeks imprisonment.

Three men were charged with perjury committed before the Nicholson Inquiry. One was acquitted at the direction of the trial judge, one pleaded guilty and was sentenced to six months imprisonment, and one was tried and convicted and sentenced to nine months. Both of these sentences were directed to be served at the Prahran Attendance Centre.

Gregory O'Connell, the nephew of the former Mayor of Richmond, was tried in the Country Court at Melbourne in April 1983 on charges of inflicting grievous bodily harm and assault occasioning actual bodily harm. The charges arose out of the alleged assaults against three men who were placing campaign material in letterboxes on behalf of independent candidates in August 1981. O'Connell was acquitted on all counts.

Prosecutions for offences relating to bribery also proved to be unsuccessful. One individual charged with receiving a secret commission of $500 was discharged by the Magistrates Court at the preliminary hearing in July 1983. Another was committed for trial on one charge of attempting corruptly to 'receive a valuable consideration' (an offence at common law). Ultimately, because the evidence against the accused was found to be unsatisfactory, a nolle prosequi was entered.

The third and final volume of the *Nicholson Report* proposed a number of amendments to the Local Government Act which were designed to improve the conduct of municipal elections.

These included the creation of a court of disputed returns, which would provide for declaring an election void if the outcome were found to have been affected by misconduct. Other recommendations included the creation of an offence of undue influence and intimidation of voters and the power for a returning officer to seek proof of identity from an intending voter. The *Nicholson Report* also called for the creation of an offence providing up to two years imprisonment for fraudulently altering any official mark or writing on any electoral paper.

In the years following the dismissal of Richmond Council, the Local Government Department was significantly restructured to provide for a new strategy of regulatory oversight. The old reactive, rulebook approach to inspection was replaced by a more diagnostic style. The provision of technical assistance became an important function of the Department. A scheme of regionalisation was introduced and a new group of specialists with expertise in accounting and financial management were appointed to disseminate guidelines and to conduct seminars for local government officials.

A new senior position of Manager for Human Resources Consultancy was created within the Local Government Department and steps were taken to assist municipalities in recruiting the best qualified personnel and in implementing modern management practices. Electoral rolls, now computer-generated by the state Electoral Office, are regularly purged of the names of those who have moved from Richmond, to terrestrial locations or elsewhere.

Shortly after the Labor government came to power in 1982 it introduced freedom of information legislation. Because of political resistance, local government matters were exempt from provisions of the Act. But steps were eventually taken to improve the accountability of local government in Victoria.

Five years after the dismissal of Richmond Council, the Victorian Government introduced a new Local Government Bill which would require that council and committee meetings be held in public. The new Bill addressed many of the shortcomings of local government addressed in the *Nicholson Report*. Requirements that the terms of proposed leases be published in advance were intended to prevent disastrous situations such as the arrangement with Protean. A term of imprisonment of up to two years was specified for making false or misleading statements to an auditor. Councillors and council staff would be required to register their pecuniary interests. The integrity of the electoral process would be protected by such provisions as six months imprisonment for communicating any information likely to defeat the secrecy of voting, six months imprisonment for multiple voting, and two years imprisonment for returning officers tampering with or fraudulently altering voting materials.

The Bill would also create municipal electoral tribunals to whom candidates or aggrieved voters could apply if they disputed the propriety of electoral processes or outcomes. The tribunal would be empowered to declare an election void if allegations in question were substantiated.

State supervision of local government activities is still intended to avoid even the appearance of paternalism. Beyond the proffering of managerial advice, actual intervention in the affairs of local government would not occur unless there were an apparent breach of the law, or serious mismanagement of financial matters.

The state government also planned to introduce a system of efficiency audits which would compare the local government agencies of Victoria on such criteria as the percentage of rate revenue allocated for administrative expenses. Authorities believe that compliance with proper administrative standards is more readily achievable by letting such facts speak for themselves rather than by overt chastisement. While recognising that municipalities are responsible for allocating their resources, audits would also look to the effectiveness of resource usage in meeting community needs.

Nearly five years after the dismissal of Richmond Council, the municipality's business remained the responsibility of an appointed administrator. There was obviously no rush to restore a democratically elected council, given the anti-democratic traditions which were so deeply engrained in the Richmond electorate. By 1987, consideration was given to restoring the democratic process, perhaps in conjunction with a merger of the local governments of Richmond and neighbouring Collingwood.

In the end, the likelihood that Richmond-style maladministration might one day recur seems extremely remote, due less to any reformist inclinations on the part of state government than to the course of history. By the late 1980s the social and demographic requisites of the city political machine had become part of Australia's urban past.

References

Barrett, B. 1979, *The Civic Frontier*, Melbourne University Press, Melbourne.

Victoria 1982, *Report of Board of Inquiry Relating to Certain Matters Within the City of Richmond*, 3 vols., (A.B. Nicholson Q.C., Board of Inquiry), Government Printer, Melbourne.

Chapter 19

CONCLUSION

The incidents and harms in question

The cases reviewed in this book illustrate some of the many ways in which citizens may be harmed by the actions of their governments. As was noted in the introduction, Australia's record in this area is relatively good by world standards. For the most part, the harms incurred at the hands of government are not catastrophic, and result from negligence rather than malice.

Such reassuring words, however, would be cold comfort to the relatives of the Electricity Trust linesmen, to the friends and relations of John Pat, and to the survivors of those Australian nuclear veterans who may have died as a result of their exposure to radiation. One doubts whether Barry Mannix or Jane Hill find it consoling to contemplate that they are living in Australia rather than South Africa. The Maralinga and Injalka peoples, whose cultures were subject to even greater threat by governmental action, have little cause to celebrate. Citizens who value the fundamental freedoms of speech and association and the right of an accused person to a fair trial are unlikely to be heartened by the normalisation of surveillance which characterises contemporary Australia. In brief, there is room for improvement in the conduct of Australia's public affairs.

The task of these concluding pages is to highlight any recurring themes which have characterised the various case studies, with a view toward reducing the likelihood of similar incidents arising in future. In the course of this discussion one will note the extent to which the Australian experience supports the theories of government illegality cited in Chapter 1. This concluding chapter will also review the various institutions and remedies which exist for controlling the Australian public sector, and will suggest means of improving their efficacy in light of the criteria by which such measures might be evaluated: deterrence, compensation, rehabilitation, and reaffirmation of the rule of law.

The harms inflicted in the course of the incidents described in this book were not trivial. More than five people died; in addition, the precise number of fatalities arising from the British nuclear tests remains obscure. Numerous people were physically beaten or otherwise menaced. If one includes the New South Wales prisoners who were systematically assaulted over a thirty-year period, the total would run into the thousands. Others were injured psychologically, if not physically.

Mismanagement of public funds entailed costs in excess of four million dollars in the Richmond case, and at least that much in the Victorian land scandals. The embarrassing pursuit of the social security conspirators cost tens of millions of dollars. Delay in the prosecution of the bottom of the harbour test case contributed to the development of a flourishing tax avoidance industry, and to the loss of hundreds of millions of dollars in tax revenues.

The British nuclear tests produced permanent environmental damage, and the Lea Tree incident saw the vandalism of one of Australia's oldest living things.

Fundamental democratic principles of privacy, freedom of association, and the right to a fair trial were violated. In the Richmond case, the democratic process itself was perverted. The legitimacy of police and correctional officials, whose very purpose is to uphold the rule of law, was tarnished.

Victims of government illegality

What kinds of people are likely to be harmed by government illegality? In some respects, governments are equal opportunity offenders. Waste and inefficiency in the expenditure of public funds cost taxpayers generally. Offences against democratic principles are offences against all citizens. But in many of the cases reported above, the victims of official misconduct tended to be drawn from the disadvantaged sections of Australian society. It is not coincidental that three of the cases involved harm to Aboriginal people, either as individuals or as a group. Throughout the European history of

Australia, Aborigines have suffered at the hands of government (Rowley 1970; Nettheim 1981). They still do.

Another group which suffers disproportionately at the hands of government are criminal defendants. Perhaps one explanation for this is the fact that the agencies which deal with suspected or convicted criminals, police and prisons departments, wield awesome power, and conduct a considerable amount of their activity free from external scrutiny. Indeed, a person in police or prison custody is in a position of total dependence and vulnerability. He is hardly a credible witness against government officials who abuse his rights.

Other case studies described the victimisation of such ordinary Australians as the ETSA linesmen, Jane Hill, the pensioners of Richmond and the staff of the Sheraton Hotel. And so, it is not the privileged members of society, but rather the young, the poor and the Black who appear to be most profoundly affected by official misconduct in Australia. It is these same groups whose members tend to have the fewest resources, whether psychological, political or financial, with which to defend themselves.

Culpability

The incidents differed widely in the degree of blameworthiness which might be attributed to the principals. In no case could the eventual injuries be regarded as completely unforeseeable. Whilst a great deal of precaution was taken in the conduct of the British nuclear tests, the very choice for a test site of what was perceived to be a remote wasteland implied an appreciation of the project's inherent risks. Failures to foresee the unfortunate consequences of one's conduct also characterised the ETSA case.

In other instances, the lack of foresight was more egregious. The risk that the ASIS raiders and their weapons might attract the attention of, and cause alarm to, the hotel management and staff should have been patently obvious. Jane Hill's superiors were advised on numerous occasions of the harassment she was experiencing in her workplace. The solicitors responsible for the bottom of the harbour prosecution failed to act, despite the encouragement received from private counsel, police and tax office officials.

By contrast, a number of cases entailed deliberate and knowing violation of the law. In those cases involving wrongful action which was intentional, the incidents in question entailed a variety of motives. The most common was the desire to 'cut corners' and achieve a goal more readily than would otherwise be the case using legitimate procedures. In some instances, such as the New South Wales telephone interceptions and the failure to disclose the nature of Special Branch activity in South Australia, it was argued that the ends of the conduct in question justified the means employed. In the Injalka case, the legitimacy of the law itself, or at least its prevailing interpretation, was challenged.

Only in isolated instances were the principals driven by pure self interest or by selfless devotion to duty. Private personal gain and political power were quite likely the sole bases for the activities described in the Richmond Council case. The normal conduct of one's job in furtherance of agency business was the setting for some of the incidents, including the Mannix and NSW telephone intercept cases. In one case - the vandalism of the Lea Tree - the misconduct was essentially expressive rather than instrumental.

The misconduct in a number of incidents was orchestrated by the agency's top management; in others, it arose from discretionary conduct by officers in the field. The incidents which were most clearly set in train by executive action included the New South Wales police telephone intercepts, the Richmond Council activities, and the Injalka case. Incidents of alleged illegality arising from a subordinate's exercise of discretion included the Mannix and John Pat cases.

Another set of cases involved flawed implementation of policies which had been formulated in general terms by senior management. Such cases would include the ASIS raid and the social security conspiracy.

Organisational pathologies

Each of the incidents was shaped by the organisational context in which it occurred. In no case can the misconduct at hand be traced to a single cause. Rather, the cases arose from a constellation of factors; some of the more influential of these require a brief summary.

Environment

Environmental influences underlay a number of the incidents under review. In their theory of organisational crime, Finney and LeSieur (1982, pp. 269-70) posit that the stronger the goal orientation within an organisation, the greater the pressure for organisational crime. Performance pressures were perhaps most salient in the Mannix, Injalka, and Asia Dairy cases. As the crucial early days of the Mannix investigation wore on, with no arrests made, pressures to solve the case were reinforced by the arrival of senior officers from Brisbane. The desire to expedite development of the Northern Territory in general, and the Barrett Drive project in particular, contributed to the minister's decision to bulldoze the Injalka site. The less than robust state of the Australian dairy industry made the retention of overseas markets of highest priority, thus contributing to the decision to pay the requested rebate to the Philippine company HOMPI. External pressures also contributed to the social security conspiracy scandal. Recall how the incoming Director General of Social Security was recruited to crack down on benefits fraud. In the eagerness to deliver the goods, the department's role in the planning and execution of 'Don's Party' could have been orchestrated with greater care.

Resource constraint

Although financial exigency in the private sector can lead to corporate crime, lack of resources made a significant contribution in but one case reviewed here - the inordinate delay of the bottom of the harbour prosecution. Staff ceilings, caseload pressures and inadequately skilled personnel led to neglect of the crucial file. By contrast, a relatively munificent environment appears to have provided the setting for a number of cases. The Victorian government was flush with funds to spend on the acquisition of land. With money as no object, few incentives to ensure efficient expenditure remained. The South Australian and New South Wales police departments were able to allocate staff resources to the tasks of physical and electronic surveillance. It might also be argued that there was an overabundance of police and an excessive preoccupation with public order in John Pat's hometown of Roebourne.

This suggests that there may be an optimum level of resources for the achievement of legitimate ends by public sector agencies. Insufficient resources can lead to the cutting of corners, or to neglect. An overabundance of resources, on the other hand, may lead to carelessness, or to the allocation of surplus means to illegitimate ends.

The double interact of control

One useful framework for the analysis of organisational pathology is what communications theorists term the double interact of control. Simply stated,

> Supervisor A gives directions to subordinate B; Subordinate B complies (or fails to comply) and the 'messages' concerning compliance and goal attainment are monitored through feedback loops leading back to A; Supervisor A assesses the results of B's performance and accordingly dispenses rewards and punishments to B (Tompkins & Cheney 1985, p. 195).

In Braithwaite's (1985) study of coal mining safety, he found those mining companies with exceptional achievements in worker safety to be characterised by clearly defined accountability for safety performance, rigorous monitoring of that performance, and systems for communicating performance feedback to managers and workers.

But not all organisations have such impressive control procedures. In each of the chapters above one may discern evidence of malfunctioning in the system of directing, monitoring, and correcting organisational activity.

Direction   Direction may be explicit, that is by command, or implicit - by suggestion or example. Social critic and consumer activist Ralph Nader once said that organisations, like fish, rot from the head down. In his study of American business executives, Clinard (1983) observed that ethical standards established by senior management were reflected in patterns of conduct throughout the company. So too do leaders of public sector organisations create a moral climate that influences the values and the behaviour of those who work for them. Direct complicity of top management in the illegal activities of the organisation were apparent in a number of cases. Perhaps the most extreme example was that of the New South Wales Police telephone interception program, initiated at the explicit direction of the Commissioner of Police. Similarly, the systematic beating of New South Wales prisoners, with special compensation of prison officers at Grafton, could only have taken place with the complicity of the comptroller general of prisons. Indeed, Mr McGeechan's management was so flawed that the Royal Commissioner called for his dismissal. Similarly, the former Town Clerk of Richmond was faulted for setting a most unsavoury example of personal conduct, not to mention his contempt for democratic principles. Senior management of the New South Wales Water Resources Commission appeared less than totally committed to principles of equal employment opportunity. Their lack of enthusiasm was not lost on the boys in the purchasing division. Executives of Tasmania's Hydro-Electric Commission placed less value on preserving nature than on conquering it. In each of these cases, the values of senior executives were shared by officers in the field, to the detriment of the public interest.

It was once traditional in the Westminster system that the acts of a public servant were regarded as those of the responsible minister. Much as the captain of a ship, a minister was in theory accountable for any wrongdoing within his or her portfolio. Such a tradition is no longer a part of Australian political culture, however. In recent years, ministerial dismissals or resignations have arisen almost invariably from personal shortcomings of the individual concerned, and not from departmental failures.

Ministers became the subject of intense criticism for their roles in the NSW prisons scandal, the failure to prosecute the 'bottom of the harbour' promoters, the social security conspiracy, and the Victorian land purchases. Only in the latter case did a resignation eventuate, and then after a considerable period of time elapsed and the minister was in fact holding another portfolio.

The durability of ministers in these cases stands in contrast to the demise of federal treasurer Philip Lynch, whose misfortune it was to profit very handsomely from a land transaction in Victoria when his state colleagues were the subject of such criticism for their profligate spending. One may also recall the young minister Andrew Peacock's tendering his resignation following the appearance of his first wife in an advertisement for bed sheets.

<u>Monitoring</u>   In those cases where the pattern of organisational misconduct has not been established by executive action, one might expect the monitoring of subordinates' behaviour to explain some variation in government illegality (Kaufman 1973). One of the more striking similarities, a common thread running through a number of otherwise widely diverse cases, was an apparent lapse of supervision on the part of middle management. The Deputy Crown Solicitor in Perth failed to review the progress of the 'bottom of the harbour' test case and to oversee the transfer of files when the original solicitor responsible left the office. The fatal accident involving Electricity Trust of South Australia linesmen occurred when their supervisor was absent from the construction site. Because of turnover resulting from illness and incapacity, three middle level supervisors between Jane Hill and senior executives in the Water Resources Commission did not protect her from victimisation or reinforce the legitimacy of her position. Activities of the Australian Dairy Corporation and its Asian subsidiaries were not closely monitored by officers of the Department of Primary Industry. The South Australian Special Branch went about its business for years without guidance from the superintendent in charge of the CIB. The officer in charge of the ASIS training exercise was strongly criticised by Mr Justice Hope for his management of the mission. The McClelland Royal Commission faulted the AWTSC for undue deference to British testing personnel and for inadequate monitoring of the testing program. Recall how the Queensland Police Tribunal faulted the officer in charge of the Broadbeach CIB for not exercising closer control of the Mannix murder investigation in its crucial early stages.

Communications   The flow of information within an organisation can be crucial to an agency's performance (Dunsire 1978, p. 169; Downs 1967, pp. 77-8, and Ch. 10). Blockage or distortion of organisational communication may not only create problems, but may compound them, once made. Communications breakdowns may take a number of forms (Billings & Cheaney 1981). On the one hand, there may be an absence of information transfer, that is when the necessary message is not transmitted at all. When information transfer does take place, the message may be incomplete or inaccurate, thereby containing insufficient information on which to base subsequent action. Alternatively, the message may be untimely, having been transmitted too late to be of assistance. Furthermore, the information may be transmitted, but may not be perceived or may be misperceived by the intended recipients.

Flawed communications played less of a role in the incidents under review than might have been anticipated. One example involved incomplete information communicated downward through an organisation.   Proper construction procedures were imperfectly communicated from the supervising engineer to the ETSA construction crew, and thus inappropriate (and ultimately fatal) materials were used. Ambiguous or erroneous information appears to have been communicated to the responsible minister in the Injalka case. By one account, officers of the Northern Territory government advised the minister that negotiations with the Injalka people had irretrievably broken down, when in fact a compromise may still have been possible. Based upon that information, the minister decided to have the site blasted. At least one example of selective filtering of upward communication occurred in the NSW prison case, when the minister was not made aware of the results of an internal investigation reflecting adversely on departmental performance. Another type of communications pathology occurs when an organisation is in receipt of ambiguous information from external sources.   The Yass Council received considerable information, much of it contradictory, from a number of agencies, and was thus disinclined to take the abatement action demanded by the State Pollution Control Commission.

<u>Plausibility of denials</u>   As the Iran-Contra hearings in the United States demonstrated, the principle of accountability can be defeated by structuring a managerial situation so that an executive can deny knowledge of misconduct occurring under his or her administration. As there is less stigma, and indeed, less culpability, attached to ignorance than to condonation or complicity, one may arrange affairs so that management remains ignorant of an ongoing procedure, or is able to plead ignorance by avoiding the creation of a record which would indicate to the contrary.

Of the cases presented above, there are three in which ministers of the crown, who might have been expected to know about misconduct within their portfolios, claimed ignorance. These were the abuse of New South Wales prisoners, the social security conspiracy, and the Asia Dairy case. In each, the plausibility of ministerial denials was called into question - by subordinates themselves in the two latter cases. Suffice it to say that there is more than a grain of wisdom in the Rae committee's injunction in the course of the Asia Dairy inquiry that written communications were superior to oral. One may also paraphrase the sage observation of a Hollywood mogul that a verbal reassurance isn't worth the paper it's written on.

<u>Corrective feedback</u>   Two cases which involved a noticeable lack of appropriate reinforcement to subordinates were the social security and special branch surveillance cases. In the former, deference to police autonomy prevented a refinement of the operation and a reduction of the number of persons charged. Committal proceedings thus continued for months before they were abandoned. In the special branch case, the Commissioner of Police failed to narrow the scope of surveillance activity, even when these excesses had become the subject of public discussion.

External oversight

The degree to which the conduct of an organisation is subject to scrutiny by external agencies may also explain its behaviour (Downs 1967, p. 148). Autonomy is a major goal of most organisations. To the extent that an organisation is able to achieve a degree of economic independence, prestige, and the ability to dictate its own policies and procedures, it becomes insulated from external control and supervision, and may even develop a separate morality (Ekland-Olson & Martin 1988). In turn, this can lead to organisational misconduct. In a number of cases reviewed here, the organisations involved enjoyed a degree of autonomy which tended to shield them from external scrutiny. Most prominent among these were the police agencies, which traditionally sought to insulate themselves from accountability and democratic control. Although ambiguities regarding the constitutional status of the South Australian police were generally regarded as having been resolved following a royal commission report some years earlier, Harold Salisbury continued to claim that he had legal grounds for misleading the government. The New South Wales Police resisted external guidance as well. In the late 1970s a number of officers engaged in a campaign of calculated insubordination and disinformation against the government's newly introduced summary offences legislation. The acute sensitivities of the police, combined with their political muscle, made governments extremely reluctant to provide the guidance and oversight which can reduce the risk of misconduct.

The non-existence or failure of external oversight mechanisms was by no means unique to police agencies. The Victorian Department of Local Government might have been more strict in its scrutiny of the Richmond Council. The excessive secrecy of the New South Wales Department of Corrective Services was criticised in the *Nagle Report*. Not only were the state's prisons beyond the scrutiny of the media and parliament, the century-old proposal of Sir Henry Parkes for an independent inspector had yet to be implemented. There seems little doubt that the absence of an external oversight body contributed to the climate in which illegality flourished.

Rapid expansion of organisational activity

In at least three cases, the rapid expansion of organisational activity provided the background for illegality. The introduction of a special operations function within ASIS involved activities outside the traditional ASIS repertoire. The desire on the part of the government of Victoria to acquire, in haste, large amounts of land for public housing led to the carelessness of the procurement process. The decision of the Commonwealth Police to embark upon a massive social security fraud crackdown proved most unwise given its lack of experience in planning and executing large scale operations.

The organisational culture of illegality

In a number of cases, the incidents in question arose not from a temporary lapse or aberration, but rather reflected practices deeply ingrained in the organisation. At one extreme, the tribal politics of the Richmond Council (where looking after one's relatives, friends and political allies was central to the natural order of things) constitute one example of how illegality becomes ingrained in the culture of an organisation. So too, albeit more for institutional than for private ends, were the beatings at Grafton Gaol, which had become routine for generations of prisoners and prison officers. The routine police practice of fabricating confessions, attributing them to a suspect, and introducing them as evidence in criminal cases, long preceded their official disclosure by the Beach and Lucas reports (Swanton 1986). The program of telephone interceptions by the New South Wales police was a common adjunct to criminal investigations, and had become institutionalised within the department over a period of nearly twenty years.

Common to all of these examples is the fact that the illegality in question had become part of the standard procedure of the agency. The rationalisation of illegality by law enforcement officers became a fact of organisational life (Skolnick 1982). Individuals within the organisation who might have been inclined to challenge the illegal practices would quite likely have done so at the risk of informal harassment and retribution, if not formal disciplinary action.

Toward a theory of government illegality

At this stage, it might be instructive to return to the theories of corporate crime and organisational deviance reviewed in Chapter 1, to determine the degree to which they are supported by the evidence from the case studies. An attempt will then be made to formulate a provisional theory of government illegality.

The explanatory power of existing theories

Kriesberg's (1976) rational actor model, which corresponds closely to Kagan and Scholz' (1984) model of the amoral calculator, would appear to characterise the decision to bulldoze the Injalka site and perhaps to begin the program of illegal telephone interceptions. Beyond these, none of the cases appears to have involved the careful assessment and weighing of the risks and benefits attending a particular course of action.

Kriesberg's model of organisational process decision-making can explain a number of incidents under review. The absence of standard operating procedures to deal with a new situation underlay the downfall of the ASIS training exercise. By contrast, the persistence of existing procedures under circumstances no longer appropriate (if ever they were) characterised the abuse of prisoners, the Special Branch surveillance, and the Mannix interrogation.

Kriesberg's model of bureaucratic politics can be applied to the social security conspiracy case. Here, three different public agencies were involved in planning the operation. When the case began to unravel, major participants hastened to dissociate themselves from the alleged improprieties, claiming that they had been insulated from knowledge of the matter in question. One may also recall the secrecy and compartmentalisation of knowledge which characterised the British nuclear testing program.

Kagan and Scholz' model of corporations as political citizens can explain a number of incidents involving alleged police misconduct. Police, perceiving their legal environment to have been excessively constraining, were moved to violate laws which they regarded as arbitrary or unreasonable. In a more overt manner, the Injalka case involved an explicit challenge to a law the validity of which had been called into question.

A number of incidents arose from what Kagan and Scholz would describe as organisational incompetence. All of the lapses in monitoring just reviewed can be so described. The carelessness which characterised the ASIS operation, the inadequate supervision and the inefficiency which underlay the stalled bottom of the harbour prosecution, and the management failure which allowed the victimisation of Jane Hill are all illustrative. Similarly, the poor planning and failure to anticipate the legal and political consequences of the social security raids were symptomatic of management failure rather than malevolence.

Finney and LeSieur (1982), Vaughan (1983; 1986), Coleman (1987) and Braithwaite (forthcoming) each emphasise the goal orientation of organisations, and suggest that when such goal orientation is intense and when legitimate means of attaining the goals in question are foreclosed, illegitimate means will be used to the extent that they are available. Such a focus on goal orientation in general transcends distinctions between private and public sectors. The preceding discussion of the environmental context of the cases under review provides considerable support for explanations of organisational deviance which are based on goal orientation. It is perhaps most apposite in the cases of the alleged rebate paid by Asia Dairy, and the telephone intercepts.

The above theorists also accord considerable importance to the degree of normative support for illegality which prevails within an organisation. The key role of leadership in setting a moral tone for the entire organisation was noted above, as was the development of an organisational culture of illegality. The organised subculture of resistance was most strikingly visible in the telephone interception case, where the officers responsible refused to co-operate with authorities until they had been granted immunity from prosecution.

Vaughan, Coleman and Braithwaite each refer to the likelihood of detection, or the perceived certainty and severity of punishment in the event of detection, as factors which would tend to inhibit government illegality. Certainly, the secrecy which traditionally surrounds many aspects of law enforcement and corrections in Australia (not to mention matters of defence and intelligence) shields them from public scrutiny, and renders less likely the detection and punishment of those offences which may occur.

Organisational complexity did not appear to figure prominently in the cases under review. Lapses in supervision and communications, which one may expect to occur more often in complex organisations, were found in relatively small agencies. It thus appears that for purposes of potential for deviance, the structure of an organisation is less important than its members.

If, as Braithwaite argues, the threat of potent shaming tends to inhibit illegality, the cases in this book suggest that the threat must be credible. Certainly, many of the incidents in question were followed by shaming which bordered on vilification: the bottom of the harbour case and the social security case were perhaps the most vivid examples. But in these and other cases, the risk of embarrassment appeared not to loom large in the consciousness of the actors before the event. Indeed, even after the event, principals in many cases remained unrepentant, or were at least able to rationalise their behaviour.

A provisional theory of government illegality

Based on the analysis of seventeen selected cases, it would be presumptuous indeed to proffer any definitive generalisations about the causes of government illegality, in Australia or elsewhere. But, with some guidance from previous theorists of organisational misconduct, it would not be inappropriate to suggest what the broad contours of a theory of government illegality might look like. A diagrammatic model is presented in Figure 19.1.

Weak institutions of external oversight

Organisations which are shielded from external scrutiny are more likely to offend than are those whose activities are subject to the attention of independent monitoring agencies. Inadequate external oversight will diminish inhibitions to offending directly, as well as through the conduct of senior and middle management.

Powerlessness of prospective victims

The greater the extent to which agencies deal with disadvantaged or otherwise marginal members of society, the

Figure 19.1

A Provisional Theory of Government Illegality

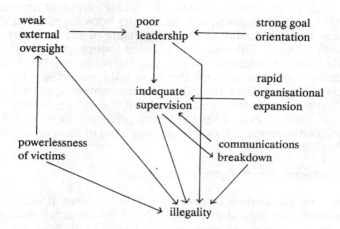

greater the likelihood of offending. Such individuals will tend to lack the resources necessary to defend themselves, and will be less able to invoke the assistance of external oversight bodies.

Poor leadership by senior management

The greater the extent to which an agency's top management condones or encourages illegal conduct, or engages in such conduct personally, the greater the likelihood that other members of the agency will follow suit.

Inadequate direction

The likelihood of illegality will increase to the extent that organisational policies and procedures are inadequately communicated to the rank and file.

Inadequate supervision by middle management

The less rigorous the monitoring of day-to-day operational routines and provision of corrective feedback by middle management, the greater the likelihood of illegality.

Rapid organisational expansion

The more rapid the growth of an organisation, in terms of size or function, the greater the likelihood of illegality. Rapid organisational growth may inhibit both effective supervision and essential communication within the agency.

Strong goal orientation

The stronger the organisation's goal orientation, the greater the likelihood of illegality. When the achievement of an organisation's ends is seen to justify illicit means, the likelihood of offending will be greater.

The task of refining (or of discrediting) this provisional theory will be left to subsequent researchers. But it is suggested that many of the relationships specified in the theory can explain a good deal of the official misconduct which occurs not only in Westminster style democracies, but in a variety of other regimes as well.

Mobilisation of law

The incidents described in the above chapters varied greatly in their initial visibility. Some were self-consciously clandestine prior to their unintended disclosure, whilst others achieved instant attention. The most common course of detection entailed the definition of the incident as wrongful by the immediate victim, who then lodged a complaint with the relevant legal authority.

Those incidents which involved sudden and violent death, the John Pat and ETSA cases, resulted automatically in coronial inquiries after initial notification of police by officials on the scene.

In only one case, the NSW police telephone interception program, was the illegality disclosed directly as the result of a leak from within. But in contrast to the classic situation of 'whistleblowing', the disclosures were made not to discredit the agency itself, but rather to embarrass a political enemy outside the organisation.

In the Asia Dairy and DCS Perth cases, the alleged misconduct was discovered by external investigative bodies. In the latter case, as the trail from the Melbourne waterfront to the solicitor's bottom drawer illustrated, the discovery was quite serendipitous.

The news media were instrumental in bringing the illegality to light in only a minority of cases. Perhaps the most successful example of investigative journalism in the detection of misconduct was the work of *The Age* in exposing the Victorian land scandals. Articles in *The Australian* newspaper finally forced disclosure of Special Branch surveillance in South Australia. And after some delay, the investigative team from *The Adelaide Advertiser* brought to public attention the unfortunate consequences of the British nuclear testing program. In a number of other cases, the news media were instrumental in setting the public agenda by keeping the alleged misconduct in the spotlight.

The most common governmental response in the aftermath of an incident's initial disclosure was the appointment of a royal commission or judicial inquiry. In some instances, most notably those in which senior government officials thought that media attention and public concern might soon fade, this occurred only after some delay. Such initial reluctance was apparent in the NSW prisons, social security, Victoria land, and Maralinga cases. When it became obvious that the incident would not 'blow over' the mobilisation of a judicial inquiry served to take the heat away from the government - at least for the time being.

Despite allegations of criminal conduct in most of the cases presented above, prosecutions were by no means automatic. Following the verdict of the Coroner, the officers implicated in the death of John Pat were tried for manslaughter. The Electricity Trust of South Australia was prosecuted under the general duties provision of state occupational health and safety legislation. The Yass Shire

300

Council was, after some delay, charged with a licence violation by the State Pollution Control Commission. A number of minor functionaries were prosecuted by Victorian authorities as a result of the land scandal and Richmond Council cases.

But in a number of other cases the criminal process was never invoked, or if so, it did not run its full course. On at least two occasions, this reflected a conscious policy decision by the government. In the NSW police tapes case, suspects were granted complete immunity by the federal government in return for their testimony before the Stewart Royal Commission. The NSW state government chose not to proceed against those prison officers who had been implicated in the abuses outlined in the *Nagle Report*.

At other times, the lack of prosecution arose from decisions by ostensibly independent tribunals or prosecuting authorities that insufficient evidence existed to enable a prosecution to succeed. Indeed, the bulk of the *Queensland Police Complaints Tribunal Report* on the Mannix case was devoted to impeaching the credibility of the complainant. In the Asia Dairy case, the Australian Federal Police concluded that a prosecution against the chairman of the Australian Dairy Corporation was unlikely to succeed.

The federal government suggested to Victorian authorities that the public interest would not be served by prosecuting the ASIS raiders. Ultimately, the state Director of Public Prosecutions concluded that evidence was insufficient to convict specific defendants of the charges in question. Inadequate evidence, the death of one of the principals, and the passage of time since the commission of the alleged offences also underlay the decision not to prosecute a number of suspects in the Richmond Council case.

Disciplinary action was taken only infrequently, and then more often against dissenters and whistleblowers than against perpetrators of government illegality. A number of those involved in the harassment of Jane Hill were eventually subject to disciplinary hearings, but the judgments were largely negated upon appeal. The unfortunate officer in the Perth Deputy Crown Solicitor's office whose wife ran an escort agency was dismissed from the Australian Public Service. The Deputy Director of the Australian Dairy Corporation was relieved of his executive responsibilities, but remained on the ADC board.

In only five cases did victims seek redress at civil law. The employees and hotelkeeper in the ASIS raid, the widows of the deceased ETSA linesmen, Jane Hill, and a number of social security beneficiaries and nuclear test veterans, each sought to recover damages. New South Wales prisoners were prevented by law from suing, and after Barry Mannix' unfortunate experience with the Queensland Police Complaints Tribunal, he may well have concluded that any further legal action was unlikely to succeed. In the remaining cases, there was either no specifiable injury to a given person or group, or the potential plaintiff's state of legal vulnerability was such that legal action was likely to have been disadvantageous. The Maralinga people chose to deal directly with the federal and South Australian governments rather than go through a formal legal process.

Outcome of the legal process

Of those criminal charges which were laid, most were unsuccessful. Charges were withdrawn in the Injalka case when it became apparent that the act did not bind the Crown. The minister, his officers and agents were thus immune from prosecution. The police who were prosecuted over the death of John Pat were acquitted of all charges. Charges were found proven against the Yass Shire Council, but no conviction was recorded.

Convictions were obtained in only three cases. The Electricity Trust of South Australia was convicted and fined $250 for negligence leading to the deaths of four men. The public servant who was found to have benefited personally from the Victorian land deals was sentenced to prison. A few minor participants in the Richmond Council affair were also sentenced to prison or to periodic detention.

Claims by victims or their surviving relatives for civil damages were somewhat more successful. The widows of the ETSA linesmen received damage awards which collectively exceeded one million dollars. Victims of the ASIS raid reached a settlement with the federal government for a sum of approximately $300,000. Jane Hill was awarded $37,000 by the New South Wales Equal Opportunity Tribunal, and the victimised social security beneficiaries received ex gratia payments which collectively approached ten million dollars.

Long term consequences

Although incidents such as the ones under review here result in considerable cost and suffering in the short term, they are not totally without benefit. Fisse and Braithwaite (1983) have shown that crises of adverse publicity experienced by private sector organisations tend to have a salutary effect on subsequent corporate conduct. A scandal in the public sector, by attracting attention to the misconduct in question and to its causes, may also serve as a catalyst for reform. Sherman (1978) and Punch (1985, p. 27) have shown this to be the case with police agencies in the United States and Europe.

Formal investigations and informed public debate may generate recommendations for improved policies and procedures. Executives of wayward bureaucracies may seek to rebuild their own public image, as well as that of their organisation, by implementing proposed reforms. The political pressures arising from a scandal may make the external imposition of reform more tolerable to otherwise resistant management. Alternatively, the clouds of scandal can assist reform-minded management to prevail over the resistance of ordinarily intransigent rank and file.

Most of the cases reviewed above have resulted in some benefit thus far. These positive outcomes will be summarised under our general evaluative criteria - deterrence, compensation, rehabilitation and denunciation of the illegality and reaffirmation of the rule of law.

Deterrence

To what extent did the reaction of governments and public to the above incidents have a deterrent effect? Are the wayward agencies less likely to inflict similar harm in future, and are others less inclined to follow in their paths? One would argue that in most cases, both recidivism and emulation are unlikely, due less to any *in terrorem* effects than to the rehabilitative impact of the interventions which took place.

There were cases, however, in which a deterrent impact was noticeable. In four instances, entire organisations or their wayward components were abolished. The Richmond Council was replaced by an administrator. ASIS no longer has an attack function. The South Australian Special Branch was disbanded, with those of its responsibilities pertaining to intelligence on political violence and terrorism given to another, more accountable unit within the police force. The functions of the New South Wales Water Resources Commission were distributed amongst local authorities or transferred to a new department of state.

Although the ASIS and special branch functions were highly specialised, one may assume that future training exercises involving law enforcement and security agencies will be planned and executed with greater rigour. Public agencies in New South Wales will be less apathetic about sexual harassment in particular and equal employment opportunity in general. Similarly, local government bodies in Victoria will remain mindful of the fate which can befall them for maladministration.

Other lessons appear to have been learned from those cases which resulted in less draconian treatment of the agencies concerned. One imagines that greater care is taken by Queensland detectives in the course of complex criminal investigations, and by Western Australian police in their dealings with Aboriginal communities. The Department of Social Security now exercises greater caution in its approaches to fraud control.

The difficulties experienced by the Deputy Crown Solicitor's office in Perth illustrate the usefulness of ridicule as an instrument of social control. The failure to prosecute the bottom of the harbour promoters received even greater public attention because of the disclosure of the peripheral activities of the escort service. The degree of embarrassment experienced in Canberra was such that similar lack of effective oversight in future became much less likely.

Rehabilitation

The majority of cases resulted in significant improvements to the organisations themselves or to their policies and procedures. In one case, an entire new organisation was created. In 1984, the federal Director of Public Prosecutions and his staff assumed the prosecutorial responsibilities of the Crown Solicitor.

Improved management procedures intended specifically to minimise the recurrence of similar incidents were instituted by the Electricity Trust of South Australia, by the Australian Attorney-General's Department and by the Department of Primary Industry. The prisons of New South Wales came under the management of a five-member Corrective Services Commission, and greater care was devoted to the recruitment and training of prison officers.

New systems of external oversight and control were introduced in the aftermath of the ASIS raid, the South Australian Special Branch revelations, the Asia Dairy affair, and the Victorian land scandals. The report on abuses within the New South Wales prison system led to the involvement of the state Ombudsman in investigating complaints by prisoners.

In one instance, the disclosures of illegality helped legitimise and institutionalise reforms which were already in train. The creation of a Police Board in New South Wales, and the more active involvement of the state Ombudsman in investigating complaints against police were both given a boost by the telephone intercept scandal.

Compensation

To what extent did those who suffered as a result of government action receive adequate compensation for their losses? If one considers the goal of compensation to be the physical, psychological and financial restoration of the victim to that state prevailing prior to the injury, one must regard the results as generally unsatisfactory. In a number of cases involving concrete, identifiable victims, most notably the Mannix, John Pat, and NSW prisons matters, no compensation was made. In others, particularly the Jane Hill, ASIS, ETSA, and social security cases, the victims or their surviving relatives received monetary damages. A few of the Maralinga test veterans were compensated for their injuries; legal action is still pending in a number of cases. Title to the Maralinga lands was vested in its traditional inhabitants, and the British and

Australian governments undertook some decontamination and
monitoring efforts. The dispute between the two nations
regarding which would bear the responsibility (and the cost) of
further decontamination will continue for years.

Certain losses, moreover, are difficult to express in
monetary terms. Violations of privacy and abridgement of
political freedom often defy costing, as does injury to the
environment.

In none of these cases can one regard the restoration of
the victim as complete - where injuries are fatal, this becomes
an impossibility. But it would appear that in the current
climate of fiscal austerity, governments will battle tenaciously
to minimise any drain on their finances, even when this may
result in some injustice. The cost of litigation for a victim of
government illegality may be prohibitive, and court awarded
damages may not be great. Victims may have to rest content
with small concessions.

Denunciation of illegality and
reaffirmation of the rule of law

Most of the incidents described in this book became the objects
of ringing denunciation. Where this occurred, it tended to be
at the hands of royal commissions, arguably the most
prestigious and authoritative voices in Australian public life.
Perhaps the most strenuous denunciations were those of the
Nagle Report on NSW prisons, the *Costigan Report* on the
failure to prosecute the 'bottom of the harbour' cases, and the
McClelland Report on British nuclear tests. Considering the
politeness of discourse which generally characterises the
Victorian legal profession, the *Nicholson Report* on the
Richmond Council might also be regarded as stern. Somewhat
less scathing in tone were the reports concerning the ASIS raid
and the NSW police tapes. Other examples of denunciation
may be seen in the Ombudsman's report on the Yass Shire
Council and in the Rae Committee's report on the Asia Dairy
case.

One takes great risks in venturing an explanation for the
variation in indignation which appears across the official
reports in response to the incidents of illegality. Public officials
vary in their capacity for outrage. Differences may reflect

individual personality and nothing more. It would seem, however, that those royal commissioners who had some considerable previous experience with the type of organisation they were investigating tended to be less vehement in their condemnation, and perhaps more understanding of the shortcomings upon which they reported. Neither Mr Justice Stewart, a former police officer and current head of the National Crime Authority, nor Mr Justice Hope, who had become immersed in security intelligence matters for a number of years, engaged in denunciation beyond detailed exposition and perfunctory criticism of the illegalities with which they were confronted. One may recall that the Queensland Police Tribunal, chaired by a former police officer, expressed as much sympathy for those police who testified before the Tribunal as they did for Barry Mannix, who had spent more than four months in prison before his father's real killers were identified.

The prevention and control of government
illegality: directions for reform

In the United States, Wilson and Rachal (1977) observed that public sector agencies were often much less amenable to control than private sector organisations. They noted that governmental entities have successfully cultivated independent sources of support which they are able to mobilise artfully when their institutional interests have been threatened. Although they refer specifically to the Veterans Administration, they note that other agencies as diverse as the Federal Bureau of Investigation and the US Army Corps of Engineers were for years virtually autonomous and quite impregnable. Australians too may ask themselves the question posed by the title of Wilson and Rachal's essay: 'Can the government regulate itself?' Indeed, we may also ask the extent to which the excesses of government are susceptible to control by citizen action.

None of the incidents described in this book was inevitable. Each would have been much less likely to occur had various institutions and countermeasures been in existence or had been functioning optimally. It will be the task of these remaining pages to review in general terms the mechanisms of control and accountability which exist in contemporary

Australia, and to suggest ways in which they may be strengthened. We will begin with a review of those institutions which exist to prevent and detect government illegality, then proceed to a discussion of remedies available once the government breaks the law.

Internal oversight

Internal oversight and control are the major bulwarks against government illegality. As many of the above cases illustrate, leadership and supervision play a major role in facilitating or inhibiting official misconduct. The ETSA accident would almost certainly not have occurred had the supervising engineer remained on site. More attentive supervision by the Crown Solicitor in Canberra and by his deputy in Perth would have prevented the bottom of the harbour file from becoming lost in the proverbial 'too hard basket'. Stricter scrutiny by senior management could have prevented the ASIS debacle.

Organisational capacity to supervise and control the behaviour of subordinates is unquestionably greater than that of outsiders. Organisations may, for example, impose obligations on their employees to identify and disclose unethical or illegal conduct. Fisse and Braithwaite (1983, pp. 168-81) refer to the extraordinarily strong policy of Exxon requiring employees to advise senior executives of any illegality coming to their attention, whether or not the illegality lies within the employee's normal domain of responsibility. A senior executive referred to the company as an organisation full of 'antennas'. Public sector organisations are no less capable than Exxon of developing such antennas.

Agencies which fail to keep their own houses in order may soon expect the attentions of outside authorities. Any public sector organisation which seeks to maximise its autonomy will develop an effective system of self-regulation. The organisational design of internal oversight has received considerable attention in both public and private sectors. The establishment of an internal compliance unit, with power to investigate all aspects of an agency's operations, has become increasingly common. Perhaps the greatest virtue of an in-house compliance unit is the potential for its personnel to develop intimate familiarity with the practices and procedures of the organisation (Downs 1967, pp. 148-51). Such inside knowledge is rarely achievable by outside inspectors. As Braithwaite notes, insiders are in the best position to know 'where the bodies are buried' (Braithwaite & Fisse 1985; Braithwaite 1987, p. 148).

It is important for the internal investigative function to be independent of line management, and answerable directly to the chief executive. In the United States, for example, each major federal agency has an Inspector General, whose responsibility it is to conduct periodic audits and to investigate and report on suspected misconduct, including fraud, abuse of power, and waste of government resources (Rosen 1982, p. 129). Inspectors-General are presidential appointees, responsible directly to the agency head, who is specifically forbidden to impede audits and investigations. Inspectors-General possess subpoena power, and are required to report semi-annually to the Congress of the United States on the audits which they have completed, the problems which they have identified, and the proposals for reform which they have made. The semi-annual report also provides follow-up information on previous recommendations and on the details and outcomes of any matters previously referred for prosecution.

Each Australian police department has an internal affairs branch with the task of investigating complaints against members of the force. These vary in terms of the number and seniority of personnel attached, the zeal with which they conduct their investigations, and their relative influence within the police organisation. By contrast, in addition to its internal affairs section, the New York City Police Department has designated integrity control officers in each precinct.

Some internal oversight bodies are entirely reactive - that is their investigations are mobilised when they receive a complaint of alleged misconduct. The more effective strategy of internal oversight combines reactive mobilisation with a preventive patrol function. That is, investigations are triggered not only by complaints but may occur as the strategic sensibilities of investigators dictate.

Such an arrangement exists within the Victoria Police Internal Investigation Department. Within this department, an Internal Security Unit may initiate its own investigations when directed by the Assistant Commissioner in charge (Horman 1987).

Internal police investigations, however, are by no means above reproach. They often entail inordinate delay, and have been faulted for lack of rigour by outside observers.

Organisational redesign

Various administrative reforms can be introduced within an organisation in order to inhibit illegality. In the aftermath of the space shuttle Challenger explosion, the National Aeronautics and Space Administration established an independent communications channel which enables officers to communicate anonymously with top agency officials through an independent office external to the agency. A similar system exists at the US Federal Aviation Administration (Wilford 1987). Other organisations have introduced programs whereby supervisors meet periodically with individuals two levels down in the hierarchy. Following the Iran-Contra scandal, the US President's chief of staff and his national security adviser undertook never to meet alone with the chief executive, in order to minimise the likelihood of deception or communications breakdown. The New South Wales Police have regionalised the criminal investigation function, making detectives accountable to regional commanders rather than to a centralised, hierarchical criminal investigation branch. Such administrative arrangements are more conducive to supervision of detective work.

Other examples of organisational structures to inhibit illegality are discussed by Braithwaite (1984, pp. 143-8). He describes how, in the pharmaceutical industry, the recommendations of quality control managers to destroy certain batches of drugs which fail to meet purity criteria may be overruled by production managers intent on meeting quotas. A number of companies require all quality control reports to be in writing, to be distributed to certain senior managers, and that any decision to overrule the recommendation of a quality control manager be made in writing, over the signature of the chief executive officer (*see also* Braithwaite 1987; Doig et al. 1984 p. 32). Accountability procedures of this type, had they been in place, would have lessened the likelihood of the financial irregularities alleged in the Asia Dairy, Victoria land, and Richmond Council cases.

External oversight

Whilst internal control mechanisms are a necessary bulwark against official misconduct, they are by no means sufficient. To ensure their efficacy, to prevent their co-option, and to guarantee their credibility by demonstrating that their role is more than symbolic, they must be reinforced by independent, external oversight bodies (Kaufman 1973, p. 33). Thus, the most effective organisational safeguards against official misconduct would entail a combination of internal control subject to external oversight.

The strategic relationship between internal and external control machinery is an important and sensitive one. Katz (1977) has argued that a natural tension exists between authority systems within and external to an organisation. Control within an organisation depends upon the support of rank and file. There is therefore a prevailing tendency within organisations to shield internal deviance from outside scrutiny. There thus may be very strong internal pressures to condone misconduct, or at least to respond in a discrete or ultimately tolerant manner.

On the other hand, the looming presence of an external oversight body, poised to identify shortcomings in internal control procedures, provides internal controllers not only with the incentives to pursue misconduct, but with the justification to deal strictly and convincingly with those insiders who resist. At the same time, the existence of an external authority which is in a position to ratify the practices and decisions of internal investigators can enhance the legitimacy not only of the internal control system, but also that of the organisation as a whole.

A variety of institutions exist in contemporary Australia to oversee the operation of the public sector. They tend to complement each other, rather than to compete. In theory, they constitute collectively a formidable set of safeguards against wayward governance. In practice, their functioning has at times been less than ideal.

Parliamentary oversight   In the Westminster system, ultimate responsibility for effective public administration rests with parliament (Cranston 1987, pp. 81-3).   Given the scope of the contemporary Australian public sector, parliaments are able to devote only selective attention to oversight of day-to-day administration.   The amount and the quality of parliamentary scrutiny, moreover, will vary across the states and territories of Australia.   Three committees of the Australian Parliament perform a general oversight function.   The Senate Committee on Finance and Government Operations, as we have seen, was instrumental in investigating the activities of the Australian Dairy Corporation and its Asian subsidiaries.   The Joint Committee of Public Accounts has been extremely critical of the performance of the federal Health Department in the prevention and control of medical benefits abuses.   The Senate Scrutiny of Bills Committee reviews pending legislation for provisions which might tend to facilitate government illegality (Haines 1987).

Not all state parliaments have equivalent committees, however.   But in some jurisdictions, matters which traditionally have escaped the attention of outsiders have recently been the subject of some scrutiny.   The Public Accounts Committee of the New South Wales State Parliament has begun to investigate such matters as the extraordinary amount of sick leave taken by the New South Wales Police, and the underutilisation and misuse of police vehicles.

None of the cases reviewed above occurred as a direct result of a lapse in parliamentary scrutiny, although greater visibility of operations of criminal justice agencies in New South Wales and South Australia would have made it more difficult for the abuse of prisoners, the illegal telephone interceptions and the Special Branch surveillance program to endure as long as they did.

More importantly, persistent scrutiny by Parliament can have the more general effect of keeping management 'on its toes', and thus reduce the likelihood of illegality by improving the quality of administration.

Ombudsmen   The institution of ombudsman exists for every Australian state and territory as well as for the federal government.   In the Yass Council case, the pressure which an ombudsman can bring to bear on an agency was quite apparent. There seems little doubt that the systematic abuse of prisoners in New South Wales over a period of decades could only have taken place in the absence of an ombudsman.

Whilst its potential contribution as a bulwark against government illegality is beyond doubt, the office of ombudsman is not without its weaknesses. Most noteworthy of these is its complaint-centred orientation. Whilst some ombudsmen have the power to investigate matters of their own motion, this is rarely used. Consequently, although the very purpose of the ombudsman is to assist the aggrieved citizen, the focus on individual service often occurs at the expense of attention to structural pathologies and their remedies (Selby 1987, p. 3).

In addition, whilst ombudsmen may make recommendations as a result of their investigations, they have no power to compel compliance on the part of government agencies. They may advise on what might be considered an appropriate amount for ex gratia compensation, but they cannot write a cheque nor require Treasury to do so. Government intransigence on this very issue was the subject of strong criticism from the Commonwealth Ombudsman in his 1986-87 annual report (Commonwealth Ombudsman 1987). The powers of the ombudsman are thus primarily persuasive, although, through the ultimate weapon of a report to parliament, an ombudsman may denounce an agency and thereby cause it (and its government) considerable embarrassment.

Another disadvantage which ombudsmen may face is lack of resources. They are dependent for their budget on the very government whose administration they are to oversee. In some cases, governments wield more than the power of the purse. Until recently, personnel and travel decisions in the New South Wales Ombudsman's office had to be ratified by the state Premier's Department.

Ombudsmen, moreover, vary in terms of their inclination to use those powers which they do have. There are hawks and doves amongst them. Governments with proverbial skeletons in the closet may well be coming to the realisation that when they appoint an energetic person as ombudsman, they do so at their peril.

The powers of the ombudsman in some jurisdictions are further constrained by strict secrecy provisions. Indeed, the New South Wales Ombudsman has noted that these restrictions have prevented him from assisting other ongoing governmental investigations. Not all of the secrecy surrounding ombudsmens' offices is externally imposed. The Commonwealth Ombudsman devoted a great deal of time and energy in seeking to thwart a freedom of information request by the victims of the social security conspiracy crackdown.

Political constraints often reduce the influence which ombudsmen could have. Recall from the John Pat case how the Western Australian Police Association successfully thwarted attempts to expand the ombudsman's powers relating to police matters. Ombudsmen have been excluded from some areas of government operations altogether, for reasons which appear to reflect the relative political power of vested interests rather than any justifications grounded in administrative efficiency. The most obvious example is, not surprisingly, law enforcement. The South Australian Police Association campaigned successfully to exclude the state ombudsman from investigating complaints against the police (Goode 1987). Separate police complaints authorities exist in Victoria and Queensland as well.

For these reasons, the institution of ombudsman cannot be regarded as the major defence against government illegality, but rather as an important institution which, at best, complements other means of social control.

Audits The office of auditor general or its equivalent exists in most modern systems of government to ensure the financial accountability of public authorities. The detection of departures from financial integrity is a goal which is worthy in itself. But as the Richmond Council and Asia Dairy cases have illustrated, financial shortcomings may occur alongside other abuses of power and may be symptomatic of more general administrative pathologies.

The Royal Commission on Australian Government Administration recommended that the function of the auditor general be expanded to include efficiency auditing in addition to financial auditing (Australia 1976). This new role entails evaluation of an agency's resource utilisation, its information systems and its management practices. Oversight of this kind almost certainly would have identified the administrative shortcomings in the Perth office of the Deputy Crown Solicitor which prevented timely prosecution of the bottom of the harbour case.

Efficiency auditing is only a recent innovation in Australian public administration. The Australian Audit Office began conducting efficiency audits of federal government agencies on a modest scale in the aftermath of the Royal Commission report, and now conducts some fifteen such audits each year. Reports of the Australian Auditor-General are accompanied by a press release, which calls attention to the shortcomings which were detected and remedies which were proposed. Such high profile reporting keeps maladministration and reform on the public agenda.

The practice of efficiency auditing exists on a more limited scale in some state jurisdictions. In New South Wales, efficiency auditing is a responsibility of the state Public Service Board. But even where efficiency auditing does exist, resources do not permit frequent regular auditing of all public sector agencies. It has been estimated that at the current rate it will take more than twenty years to subject each federal government program with a value exceeding ten million dollars to an efficiency audit (Lidbetter 1987, p. 23).

Police complaints authorities: controlling wayward police The problem of police misconduct and its control is one of the most difficult and contentious issues in the entire domain of public sector accountability. Its importance hardly needs emphasis. By virtue of their unique role in Australian society, police experience both substantial opportunity to inflict unlawful harm, and a great risk of so doing. The control of police illegality is of even greater importance because of their special role of moral exemplars. It may well be argued that of all government officers, the ones who should be held to the highest standards of integrity are those whose very job it is to uphold the law.

That police in Australian society have fallen short of this ideal invites some consideration of how the gap might be narrowed. Controlling police illegality is made difficult by organisational characteristics of the police agency and by properties of the environment in which they operate (Punch 1985). Noticeable characteristics of the police organisation are in-group solidarity and distrust of outsiders. Like many professions, police have a relatively high tolerance for deviance by their peers, and a great reluctance to discuss publicly their own individual or collective shortcomings.

The control problem is compounded by the fact that police possess political and industrial muscle which, with the possible exception of that wielded by the business community, is unrivalled in contemporary Australia. Australian police have generally succeeded in becoming identified in the public mind as the embodiment of law and order. The argument that public security can best be achieved by increasing police staffing levels and by enhancing police powers has, regardless of its basis in fact, become received wisdom. In a period when no Australian government enjoys an electoral majority which is comfortable enough to enable it to look beyond the next election, and with parliamentary oppositions poised to attack governments for 'placing handcuffs on police', critical discussion of police issues does not take place.

Arrangements for external oversight of police in Australia are varied (Freckelton & Selby 1987; 1989). In New South Wales (since 1983), the Northern Territory (since 1978) and Western Australia (since 1985) ombudsmen have the authority to investigate a complaint against the police if they are not satisfied with the outcome of the police internal investigation. The Queensland Police Complaints Tribunal, established in 1982, receives complaints of alleged police misconduct and may investigate complaints itself or require police to conduct an internal investigation and report its results. Specialised police complaints authorities were established in South Australia in 1985 and in Victoria in 1986. Pressure from the Police Association and an impending election saw the abolition of the latter within two years (Freckelton & Selby 1989).

The operations of these agencies do not always inspire the confidence of prospective complainants. The Queensland Tribunal appeared to devote more energy to discrediting Barry Mannix than to addressing the misconduct which he alleged. Moreover, the powers of each of these independent authorities are limited, and the argument has been made that the function of police oversight might best reside with the ombudsman on grounds of administrative efficiency and greater stature inherent in the office of ombudsman.

<u>Judicial oversight</u>   Police misconduct may also come to the attention of a judge or magistrate in the course of a prosecution (Applegarth 1982). Judicial officers are, of course, free to denounce questionable police conduct, as occurred during the social security conspiracy committal. In addition, they have a discretionary power to exclude evidence which has been illegally obtained, or they may even prevent a prosecution from proceeding in the event of egregiously oppressive misconduct on the part of the prosecution (Hunter 1985).

The judiciary of Queensland had been sensitised to the risk of police fabricating evidence since the Lucas Inquiry. How the trial of Barry Mannix might have progressed had not the real offenders confessed is a haunting and unanswerable question.

The importance of judicial oversight of police misconduct is that much greater when alternative external and internal control processes are not functioning properly. A law which automatically precluded the admissibility of illegally obtained evidence would constitute an even stricter safeguard against police illegality.

<u>Political processes</u>   Whilst it might be hoped that one solution to the excesses of government lies in the democratic political process, the ability of aggrieved citizens to obtain redress through political representation is limited. The political process is most sensitive to the concerns of the majority and to the interests of elite minorities. Whilst the institutions of government might protect such fortunate souls from injury in the first instance, they are less helpful to those disadvantaged and peripheral members of society who, as many of the above cases have illustrated, are perhaps most vulnerable to the excesses of government. In the United States, the existence of a Bill of Rights and the availability of legal resources with which to enforce it have long been recognised as an important shield for the citizen of an otherwise powerful state.

Just as the institution of neighbourhood watch has been heralded as successful in the fight against street crime, so too can community groups exercise vigilance against official misconduct. Monitoring groups in the United Kingdom have contributed to the control of police misconduct by providing advice and support to those with grievances against police, and by serving as an information resource. Established with the financial support of local government, such groups keep abreast of legislation and policy relating to law enforcement, and raise public awareness by publicising certain cases and issues (Greater London Council 1982-85; London Strategic Policy Unit 1986-87). One London organisation, Inquest, is specifically concerned with deaths in police custody, and has canvassed a number of policy options to reduce these fatalities (Ward 1986).

Political agitation by citizens' groups in Australia has occasionally succeeded in focusing attention on matters of alleged government illegality. Such activity may be ad hoc, or on a continuing basis. The New South Wales Council for Civil Liberties was founded in the early 1960s in response to police abuses in Sydney. Perhaps the most obvious example in recent years is the campaign regarding Aboriginal deaths in custody, inspired in part by the John Pat case. But such a sustained campaign, and the official reaction which it has thus far elicited, are exceptional.

<u>Freedom of information</u>   When the Australian government introduced the *Freedom of Information Act 1982* (Cwlth), it was heralded as an instrument to improve the quality of public administration by making the processes of government more visible to the citizenry. Ideally, decisions would be reached with greater care and deliberation. Evidence of wrongdoing would be more readily detectable, and the conduct of public officers would be that much more improved (Harrison 1987). If any improvement in the quality of governance has been realised since the early 1980s, however, it is quite likely attributable to something other than freedom of information legislation. Governments, which spend hundreds of millions of dollars generating information which the public does not want, are extremely reluctant to implement a program which would enable people to obtain the information which they do want.

As of 1988, statutory freedom of information (FOI) existed in only two jurisdictions - the federal government and the state of Victoria. In both jurisdictions, the legislation was watered down substantially. Exemptions are numerous, and the imposition of fees and other costs for making FOI requests discourage not only the frivolous, but also the disadvantaged. Australian government departments have also delayed honouring FOI requests until the applicant is almost literally on the steps of the Administrative Appeals Tribunal. The remaining states and territories have shown a distinct lack of enthusiasm for following in the footsteps of those with FOI, and their disinclination, moreover, is reinforced by the negative comments emanating from the governments of those jurisdictions where FOI exists even in its tepid form.

The ideal of freedom of information is fundamentally inconsistent with the paramount goals of bureaucracy - growth and autonomy. It is not coincidental that freedom of information is most strenuously opposed by those whose behaviour would be subject to stricter scrutiny as a result. One might also note Thompson's (1985, p. 222) ironic insight that in our free enterprise society, failure to disclose material information to investors can be a crime, but refusing to reveal information to citizens in the democratic political arena is often *required* by law.

Of the cases reviewed above, the Richmond Council matter would have been most amenable to detection through a freedom of information request. The availability of limited freedom of information provisions might even have prevented the excesses canvassed in the Special Branch and nuclear testing cases. Whilst perhaps beyond the imagination of Australian political officials, FOI was invoked during the Reagan administration to document the fact that the US Federal Bureau of Investigation had been monitoring the activities of citizens who had expressed public disagreement with the administration's policies in Central America. It would thus appear that freedom of information legislation can contribute to curbing the excesses of law enforcement and intelligence agencies without jeopardising the national security.

News media   In democratic societies, one of the most important bulwarks against the abuse of power is a free press. The ability of journalists to detect and to expose government wrongdoing can be a powerful deterrent. Sustained media criticism can be a very effective means of inspiring otherwise intransigent politicians to undertake reforms. The potential contribution to be made by journalists to public debate about official misconduct and its control can be a great one. Whilst the Australian media have devoted considerable attention to issues of government illegality in the past, its performance has been less than flawless. Two major factors inhibit open and robust debate on official misconduct in Australia today - the political economy of the Australian media and the law of defamation.

To an unprecedented extent, the Australian media are controlled by conglomerates. These controlling interests are thus dependent upon the largesse of either state or federal government for a myriad of favours which facilitate doing business in Australia and which ultimately affect corporate profitability.

Inhibitions of a different nature characterise media coverage of police affairs. Most media organisations depend upon police for a regular supply of news, and are reluctant to direct sustained criticism at police for fear of alienating their sources. Police 'black bans' on news organisations are not uncommon. Critical questioning of police may not be as risky for the media as it is for elected officials, but it is hardly cost-free.

Another significant constraint faced by the Australian media is the law of defamation. Australian laws stem from the English legal tradition where criticism of government and public officials was once punishable as seditious libel (Pullan 1984). Contemporary Australian defamation laws are weighted more toward protecting public officials than their critics.

The ambiguities and uncertainties of defamation law in the various states and territories have been addressed by the Australian Law Reform Commission (1979) and by Armstrong, Blakeney, and Watterson (1983). Suffice it to say for present purposes that Australian public officials have received significant damage awards, sufficient to inhibit free and open discussion about the way Australia is governed. At least one state premier had officers monitor media coverage of his administration with a view toward referring defamatory statements to the Crown Law Office or to his personal solicitors.

Elected officials are not the only people who use the threat or reality of defamation writs to discourage open discussion on matters of public policy. One New South Wales judge succeeded in bringing about the withdrawal from sale of a book which referred to his attitude as sexist. The threat of defamation action was raised by the Queensland police union in conjunction with allegations arising from the Mannix investigation. In 1985, the Northern Territory Police Association was reported as having sought legal opinion with a view to defamation action against citizens who were calling for a judicial inquiry into the shooting of two Aborigines by police five years earlier. The officer accused of the shooting had been acquitted of all charges (*Northern Territory News*, 19 November 1985).

Whistleblowing

Australia lacks a great tradition of whistleblowing - public disclosure of organisational misconduct by a person within the organisation. Cultural inhibitions against 'dobbing in one's mates' aside, the explanation is simple. The risks are great and the potential benefits are few.

Perhaps the most celebrated whistleblower of the early 1970s in Australia was Detective Sergeant Philip Arantz of the New South Wales Police. Arantz disclosed that official police statistics of reported offences were actually understating the incidence of crime. For his efforts, he was committed to a psychiatric hospital and later dismissed from the force. Ten years passed before he received any compensation for his dismissal. As a condition of the modest compensation payment which he did receive, Arantz was required to give an undertaking to refrain from further public comment on the matter.

A few officers of the organisations discussed in this book may have been tempted to blow the whistle. Those who made an effort gained few rewards and many headaches. One officer of the Richmond Council lost his job, a New South Wales prison officer who called for a royal commission was dismissed, although he was eventually reinstated at a lower rank. Four prison psychologists who complained to the Comptroller

General about systematic and calculated brutality were threatened with reassignment and eventually left the prison service.

In addition to the use of incentives such as rewards for disclosing criminal conduct, structures may be developed to facilitate whistleblowing. The US General Accounting Office, roughly the equivalent of the Australian Audit Office, has a twenty-four hour toll-free hotline to encourage the reporting of any abuses relating to US government expenditures.

Whistleblowing can be an important deterrent to government illegality, particularly in those organisations which normally have a low profile or whose operations may not enjoy the benefit of rigourous external oversight (Doig et al. 1984, p. 32).

Given whistleblowers' vulnerability to reprisals, some form of protection against subsequent victimisation is essential. Ample precedent exists overseas for legislative protection (Vaughn 1982; Wood 1984; Near & Micelli 1987). Until appropriate structures are created to encourage principled organisational dissent in Australia, the likelihood that whistleblowing can serve as an effective countermeasure against government illegality is remote.

Criminal prosecution

The criminal sanction is perhaps the most forceful instrument of responses to government illegality. The threat of being labelled a criminal is a powerful deterrent to wrongdoing by anyone holding a position of public trust. The authoritative determination of guilt on the part of a public official is the most awesome statement of denunciation available in a secular society.

In the Anglo-Australian system of justice, the criminal law is reserved for those acts which are most morally blameworthy. Harms arising from simple negligence are left to the civil law. Those where the negligence was extreme, or when the harms in question arose from the conscious disregard of the risks posed by official actions, can be dealt with by the criminal process, as are the intentional commission of acts known to be unlawful.

In addition to its limited applicability, the use of the criminal law is constrained by the formidable evidentiary burdens which exist, and the necessity of proving the guilt of the accused beyond reasonable doubt. Thus, the criminal law is hardly a panacea for government illegality. The criminal process is but one of a number of instruments for controlling wayward governance. Indeed, there are many instances when its use would not meet the criteria for ideal response. In particular, its compensatory and rehabilitative capabilities are limited.

Nevertheless, the criminal sanction has been underutilised as a weapon against public sector illegality. In particular, it can be used more selectively and more creatively than has been the case thus far. Governments are loath to mobilise the criminal law against individual public servants, especially for conduct in furtherance of government policy. Such reluctance is particularly noticeable when the offenders are police, prison officers or intelligence agents.

In addition to the substantial legal burdens which must be met in order to prosecute successfully, there are certain structural inadequacies in the criminal law. One of the most significant of these is what Fisse (1987) has called its individualist bias. The criminal law evolved over hundreds of years to control individuals, not organisations. Central to the determination of guilt in criminal jurisprudence has been the individual's state of mind. Only recently have commentators begun to recognise that much criminal behaviour has an organisational as well as a psychological basis (Stone 1975; 1980; Coffee 1977).

Where the doctrine of crown immunity prevails, government agencies are beyond the reach of the criminal law. In those relatively infrequent occasions when the criminal law has been mobilised against organisations, the judicial response has been modest indeed. Criminal penalties against private sector corporate offenders in Australia have been criticised as trivial (Grabosky & Braithwaite 1986). Although charges were laid against organisational defendants in the ETSA and Yass Council cases discussed above, a trivial fine was imposed in the former, and no conviction recorded in the latter. Such exceedingly modest judicial responses would seem to neutralise whatever benefits might otherwise flow from the stigmatising effect of criminal conviction.

The first strategic choice in mobilising the criminal law in the aftermath of public sector illegality is whether to prosecute the agency, the individual, or both. No one alternative is automatically preferable. Fisse (1987) calls for a mixed strategy of organisational and individual criminal liability. Thus, Braithwaite and Fisse (1985) would argue that the application of the law should be consistent with the context of the decision which led to its breach. Stone (1985) identifies three basic situations - those in which the individual alone should be liable, those in which liability rests with both the individual and the organisation, and those in which the organisation alone is liable.

Where the illegal conduct is that of the individual, and where the conduct lies beyond the agency's ability or opportunity to control, criminal liability rests with the individual alone.

Where the conduct is essentially individual, but where there is also an underlying organisational pathology, both the individual and the organisation should be liable. Consider, for example, a police officer with a reputation for aggressiveness who had been the subject of previous complaints relating to violent conduct. If this officer were to use excessive force in restraining a suspect, and in the process inflict an injury, he/she should be liable to a charge of assault. The department should also be liable, however, since it was in a position to prevent the misconduct in question. The flawed personnel screening and deployment practices created a substantial likelihood of injury to a member of the public.

Where the offence arises essentially from an organisational, rather than an individual lapse, liability should rest with the agency and not with any person. Incidents arising from collective decisions, or from situations in which responsibility is diffused amongst members of an organisation, make it difficult for individuals to be held criminally responsible. Consider, for example, a police raid on a premises whose occupants were suspected of harbouring a fugitive. Assume that all aspects of the operation were executed strictly according to standard procedures, but through careless transcription or communication, the officers arrived at the incorrect address, guns drawn, to the serious alarm and affront of the occupants therein. Criminal liability should rest with the department rather than with the officers concerned.

It might also be added that organisational liability is appropriate for those cases in which the judicial determination of a perpetrator's identity may be difficult. Such uncertainty contributed to the decision not to prosecute the ASIS raiders.

Under what circumstances might the senior executives of an organisation be prosecuted for the sins of their subordinates? At one extreme, an executive might be held strictly liable for offences committed by members of the organisation. Such strict liability would offend those principles of justice which require knowledge of and intention to commit a wrongful act in order to frame criminal charges. Many competent and dedicated executives might be reluctant to expose themselves to such risk. Indeed, such vulnerability may well invite deceit in the form of subterfuge and cover-up.

Alternatively, criminal liability of an executive would certainly seem appropriate when the misconduct was set in train by executive decision. Thus, the commissioner of police who establishes a program of illegal telephone surveillance is no less culpable than the senior detective who orders a tap, the technician who installs one, or the officer who does the actual listening.

Similarly, executive liability should apply to situations in which the senior official is aware of or wilfully blind to subordinates' misconduct but fails to take corrective action. Thompson (1985) has argued that in some cases, executives who could be expected to know about the misconduct within their organisation could be properly subject to criminal sanctions. To cite an example from the private sector in the United States, the president of a large national supermarket chain was held liable for persistent unsanitary conditions in one of the company's warehouses, even though he had no personal involvement in managing the warehouse (*United States v. Park*, 421 U.S. 658 [1975]).

Such liability in the Australian public sector would no doubt serve to enhance managerial vigilance. Executives who stand to be prosecuted are also more likely to activate a more rigorous system of internal control within the organisation.

The deterrent potential of organisational criminal liability should not be underestimated. Organisations themselves possess formal and informal resources to compel compliance which, because of their flexibility, are often superior to the criminal law. When the threat of criminal prosecution serves to mobilise the organisation's own deterrent capabilities, the goal of deterrence can be more efficiently achieved.

Another utilitarian justification for the use of criminal sanctions against organisations is their rehabilitative potential. This potential has yet to be realised, however, as those infrequent occasions when public sector agencies have been convicted of an offence tend to result in the imposition of a fine.

Not only are trivial fines devoid of any salutary impact, they may actually breed contempt for the law. Severe monetary fines, on the other hand, can be counterproductive. At best, the right hand of government may be seen to be paying the left hand (Stone 1982, pp. 1469-70). At worst, where a fine imposes an actual burden on an agency, there may be a spillover effect. Thus, a burden may be shifted to clients or to organisations with less political influence. It might strike some people as unjust to see welfare recipients pay the costs of police misconduct.

As an alternative to traditional criminal penalties, Fisse (1987) has proposed sentences of corporate probation, with specified conditions of a probation order directed at improving the organisation. If, for example, an incident of government illegality arose from inadequate training of personnel, a probation order might call for the restructuring of the agency's training program. If illegality could be traced to inadequate disciplinary practices within the agency, it could be required to introduce a new system of internal control. In general terms, an offending agency might be sentenced to design a compliance program subject to the approval of the court. It might then be required to file periodic reports detailing the progress of the program's implementation.

Other imaginative strategies might include the design of a program to facilitate whistleblowing, or the drafting and implementation of a whistleblowers' protection plan.

Civil litigation

Civil litigation may be a more advantageous alternative to the criminal process for a number of reasons. The limited applicability of the criminal sanction and the reluctance of governments to mobilise it were noted above. Civil action resulting in an award of damages can best achieve the goal of compensation to the victim of government illegality. Public agencies, by virtue of their size, insurability, capacity to spread losses and ability to control risks are better situated overall to minimise the costs of official misconduct (Schuck 1983, p. 51). Moreover, the threat of having to pay substantial damage awards can be a powerful deterrent to a potentially errant agency or public official. Unlike the criminal process, it can be directly mobilised by the injured party (private prosecutions do exist, but occur very infrequently). In the United States, the availability of punitive damages over and above an award made by way of compensation enhances this deterrent threat.

Civil litigation may provide a diagnostic benefit as well, in the form of feedback about where negligent conduct may occur within an organisation (Mashaw 1978).

Much as the personal threat of criminal sanctions can induce an executive to 'run a tight ship', civil liability of public sector executives can also have a salutary systemic impact on an organisation. Officials who can be held legally responsible for failure to rectify situations likely to lead to illegality will be more inclined to see to it that appropriate safeguards and preventive measures are in place (Doig et al. 1984, p. 48).

An additional advantage over the criminal process is a lesser burden of proof. In order to succeed in a civil action, a plaintiff must establish proof on the balance of probabilities rather than beyond reasonable doubt.

The use of civil litigation by victims of police illegality in Australia may be relatively infrequent, but it is not without precedent. An incident involving the fatal shooting of one Aboriginal man and the wounding of another resulted in civil action against a police constable and the Northern Territory government. The surviving victim settled for an undisclosed amount, and the widow was paid $15,000 plus costs. The plaintiffs agreed to discontinue their actions against the police officer, who had been acquitted of criminal charges arising from the matter (*Northern Territory News*, 19 November 1985).

Australian prison officials have also been held liable for negligently failing to supervise prisoners properly. A prisoner on remand, who was made to share the same cell overnight with prisoners under sentence, was sexually assaulted. He brought a successful action against prison authorities (*L. v. Commonwealth* [1976] 10 ALR 269).

But indiscriminate civil litigation has its disadvantages as well. Just as individual criminal liability might in some cases be regarded as unduly harsh, so too can individual civil liability. Most individual public servants would be reduced to financial ruin by an award of significant damages against them. Thus, individual civil liability could tend to produce excessively cautious public administration, to the point of paralysis. Indeed, just compensation for the harms occasioned by government illegality may be beyond the financial means of the responsible public official. The burdens of civil litigation are thus best borne by the government. So it is, in the United States, that many public officials enjoy a degree of immunity for damages resulting from simple negligence, whilst they remain liable for damages resulting from knowing violation of the law or from malicious intent (Woolhandler 1987; Balcerzak 1985). Some Australian jurisdictions have erected shields of immunity for their officials. For example, the South Australian Police are specifically indemnified against actions for damages arising from conduct undertaken in good faith in the course of duty.

One inhibition to the use of civil litigation is cost. Not every Australian is able to afford legal representation, and public funds for legal assistance are limited. Moreover, it is common practice in Australia for the unsuccessful party to civil actions to compensate the victor for costs incurred. A plaintiff thus takes a calculated gamble. Whilst recipients of legal aid in New South Wales are indemnified against costs being awarded against them, prospective litigants in the federal courts and in other state and territory jurisdictions have no such assurances. Litigation resources of governments, moreover, are considerable. Individual plaintiffs are understandably daunted by the prospects of confronting the legal might of the state. Indeed, an unsuccessful outcome for them could result in bankruptcy. Such risk hardly invites aggrieved citizens to seek redress through the courts.

In contrast to the United States, English and Australian legal systems are less accessible to aggrieved citizens (Birkinshaw 1985, p. 181). There exist no constitutionally enshrined rights whose abridgement by state officials can serve as the basis for legal remedies in federal courts. Another impediment to the use of civil litigation in Australia is the law of standing. Simply stated, in order to gain access to the courts a citizen must demonstrate a tangible personal stake in the issue at hand. It is not sufficient to be a concerned citizen. In the 1970s a group of environmentalists sought to challenge the legality of the flooding of Lake Pedder by the Hydro-Electric Commission of Tasmania. They were denied access to the courts for lack of standing. The Australian Law Reform Commission has called for a broadening of the law of standing (Australian Law Reform Commission 1985), but action has yet to be taken on their recommendations.

A further limitation of the use of civil litigation is the problem of causality. To prove that harm to a plaintiff was caused by breach of duty on the part of the government is rarely an easy task. It is, for example, extremely difficult to prove, even on the balance of probabilities, that a given disability arose from exposure to Agent Orange in Vietnam. Indeed, a number of Australian nuclear veterans have found it difficult to prove that their illnesses arose from exposure to radiation from the atomic tests, rather than from some other cause. Similarly, had the downstream residents of Yass chosen to sue the Shire Council, they would have been required to prove that the eutrophication of the river arose from the sewage outflow and not runoff from pastures upstream.

In addition to civil litigation serving as the means of compensating victims of government illegality, it can also be a catalyst for reform. Civil litigation has inspired both legislative change and internal reforms in the United States public sector. One victim of domestic violence, whose complaints to the police went unheeded and who subsequently sustained crippling injuries at the hands of her husband, sued the police for negligence and received US$1.9 million in damages. The state then enacted a new law which required police to make an arrest in cases of probable domestic assault (Johnson 1986).

Stricter controls on the use of firearms by police were also inspired in part by the reality or threat of legal action by victims or their surviving relatives. The controls were credited for reducing the incidence of police shootings by 50 per cent over a thirteen year period (Sherman & Cohn 1986). Governments in the United States are liable for negligence resulting in the deaths of prisoners in custody. The threat and reality of damage awards running into the millions have induced governments to undertake special suicide prevention measures (Rowan 1988).

The rehabilitative potential of the civil law is most clearly manifest in the injunction. Through injunctions, a court may order a bureaucracy to refrain from specified conduct or to perform certain specified acts. In contrast to the award of damages, the injunction is essentially prospective in orientation.

A more intrusive use of the civil law would involve structural injunctions. These remedies, which stipulate certain large scale changes in organisational practice and procedure are without precedent in Australia, but common in the United States (Schuck 1983, Ch. 1) where federal judges have placed entire state prison systems in receivership, specifying in considerable detail such conditions of detention as opportunity for exercise, bathing, and the caloric intake of prisoners. The structural injunction is thus a much more intrusive remedy than an award of monetary damages. Its major function is rehabilitative rather than compensatory.

Whilst some Australian judges might resile from an administrative role, there exists ample precedent for the use of special masters to manage private sector organisations in receivership. It should again be emphasised, however, that the legal basis for such judicial activism in the United States is an enforceable bill of rights, an idea yet to receive widespread support in Australia.

Participatory democracy

A democratic society is best able to prevent and control government illegality. When the processes of government are visible and subject to open and robust public discussion, when the excesses of government are subject to the scrutiny of a free and diverse press and through it, the public which government exists to serve, both the inclination and the opportunity to violate the public trust will be that much less. Our challenge lies in replacing a tradition of secrecy and cover-up in public affairs with an activist democratic culture, a new tradition of candour, openness, and self-assessment.

The first draft of this conclusion was written in July 1987, when a joint select committee of the United States Congress was holding public hearings on the Iran-Contra affair. Only a few months before, the report of the President's Special Review Board (the Tower Commission) had criticised White House procedures for formulating and implementing foreign policy (Tower, Muskie & Scowcroft 1987). The report was published in paperback, and sold in bookstores and newstands across the United States. The Iran-Contra hearings themselves were given continuous live coverage on two television networks nationwide. In the course of the hearings, the incumbent Secretaries of State and Defense were openly critical of the organisation and management of the White House staff and the National Security Council.

There were those who sought to argue that such openness in government stood to weaken the position of the United States in world affairs. Others, however, regarded the hearings and the public discussions which they inspired as an important learning experience, a lesson in constitutional democracy which would lead not only to a more informed citizenry, but would also lessen the likelihood of recklessness and illegality in the future conduct of United States foreign policy.

Regardless of developments overseas, the public sector seems destined to continue to play a major role in the lives of all Australians. Accordingly, the potential for government illegality will persist. Mistakes will be inevitable, and some risk of venality will remain. One hopes that the lessons learned from the incidents described in this book will minimise the likelihood of such harms in future.

References

Applegarth, Peter 1982, 'Police Malpractice: A Judicial Response' in *The Criminal Injustice System*, eds John Basten et al., Australian Legal Workers' Group and Legal Service Bulletin, Sydney, pp. 272-87.

Armstrong, Mark, Blakeney, Michael, & Watterson, Ray 1983, *Media Law in Australia*, Oxford University Press, Melbourne.

Australia 1976, *Royal Commission on Australian Government Administration, Report*, Australian Government Publishing Service, Canberra.

Australian Law Reform Commission 1979, *Unfair Publication: Defamation and Privacy*, Australian Government Publishing Service, Canberra.

Australian Law Reform Commission 1985, *Standing in Public Interest Litigation*, (Report No. 27), Australian Government Publishing Service, Canberra.

Balcerzak, Stephanie 1985, 'Qualified Immunity for Government Officials: The Problem of Unconstitutional Purpose in Civil Rights Litigation', *Yale Law Journal*, vol. 95, pp. 126-47.

Billings, C. & Cheaney, E. (eds) 1981, *Information Transfer Problems in the Aviation System*, NASA Technical Paper 1875, Moffett Field, California.

Birkinshaw, P. 1985, *Grievances, Remedies and the State*, Sweet & Maxwell, London.

Braithwaite, John 1984, *Corporate Crime in the Pharmaceutical Industry*, Routledge and Kegan Paul, London.

------------ 1985, *To Punish or Persuade*, State University New York Press, Albany.

References

------------ 1987, 'Self Regulation: Internal Compliance Strategies to Prevent Crime by Public Organisations' in *Government Illegality*, eds Peter Grabosky & Irena Le Lievre, pp. 145-70.

------------ (forthcoming), 'Toward a Theory of Organizational Crime', submitted to *Criminal Justice Quarterly*.

Braithwaite, John & Fisse, Brent 1985, 'Varieties of Responsibility and Organisational Crime', *Law and Policy*, vol. 7, no. 3, pp. 315-43.

Clinard, Marshall 1983, *Corporate Ethics and Crime*, Sage Publications, Beverly Hills.

Coffee, John C. Jr. 1977, 'Beyond the Shut-Eyed Sentry: Toward A Theoretical View of Corporate Misconduct and Effective Legal Response', *Virginia Law Review*, vol. 63, pp. 1099-78.

Coleman, James W. 1987, 'Toward an Integrated Theory of White Collar Crime', *American Journal of Sociology*, vol. 93, no. 2, pp. 406-39.

Commonwealth Ombudsman 1987, *Annual Report 1986-87*, Australian Government Publishing Service, Canberra.

Cranston, Ross 1987, *Law, Government and Public Policy*, Oxford University Press, Melbourne.

Dimelow, Mark 1982, 'Police Verbals in N.S.W.' in *The Criminal Injustice System*, eds John Basten et al., Australian Legal Workers Group and Legal Service Bulletin, Sydney, pp. 88-97.

Doig, Jameson W., Douglas E. Phillips & Tycho Manson 1984, 'Deterring Illegal Behavior by Officials of Complex Organizations', *Criminal Justice Ethics*, vol. 1, pp. 27-56.

Downs, Anthony 1967, *Inside Bureaucracy*, Little Brown, Boston.

References

Dunsire, Andrew 1978, *Control in a Bureaucracy*, Martin Robertson, Oxford.

Ekland-Olson, Sheldon & Martin, Steve 1988, 'Organizational Compliance with Court-Ordered Reform', *Law and Society Review*, vol. 22, no. 2, pp. 359-84.

Finney, Henry & LeSieur, Henry 1982, 'A Contingency Theory of Organizational Crime' in *Research in the Sociology of Organizations*, ed. S. Bacharach, JAI Press, Greenwich, Conn., pp. 255-99.

Fisse, Brent 1987, 'Controlling Government Crime: Issues of Individual and Collective Liability' in eds Grabosky & Le Lievre pp. 121-44.

Fisse Brent & Braithwaite, John 1983, *The Impact of Publicity on Corporate Offenders*, State University of New York Press, Albany.

Freckelton, Ian & Selby, Hugh 1987, 'Police Accountability: How Serious the Commitment?', *Legal Service Bulletin*, no. 2, pp. 66-70.

------------ 1989, 'Piercing the Blue Veil: An Assessment of External Review of Police in *Australian Policing: Contemporary Issues*, eds Duncan Chappell & Paul Wilson, Butterworths, Sydney.

Goode, Matthew 1987, 'Controlling Police Misconduct, Complaints Against Police, and the Process of Law Reform: As It Happens - An Academic War Story' in eds Grabosky & Le Lievre, pp. 51-76.

Grabosky, Peter & Braithwaite, John 1986, *Of Manners Gentle: Enforcement Strategies of Australian Business Regulatory Agencies*, Oxford University Press jointly with the Australian Institute of Criminology, Melbourne.

References

Grabosky, Peter & Le Lievre, Irena (eds) 1987, *Government Illegality*, Seminar Proceedings No. 17, Australian Institute of Criminology, Canberra.

Greater London Council 1982-85, *Policing London*, (fortnightly), Greater London Council, London.

Haines, Janine 1987, 'Parliamentary Committees' in eds Grabosky & Le Lievre, pp. 45-50.

Harrison, Kate 1987, 'Freedom of Information: A Remedy for Government Illegality?', in eds Grabosky & Le Lievre, pp. 171-86.

Horman, William 1987, 'Victoria Police Internal Investigation Department', in eds Grabosky & Le Lievre, pp. 77-88.

Hunter, Jill 1985, '"Tainted" Proceedings: Censuring Police Illegalities', *Australian Law Journal*, vol. 59, pp. 709-16.

Johnson, Dirk 1986, 'Abused Women Get Leverage in Connecticut', *New York Times*, 15 June, p. 8E.

Katz, Jack 1977, 'Cover-up and Collective Integrity: On the Natural Antagonisms of Authority Internal and External to Organizations', *Social Problems*, vol. 25, pp. 3-17.

Kagan, Robert & Scholz, John 1984, 'The "Criminology of the Corporation" and Regulatory Enforcement Strategies' in *Enforcing Regulation*, eds Keith Hawkins & John Thomas, Kluwer-Nijhoff, Boston, pp. 67-96.

Kaufman, Herbert 1973, *Administrative Feedback; Monitoring Subordinates' Behavior*, The Brookings Institution, Washington.

Kriesberg, Simeon 1976, 'Decisionmaking Models and Corporate Crime' *Yale Law Journal*, vol. 85, 1091-129.

Lidbetter, Peter 1987, 'Role of Auditors General' in eds Grabosky & Le Lievre, pp. 13-24.

References

Mashaw, Jerry 1978, 'Civil Liability of Government Officers: Property Rights and Official Accountability', *Law and Contemporary Problems*, vol. 42, no. 1.

Near, Janet & Micelli, Marcia 1987, 'Whistle Blowers in Organizations; Dissidents or Reformers', in *Research In Organizational Behavior*, eds L Cummings & B. Staw, vol. 9, JAI Press, Greenwich, Conn. pp 321-68.

Nettheim, Garth 1981, *Victims of the Law: Black Queenslanders Today*, George Allen & Unwin, Sydney.

Pennock J. R. & Chapman, J. (eds) 1985, *Nomos XVII*, New York University Press, New York.

Punch, Maurice 1985, *Conduct Unbecoming: The Social Construction of Police Deviance and Control*, Tavistock Publications, London.

Rosen, Bernard 1982, *Holding Government Bureaucracies Accountable*, Praeger Publishers, New York.

Rowan, Joseph 1988, *Manual on Detection and Prevention of Suicides in Jails and Lockups*, Juvenile and Criminal Justice International, Inc., Roseville, Minnesota.

Rowley, C.D. 1970, *The Destruction of Aboriginal Society*, Australian National University Press, Canberra.

Schuck, Peter 1983, *Suing Government: Citizen Remedies for Official Wrongs*, Yale University Press, New Haven.

Selby, Hugh 1987, 'Ombudsman, Inc.: A Bullish Stock with a Bare Performance', Paper presented to a seminar of the Royal Australian Institute of Public Administration, Australian National University, Canberra.

Sherman, Lawrence 1978, *Scandal and Reform*, University of California Press, Berkeley.

References

Sherman, Lawrence, & Cohn, Ellen 1986, *Citizens Killed by Big City Police*, Crime Control Institute, Washington, D.C.

Skolnick, Jerome 1982, 'Deception by Police' *Criminal Justice Ethics*, vol. 1, no. 2, pp. 40-50.

Stone, Christopher 1975, *Where the Law Ends: The Social Control of Corporate Behavior*, Harper and Row, New York.

------------ 1980, 'The Place of Enterprise Liability in the Control of Corporate Conduct', *Yale Law Journal*, vol. 90.

------------ 1982, 'Corporate Vices and Corporate Virtues: Do Public/Private Distinctions Matter?', *University of Pennsylvania Law Review*, vol. 139, pp. 1441-509.

------------ 1985, 'A Comment on "Criminal Responsibility in Government"' in eds Pennock & Chapman, New York University Press, New York.

Swanton, Bruce 1986 (unpub), 'Fabrication of Confessional Evidence: A General Look at Verballing', Australian Institute of Criminology, Canberra.

Thompson, Dennis 1985, 'Criminal Responsibility in Government' in eds Pennock & Chapman, pp. 201-40.

Tompkins, P. & Cheney, G. 1985, 'Communication and Unobtrusive Control in Contemporary Organizations', in *Organizational Communication: Traditional Themes and New Directions*, eds R. McPhee & P. Tompkins, Sage Publications, Newbury Park, California.

Tower J., Muskie E. & Scowcroft B. 1987, *The Tower Commission Report, the Full Text of the President's Special Review Board*, Joint Publication of Bantam Books and Times Books, New York.

Vaughan, Diane 1983, *Controlling Unlawful Organizational Behavior: Social Structure and Corporate Misconduct*, University of Chicago Press, Chicago.

References

------------ 1986, 'Organizational Misconduct: The Connection Between Theory and Policy', Paper presented at the Annual Meeting of the Law and Society Association, Chicago, Ill., May 29-June 1.

Vaughn, Robert 1982, 'Statutory Protection of Whistleblowers in the Federal Executive Branch', *University of Illinois Law Review*, 1982, vol. 3, pp. 615-67.

Ward, Tony 1986, *Death and Disorder: Three Case Studies of Public Order and Policing in London*, Inquest, London.

Wilford, John Noble 1987, 'New NASA System Aims to Encourage Blowing the Whistle', *New York Times*, 5 June, p. 1.

Wilson, James Q. & Rachal, Patricia 1977, 'Can the Government Regulate Itself?', *The Public Interest*, vol. 46, pp. 3-14.

Wood, John 1984, 'Whistleblower Protection Legislation', *Rupert Public Interest Movement Journal*, vol. 10, no. 26.

Woolhandler, Ann 1987, 'Patterns of Official Immunity and Accountability', *Case Western Reserve Law Review*, vol. 37, pp. 396-483.

INDEX

339

344